New Directions in Communications Policy

New Directions in Communications Policy

Edited By

Randolph J. May

Carolina Academic Press

Durham, North Carolina

Library of Congress Cataloging-in-Publication Data

New directions in communications policy / The Free State Foundation.
p. cm.
Includes index.
ISBN 978-1-59460-673-1 (alk. paper)
1. Telecommunication--Law and legislation--United States. I. Free State Foundation, Inc. II. Title.

KF2765.N49 2009
343.7309'94--dc22

2009019316

Carolina Academic Press
700 Kent Street
Durham, North Carolina 27701
Telephone (919) 489-7486
Fax (919) 493-5668
www.cap-press.com

Printed in the United States of America

For Laurie

Contents

Foreword

Randolph J. May

In enacting the Telecommunications Act of 1996, the most significant amendment to the Communications Act of 1934 since passage of the original act, Congress declared the statute's intent "to promote competition and reduce regulation."[1] Consistent with the statutory language, the conference report stated the legislation was intended "to provide for a pro-competitive, deregulatory national policy framework."[2]

In signing the bill into law, President Bill Clinton's rhetoric was soaring: "With the stroke of a pen, our laws will catch up with the future. We will help to create an open marketplace where competition and innovation can move as quick as light."[3] For good measure, he called the 1996 Act "truly revolutionary legislation."[4]

Whether or not the 1996 Act was really "pro-competitive" and "deregulatory," as Congress said it intended, or "truly revolutionary" as President Clinton characterized it, has been much debated by scholars and policymakers. And whether or not the act itself was deregulatory or revolutionary is a separate issue, at least to some extent, from questions relating to how the Federal Commu-

1. Telecommunications Act of 1996, Pub. L. No. 104-104, 110 Stat. 56, 56 (preamble).

2. H.R. CONF. REP. No. 104–458 at 113 (1996), *reprinted in* 1996 U.S.C.C.A.N. 124, 124.

3. "Remarks by the President in Signing Ceremony for the Telecommunications Act Conference Report," Library of Congress, White House Press Release, Washington, DC, February 8, 1996.

4. Id.

nications Commission ("Commission" or "FCC") implemented the statute. For there is little doubt the 1996 Act's ambiguity left the FCC with a large measure of regulatory discretion.

As Justice Antonin Scalia famously put it in the first post-1996 Act case to reach the Supreme Court, "[i]t would be a gross understatement to say that the 1996 Act is not a model of clarity. It is in many important respects a model of ambiguity or even self-contradiction."[5] Under the Supreme Court's *Chevron* test, the agency is traditionally accorded a large measure of administrative discretion in interpreting opaque provisions.[6] Moreover, the broad discretion accorded to the FCC also stems from the fact that, even after the supposedly deregulatory 1996 Act amendments, the Communications Act still has nearly one hundred statutory provisions that delegate authority to the agency to act in the "public interest."[7] At one time, it might have been thought that such an indeterminate standard would fail to pass muster under the constitutional nondelegation doctrine that requires that congressional delegations of authority contain an "intelligible principle" to guide the agency.[8] But such a thought would be wrong. The Supreme Court has refused to hold unlawful the public interest standard, and, consequently, the Commission has been able to use its inherent indeterminateness to support broad notions of administrative authority.[9]

---

5. AT&T Corp. v. Iowa Utilities Board, 525 U.S. 366, 397 (1999).

6. Chevron U. S. A. Inc. v. Natural Resources Defense Council, 467 U.S. 116 (1985) (If a statutory provision is ambiguous and if the implementing agency's interpretation is reasonable, a federal court is required to defer to the agency's interpretation, even if it differs from one the court deems better.) For a recent Supreme Court decision upholding the FCC's broad administrative discretion when interpreting an ambiguous statutory provision, see Nat'l Cable & Telecomms. Ass'n. v. Brand X Internet Serv., 545 U.S. 967 (2005).

7. *See* Randolph J. May, *The Public Interest Standard: Is It Too Indeterminate To Be Constitutional?*, 53 Fed. Comm. L. J. 427 (2001), Appendix A.

8. Id., at 443–452; see also Randolph J. May, *A Modest Plea for FCC Modesty Regarding the Public Interest Standard*, 60 Admin. L. Rev. 895, 898–901 (2008).

9. The seminal case, NBC, Inc. v. United States, 319 U.S. 190, 227 (1940), is almost seventy years old, but it remains good law and is still oft-cited.

In any event, my purpose here is not to define the contours of the FCC's discretion, but rather to drive home the point that the agency continues to possess broad leeway in carrying out many of its regulatory activities. As with the debate surrounding the statute itself, there has been much debate concerning whether the Commission has implemented the 1996 Act in the deregulatory manner Congress, at least ostensibly, intended. In my view, it has done so only in fits and starts, and without consistency and coherence.

But we are where we are. So the distinct emphasis of this book is forward-looking. Hence the title, *New Directions in Communications Policy*. In this volume, looking backwards is reserved primarily for the purpose of learning from past mistakes in the vein of Santayana's famous axiom: "Those who do not remember history are condemned to repeat it." Consistent with the "New Directions" theme, each essay contains at its end a "Recommendations and Conclusions" section. There the chief suggested new policy initiatives are summarized.

In highlighting the recommendations at each chapter's end, I need to be careful not to minimize in any way the breadth and depth of the scholarship contained in the entirety of each essay. The authors are among the nation's most preeminent law and economics scholars. They are widely-published, well-respected academics in the communications law and policy field. Many have had hands-on experience in high-ranking policy positions. I am proud to say that each essay author is a member of the Board of Academic Advisors of the Free State Foundation, the nonprofit think tank I founded in 2006 and of which I serve as president. And I am grateful that these busy teachers and thought leaders have lent their time and energy in advising the Free State Foundation and participating in its educational activities.

One more word about "revolution" before briefly introducing the individual essays. The notion that the Telecommunications Act of 1996 was "truly revolutionary," as President Clinton suggested, is, in my opinion, hyperbolic. Nevertheless, there truly has been a revolution in the communications marketplace environment since 1996, one owing much to the ongoing rush of technological developments. Sometimes ill-conceived policies may have slowed the dramatic marketplace changes, but they could not completely throttle them.[10] The Internet was still in its early adolescent phase in 1996, with the World Wide Web only recently having made its appearance in rudimentary form. Cable television companies didn't provide phone service, and telephone companies didn't provide video services. We didn't have hundreds of choices of video channels available from the cable, satellite, or telephone providers. Cell phone service was no more than a complement to traditional wireline services, not a rapidly increasing replacement. And, of course, you couldn't watch your favorite soap opera or other television show on your portable wireless device. You can now. And with today's Internet, we can all instantaneously be publishers or recipients of content from around the neighborhood or around the world. Many of the individual essays contain information describing various aspects of this revolution in the communications marketplace, so there is no need to belabor the point here.

The book begins appropriately with a broad-ranging essay by Dennis Weisman and Glen Robinson titled, "*Lessons for Modern Regulators from Hippocrates, Schumpeter and Kahn*." That would be Hippocrates of "First, do no harm" fame; Joseph Schumpeter, best known for his description of the process of "creative destruction" that is at the heart of his theory of dynamic capitalism; and Alfred Kahn, whom the authors appropriately call "one of the foremost contemporary scholars of regulated industries, as well as one of the most distinguished regulators (both at state and federal levels)." Drawing on lessons learned from the learned three, Professors Weisman and Robinson conclude that "[t]he centripetal model of command-and-control regulation of the

10. Indeed, not long after the 1996 Act's passage, then FCC Commissioner, later FCC Chairman Michael Powell wrote: "We are in the throes of a revolution. This statement is not intended to be melodramatic, but rather descriptive of the breathtaking moment in which we in the communications field find ourselves." Michael K. Powell, *Communications Policy Leadership for the Next Century*, 50 FED. COMM. L. J. 529, 529 (1998).

past that put in place strict rules to elicit a uniformity of market outcomes must now yield to a centrifugal model of regulation in which the regulator becomes less of a controller and more of an enabler." They assert that the FCC's implementation of the 1996 Telecom Act suffered from the fact that, despite changes in the marketplace environment, the agency continued to default "to its traditional regulatory mode in which it substituted its judgment for the marketplace when its task was to unleash the power of these burgeoning markets in a manner that would enable market forces to provide the requisite discipline."

As case studies, Professors Weisman and Robinson examine the most controversial topical communications policy issues: net neutrality regulation and broadcast ownership restrictions. After considering all the claims put forward to justify imposing neutrality mandates on broadband Internet providers and applying lessons from the three sages, they urge policymakers to exercise caution before accepting any of the pro-regulatory rationales. As for the broadcast ownership restrictions, the authors show that for decades there has been a mismatch between the claimed rationale that the regulations support program diversity and the means devised to achieve the supposed objective. At bottom, Professors Weisman and Robinson conclude: "While there may be some legitimate role for regulation to play in facilitating the transition from monopoly to competition, we think it is one that poses great risks of undermining the very competition it is supposed to foster."

From the broad sweep of the first chapter, with its erudite discussion of the ideas of Hippocrates, Schumpeter, and Kahn, as they relate to the political economy of communications regulation, the focus in the ensuing chapters narrows somewhat as topics are addressed more specifically. The essays of Professors Speta, Yoo, and Epstein begin a threesome, each focusing to a greater or lesser extent on probably the most contentious issue of the day: network neutrality. To attempt to define "net neutrality" here not only would be impossibly difficult—difficulty of definition is a major problem, in my view, with the notion of adopting net neutrality mandates—but it also would preempt some of the most useful discussion in the essays that follow. By way of the briefest of introductions, suffice it to say that net neutrality regulation has to do with government mandates purporting to require that broadband service providers, such as Verizon or Comcast, do not block, impair, or degrade access to any Internet site or discriminate against any unaffiliated applications, content, or equipment providers that make use of the providers' broadband services.

In "*Redefining the Landscape of Internet Regulation*," Jim Speta recommends that the Obama Administration order a systemic, substantive inquiry into Internet policy, especially in light of the uncertainties created by the FCC's August 2008 order holding that Comcast acted unlawfully by interfering with certain bandwidth-intensive peer-to-peer video applications.[11] According to Professor Speta, in rejecting Comcast's argument that its actions impacting the flow of peer-to-peer traffic constituted reasonable network management practices, the *Comcast Order* suggests a fundamental and ill-conceived departure from the "non-regulation" of the Internet that the FCC had long practiced and which many experts had regarded as having been successful. He criticizes the FCC for articulating a vision of its regulatory authority over broadband Internet services that is as broad as the agency's authority over traditional common carrier services. Professor Speta says the FCC's *Comcast Order* suggests economic regulation of Internet services could be part of the agency's agenda. Before going any further down this regulatory road, and given the importance of communications to the economy and our polity, he argues that we need a rigorous investigation of Internet markets, Internet economics, and Internet regulatory possibilities with the aim of developing a clearly articulated set of policies.

Also taking the FCC's *Comcast Order* as his departure point, Christopher Yoo casts a wary eye on proposals to impose net neutrality restrictions. In "*Network Neutrality after Comcast: Toward a Case-by-Case Approach To Reasonable Network Management*," Pro-

11. Formal Complaint of Free Press and Public Knowledge Against Comcast Corporation for Secretly Degrading Peer-to-Peer Applications, 23 F.C.C.R. 13028 (2008) ("Comcast Order").

fessor Yoo recognizes the merit of the case-by-case adjudicatory approach that seems to characterize the agency's action in the Comcast case. He explains that this approach, with its emphasis on the facts of a specific complaint, is superior to the adoption *ex ante* of categorical rules that almost always are "blunt instruments that do not permit fine distinctions."

While sympathetic to case-by-case adjudication as a methodological approach, Professor Yoo has considerable worries about the harms that might result if such an approach were to lead to the adoption of net neutrality mandates. Using his keen knowledge of antitrust jurisprudence and the economics of network industries, Professor Yoo explains why consumer welfare may be adversely affected by regulations that purport to prohibit all "discrimination" by broadband Internet service providers. Forced standardization makes it more difficult for providers to innovate and respond to consumer demand for new products. In effect, neutrality mandates that purport to prohibit discrimination do discriminate—they have the practical effect of discriminating against innovations that depend on new network designs that deviate from standard protocols. And the seeming restriction on pricing flexibility that is implicit, if not explicit, in most net neutrality proposals would make it more difficult for Internet service providers to recover the costs of building out more broadband facilities. In other words, according to Professor Yoo, by enforcing standardization that inhibits the development of network innovation and by restricting pricing flexibility that allows recovery of more network costs from premium content and applications services, net neutrality mandates end up harming overall consumer welfare.

Through the looking glass of an earlier FCC decision involving broadcast licensing, Richard Epstein, with his usual intellectual incisiveness, sees distinct perils in government adoption of net neutrality regulations. In "*What Broadcast Licenses Tell Us About Net Neutrality: Cosmopolitan Broadcasting Corporation v. FCC*," Professor Epstein recounts the FCC's rejection of Cosmopolitan Broadcasting's plan to sell broadcasting time slots to various foreign language programmers to use the time as the "sublicensees" saw fit. In this now mostly forgotten case, the agency decided the licensee had given up too much control over the station's programming in brokering the time slots. In the FCC's view, this lack of control was inconsistent with the "public interest," the ubiquitous, vague standard that guides most of the agency's regulatory activities. Calling on his deep knowledge of the Progressive and New Deal eras, including the FCC's own early regulatory history, Professor Epstein explains how the Communications Act came to be interpreted—wrongly in his view—to give the regulators such broad administrative power. The views of Felix Frankfurter sanctioning broad agency discretion to dictate detailed command-and-control regulations under the public interest standard prevailed over any Hayekian notions that marketplace dictates might best serve consumers.

While many others might miss the connection, Professor Epstein asserts that the same mode of thinking that led the FCC to dismiss the contention that broadcast sublicensees might be in a better position than the agency bureaucrats to determine what programming consumers prefer likely will cause the agency to take an unduly expansive view of net neutrality regulation. Pleas to prohibit "discrimination," like pleas to promote "diversity" through broadcast regulation, may sound benign. But Professor Epstein asserts that history teaches—indeed, the FCC's actions in *Cosmopolitan* and other broadcast cases teach—that "the parties who seek to develop sophisticated and sensible schemes for state control quickly lose control over the administrative process to persons whose ambitions for state control are not bound by any fine-grained rationale." In a wonderful (under)statement of the perils of government action that do not comport with sound economic principles such as those that infuse antitrust jurisprudence, Professor Epstein says, "the expected rate of depreciation of sound public norms that rely on administrative discretion is high." Such being the case, in no uncertain terms Professor Epstein concludes: "Keep private control over broadband pipes by abandoning the siren call of net neutrality."

The next chapters turn to issues relating to reform of the archaic "universal service" and "intercarrier compensation" regimes. These subjects create nearly as much controversy as those relating to net neutrality. One difference, however, is that proposals to change universal service and intercarrier compensation have been around for more than a decade, while net neutrality, at least in its current iteration, for only half that time. In shorthand, intercarrier compensation has to do with the regulatory regime that governs the rates, terms, and conditions upon which interconnecting telecommunications service providers originate and terminate traffic on each other's networks. Universal service has to do with a regime composed of various forms of subsidies—some of which are derived from explicitly above-cost intercarrier compensation rates—designed to assure that telephone service is affordable and ubiquitously available.

John Mayo and Gerald Brock take us from my shorthand to a deep understanding of the reasons why each of these interrelated legacy regulatory regimes, developed in a much more monopolistic era, must now be reformed to account for new marketplace competition and technological developments. Professor Mayo's contribution is entitled, "*Universal Service: Can We Do More with Less?*" His answer is an emphatic "yes," but not before taking a close look at the way subsidies for so-called "high cost" areas have grown rapidly in recent years and the moral hazard created by the high cost support program. Professor Mayo concludes that "the now century-old effort to promote universal service remains woefully antiquated, misdirected and, from an economic perspective, massively bloated." While Professor Mayo is not averse to the notion that some subsidies should be redirected from the support of narrowband to broadband communications, he urges this not be done before the regime is reformed in line with the economic principles he articulates.

Professor Brock does an admirable job of explaining, demystifying really, the truly complex compensation system that governs —largely by regulatory fiat—the payments made by one carrier to another for traffic that transits two or more networks. His essay, "*Unifying the Intercarrier Compensation Regime*," explains the irrationality inherent in the way the regulations treat various types of traffic based on legacy classifications or jurisdictional considerations that have no relevance to the economic cost considerations that ought to prevail in a competitive environment. If Professor Brock's essay did nothing else, it would have performed a useful service. But, indeed, it does much more. He argues for the replacement of the current regime, with its compartmentalized sub-regimes, with a single unified compensation framework that is neutral with regard to technology, industry structure, and pricing plans. Conceptualizing a new framework more closely aligned with economic costs and competitive realities is one thing, but wrestling with the difficulties, as a matter of political economy, of getting from here to there is another. In this regard, Professor Brock puts forward an innovative proposal for a new regime based, to the extent possible, on private bargaining, but with arbitration by industry experts as a backstop. His piece is made even more valuable for the detail he provides concerning how the arbitration process should be designed and how it should work in practice.

The next three essays relate to mass media policy. As with telecommunications, if we can use that term here to refer to one-to-one communications, the mass media marketplace—that of one-to-many communications—is also being transformed dramatically by the digital broadband revolution. Where once there was radio, and then over-the-air broadcast television, suffice it to say there are now, alongside them, cable and satellite television services that offer subscribers hundreds of different channels. And there are mobile devices that deliver not only voice calls, but text messages and the latest video offerings. And, of course, the Internet is the ultimate—well, not likely the ultimate—but the latest, one-to-many mass media communications medium.

In his penetrating essay, *"Delivering Media Content in a New Technological Environment: An Exploration of Implications for Television Policy,"* Steven Wildman examines one particular way in which technological change is altering the media landscape. He argues that the economics of server-based distribution systems, video systems that allow viewers to select and play programs stored on a video server at times of their choosing, undermines two of the basic policy tenets that prevailed in what he calls television's linear era of prescheduled appointment viewing. The first tenet undermined is that lawmakers and regulators can influence the mix of programs supplied to viewers through regulations aimed at influencing content choices made by owners of local television distribution facilities. The second is that the bandwidth employed to distribute television programs is a scarce resource limiting the supply of programs to viewers. Professor Wildman explains how the undermining of these two tenets should cause lawmakers and regulators to address whatever legitimate concerns they may have about the undersupply of program content through means less directly regulatory than the traditional dictation of program content.

Diane Disney, on the other hand, is concerned that, whatever marketplace and deregulatory changes already have occurred, have had the effect of reducing the amount of local broadcast programming, especially traditional public service announcements. Her essay, "*Public Affairs and Private Employment: Some Unintended Consequences of the 1996 Telecommunications Act*," does double duty in that it also examines some of the downside effects on employment that, in her view, followed consolidation in the telecommunications marketplace. Professor Disney is skeptical whether what others see as the increased consumer choice made available by new technologies and new entrants is really meeting the needs of the public, especially local communities. For her, broadcasters are failing in their public service obligations as licensees. While shying away from proposing outright a reinstatement of the Fairness Doctrine, at least labeled as such because she says the term generates such strong stereotyped reactions, Professor Disney proposes some kind of "Nonprofit Access Mechanism" regulation applicable to broadcasters as a way to bring local interests and local problem-solving organizations back to visibility in their communities. Readers can decide for themselves whether or not the new name is a distinction without a meaningful difference.

The next essay, "*Charting a New Constitutional Jurisprudence for the Digital Age*," is mine. It will be easy enough there to discern that I have a much more positive view of the impact of the technological and marketplace changes that have occurred than does Professor Disney. As I see it, as the transition from the analog to digital age nears completion, we have entered an age characterized by media abundance. The availability of so much content through alternative platforms in and of itself is reason enough, as a matter of policy, for jettisoning almost all legacy regulations that have the government dictating carriage of some content and suppression of other programming.

But my essay focuses on a reason more compelling than policy for doing so: conformance with the Constitution. I review the landmark First Amendment cases, such as *NBC*,[12] *Red Lion*,[13] *Pacifica*,[14] and *Turner Broadcasting*,[15] recognizing that the Supreme Court upheld the curtailment of free speech challenged in each of those cases, whether based on notions of spectrum scarcity, the unique pervasiveness of the broadcast media, or the existence of media bottlenecks. In light of the then-prevailing less competitive marketplace and less dynamic technological environment, I concede that perhaps it was predictable that the First Amendment's protections would be substantially limited in the analog age. I hope I make a persuasive case that it is time for the Court to adopt a new constitutional jurisprudence that is much more protective of free speech values than is the existing jurisprudence. As I say in closing, "now, in the face of proliferating competitive alternatives and media outlets spurred by profound marketplace and technological changes, it ought to be considered predictable, and, yes, even likely, for the Court to establish a new First Amendment jurisprudence befitting the media abundance of the twenty-first century's digital age."[16]

Bruce Owen's essay, "*A Fresh Start in Communications Policy*," closes the volume. Because of the breadth of its sweep, it makes a perfect bookend to the broad sweep of the opening essay by Professors Weisman and Robinson that invokes Hippocrates, Schumpeter, and Kahn. In part, Professor Owen's essay is a brief primer on the political economy of American government decisionmaking, with special emphasis on the role played by Madisonian factions in shaping policy. In this regard, Professor Owen states, "[o]ur system is structured to reward politicians who respond to

---

12. National Broadcasting Co. v. United States, 319 U.S. 190 (1943)

13. Red Lion Broadcasting Co. V. FCC, 395 U.S. 367 (1969).

14. FCC v. Pacifica Foundation, 438 U.S. 726 (1978).

15. Turner Broadcasting System, Inc. v. FCC, 512 U.S. 622 (1994).

16. I was gratified that Justice Thomas cited an earlier version of this essay in his concurring opinion in FCC v. Fox Television Stations, 129 S. Ct. 1800, where he expressed his willingness to reconsider the existing First Amendment jurisprudence applied to the electronic media.

the incentives created by interest group competition and the art of compromise." Compromise is not inherently a bad thing. Indeed, compromises are necessary, at least at certain times, if government is to function. But focusing on the somewhat insular communications policymaking community, Professor Owen asserts that the need of the various special interests to engage in compromises and trade-offs has led to the adoption of the community's own "foundational myth," the notion that "the enterprise is concerned directly with the public interest, as opposed to the political regulation of economic advantage." Of course, the prevalence and prominence of the vague public interest standard in the Communications Act facilitates, and provides easy cover for, this foundational myth.

Having in mind the persistence of the public interest foundational myth and the very real history of mission creep that has characterized communications regulation from the outset, Professor Owen offers two specific recommendations, one substantive and one process-oriented, for achieving fundamental change. He recommends permitting spectrum licensees to use or sell their spectrum for any purpose whatsoever that does not interfere with other licensees. This would be a bold break with the still too prevalent "command and control" approach to spectrum regulation that always has prevailed and that has led to substantial underutilization of this valuable resource. Perhaps no other suggested change would constitute such a substantive "new direction" in communications policy.

The second, more process-oriented recommendation is for the establishment of a meaningful sunset regime for all existing and future communications statutes and rules. Professor Owen shows that many of the existing statutes and rules have outlived whatever usefulness they once may have had. He suggests creating a legal presumption that all regulatory provisions would become defunct after a number of years fixed at the time of enactment, unless those who believe a particular provision should remain in effect can convince a majority of the then current decisionmaking body that the provision continues to makes sense. While adoption of such a sunset regime may not be on the near-term horizon, Professor Owen makes a persuasive case for his recommendation. It would impact the long-term sustainability of the regulations built on the traditional public interest foundational myth. With a lessening of the hold of the foundational myth, new directions in communications policymaking would follow more easily.

That brings me back full circle to this volume's principal purpose: To point the way forward, in the midst of tremendous marketplace and technological change, to concrete new policy directions that take account of digital age realities. I am confident that the scholars have accomplished this central purpose. They have offered concrete recommendations on today's most important issues. These recommendations, and the supporting rationales, should be considered carefully by all regulators and policymakers with responsibilities for establishing communications policy. In addition to regulators and policymakers, the book, with its wealth of background information on the theory and practice of communications regulation, will prove valuable to any person interested in communications law and policy, no matter whether a new student or teacher of the subject, or an experienced practitioner.

I am grateful to all the contributors for the care and diligence they exhibited throughout the preparation of their essays. Their willingness to comply with my sometimes stringent deadlines has ensured that the content of the book remains as timely as I envisioned it would be when, together, we embarked on the project. Such timeliness, in turn, ensures the book will be impactful.

I want to thank Laurie May, Len Lazarick and Elaine Orr for their editorial assistance in preparing the manuscript. I also want to thank Susan Reichbart, the Free State Foundation's Events Coordinator, for her assistance in making the February 2009 "New Directions in Communications Policymaking" conference in Washington, D.C. so successful. At the conference, several of the contributors to this volume had an opportunity to present some of the ideas they developed for this book.

In closing, I have no hesitancy in affirming my conviction that many of the "new directions" suggested in this volume will one day be considered important, even noncontroversial, elements of sound communications policy.

Potomac, Maryland
May 2009

New Directions in Communications Policy

CHAPTER 1

Lessons for Modern Regulators from Hippocrates, Schumpeter and Kahn

*Dennis L. Weisman and Glen O. Robinson**

Introduction

More than 70 years ago John Maynard Keynes lamented that accepted economic theory was not up to the task of responding to the pressing economic problems of the day. The most fundamental challenge, he thought, was not in developing new ideas, "but in escaping from the old ones, which ramify, for those brought up as most of us have been, into every corner of our minds."[1] The same challenge confronts the modern-day regulator in overseeing the market and technological upheavals that have transformed the telecommunications marketplace.

The New Webster Encyclopedic Dictionary of the English Language defines the terms "regulate" and "regulator," respectively, as follows:

> To adjust by rule or established mode; to govern by or subject to certain rules or restrictions; to direct; to put or keep in good order; to control and cause to act properly.

---

* The authors are grateful to Alfred Kahn, Randy May, and Charles Zielinski for constructive comments and discussions on an earlier draft of this manuscript.

1. John Maynard Keynes, The General Theory of Employment, Interest and Money viii (New York, Harcourt Brace and World 1935).

> One who or that which regulates; a device or contrivance of which the object is to produce uniformity of motion or action.

The term "regulator" probably describes fairly accurately what was traditionally asked of public utility commissioners. We wanted them to "keep the trains running on time"—to ensure that consumers had reliable access to public services (e.g., electric power, natural gas, telephone, and water) of acceptable quality at reasonable prices. The homogeneity of the service itself mapped well into the uniformity of action attribute, and there was probably limited scope for *innovation* in the sense in which we use that term today. The problem is that the uniformity of action that we valued in regulators of the past is increasingly at odds with what is required of "regulators" today in addressing the pressing issues of the times.

The centripetal model of command-and-control regulation of the past that put in place strict rules to elicit a uniformity of market outcomes must now yield to a centrifugal model of regulation in which the regulator becomes less of a controller and more of an enabler. We have transcended the limited objective of keeping the trains running on time; the present regulatory challenge is to enable competing technological platforms that are increasingly capable of providing the requisite discipline from within—competitive discipline of the real kind rather than the emulation thereof at the hand of the regulator.[2,3] This necessarily entails a corresponding shift in regulatory emphasis from one of controlling

---

2. Professor Kahn observes that "the single most widely accepted rule for the governance of the regulated industries is regulate them in such a way as to produce the same results as would be produced by effective competition, if it were feasible." Alfred E. Kahn, The Economics of Regulation: Principles and Institutions Vol. I, 17 (New York, John Wiley and Sons 1970).

3. Professor Bonbright observes that "Regulation, then, as I conceive it, is indeed a substitute for competition; and it is even a partly imitative substitute." James C. Bonbright, Principles of Public Utility Rates 107 (New York, Columbia University Press 1961).

market power to one of unleashing the power of markets.[4] The centrifugal regulatory model must be fluid in interpretation and yet rigid in the principles that inform that interpretation. The new "centrifugal regulator" must be prepared to referee the struggle between competing interests while recognizing that his role is a limited one.[5]

In learning just what that limited role is we suggest our regulator take some guidance from three inspirational teachers of medicine, economics and regulation: Hippocrates, Schumpeter, and—in our own day—Alfred Kahn. No doubt it will seem paradoxical that in advocating the need to escape from "habitual modes of thought and expression" we should draw on one teacher who died more than two millennia ago, and another who died nearly 60 years ago. We take comfort in the knowledge that our third teacher is still actively teaching the lessons of the other two. Some lessons endure.

Hippocrates, the father of modern medicine, is popularly known today for his famous oath, "First, do no harm."[6] It is a wise admonition not only for physicians but for all persons charged with responsibility for the well being of others, public regulators included. For the regulator we translate the lesson from Hippocrates into a basically conservative admonition not to invent a solution to a problem that doesn't exist (or at least one that will persist long enough to justify the investment of energy to solve it).

---

4. See Dennis L. Weisman, *On Market Power and the Power of Markets: A Schumpeterian View of Dynamic Industries in* Perspectives from FSF Scholars Vol. 3(5) (The Free State Foundation, February 26, 2008) at http://www.freestatefoundation.org/images/Power_of_Markets.pdf.

5. Joel I. Klein, *The Importance of Antitrust Enforcement In The New Economy*, 12 before the New York State Bar Association, Antitrust Law Section Program, New York, NY, January 29, 1998.

6. The currently known phrase is slightly inaccurate. What Hippocrates said was that physicians should regulate their treatment so as "to do good, or at least do no harm." Francis Adams, The Genuine Works of Hippocrates, (translated from the Greek), Vol. I, 20 (London, Sydenham Society, MDCCCXLIX).

Joseph Schumpeter is best known today for his theory of dynamic capitalism, reflected in his famous description of competition as a struggle among firms to capture the market by a process of "creative destruction."[7] Schumpeter believed that regulators should seek to foster the competitive process rather than mandate the competitive outcome.

Alfred Kahn is one of the foremost contemporary scholars of regulated industries, as well as one of the most distinguished regulators (both at state and federal levels).[8] In both capacities he has been a leading proponent/practitioner of deregulation.[9] In his scholarship and in his practice as a regulator, Kahn has built on the principles of Hippocrates and Schumpeter. Borrowing from the former he has emphasized that regulatory intervention in the competitive process could create more harm than good, and from the latter Kahn viewed competition within a framework of dynamic processes over time.

Admittedly the lessons to be learned from these three luminaries are at a very high level of generality, which means that it is not a simple matter to know how to translate them into guidance on specific policy issues. Even so, we think it is possible to point to concrete examples where they tell us something interesting and useful about contemporary regulatory issues in the field of communications regulation. To illustrate, in the next three sections, we address, respectively, the FCC's inertial tendencies toward centripetal regulation in implementing the 1996 Telecommunications Act, the slippery slope of the network neutrality debate, and the shifting rationales for regulating broadcast media ownership.

---

7. Joseph A. Schumpeter, Capitalism, Socialism and Democracy 81–86 (1942). For more on Schumpeter, his life, his theory of capitalism and his place in modern economics, see Thomas K. McCraw, Prophet of Innovation (2007).

8. His two-volume treatise on the economics of regulation remains a classic reference. Alfred E. Kahn, The Economics of Regulation: Principles and Institutions Vol. I, Economic Principles; Volume II, Institutional Issues (1970 and 1971).

9. Thomas K. McCraw, Prophets of Regulation 222–299 (1984).

Opening Local Telecommunications Markets to Competition

The Paradigm Shift in Telecommunications Markets

It is commonplace knowledge that the telecommunications industry has undergone a radical transformation in the past score of years. Today, consumers can choose from a number of different technological platforms for their telecommunications services,[10] including broadband and wireless.[11] The black rotary-dial telephone that was big and heavy enough to use as a doorstop (and which until the 1970s could only be leased from AT&T), has morphed into an array of multi-purpose information and communications devices that can be put in a pocket (and purchased at grocery stores). Providing a dial-tone is almost the least of the functions provided by the modern cell phone. And the telecommunications service providers have morphed into multi-purpose entertainment and information companies.

The technology has changed, the business culture and philosophy have changed, even the organization of the industry has changed. AT&T once strode the world of telecommunications like a colossus. Until at least the late 1970s, the U.S. telecommunications industry for all practical purposes *was* AT&T. AT&T is still a huge firm, to be sure, but it no longer dominates the industry as it once did.[12] The introduction of competition, along with the

---

10. See, for example, JONATHAN E. NUECHTERLEIN AND PHILIP J. WEISER, DIGITAL CROSSROADS, AMERICAN TELECOMMUNICATIONS POLICY IN THE INTERNET AGE (2005).

11. See, for example, U.S. DEPARTMENT OF JUSTICE, VOICE, VIDEO AND BROADBAND: THE CHANGING COMPETITIVE LANDSCAPE AND ITS IMPACT ON CONSUMERS (2008), *available at* http://www.usdoj.gov/atr/public/reports/239284.pdf.

12. The succession of mergers among the Bell Operating Companies, and the 2005 acquisition of AT&T by SBC in 2005, followed by the 2007 acquisition by AT&T (formerly SBC) of BellSouth has led to speculation that the old AT&T is being reconstructed. While the acquisition by SBC did rescue a declining if not dying AT&T, it did not come close to restoring its former dominance. In 1983

growth of new technologies, has seen to that. In this new environment the once colossus of the industry initially proved to be less adroit than in the heyday of regulated natural monopoly—an elephant on ice skates, as it were. The business model that enabled AT&T to thrive under the yoke of regulation proved to be particularly ill-suited for a marketplace that requires its managers to work without a net. This is not all that surprising; managing the regulatory process requires different skill sets than managing the competitive process. The old AT&T rarely hired senior managers from outside its ranks, and when it did the cultural barriers were seemingly impenetrable for these foreign born.[13] Today, growing up in the "Bell System" (and many employees had parents and grandparents that worked for Ma Bell) has arguably become more of a liability than an asset. The centripetal thought process of the old Bell System has been cast aside in favor of the centrifugal thought process—thinking outside the box, or at least outside the mindset of the proverbial Bell-shaped head.[14] There was a day when a position in the regulatory department of the Bell System was a considered a plum position, a fast track up the corporate ladder.[15] Today, when you open the annual report of a Bell Operat-

---

AT&T accounted for 82.3% of the telecommunications service industry's operating revenues of $84.175 billion. U.S. Statistical Abstract, Tables 926–927 (1985). In 2005 the industry's revenues were $449.3 billion. *Available at* http://www.census.gov/svsd/www/services/sas/sas_data/ 51/2005_NAICS51.pdf. In that year the combined revenues of AT&T and BellSouth were $64.5 billion or 14.3% of the total. *Available at* http://money.cnn.com/magazines/fortune/ fortune500/2006/snapshots/1182.html, and http://money.cnn.com/magazines/ fortune/fortune500/2006/ snapshots/191.html. So, even after the AT&T-BellSouth merger AT&T remains a shadow of its former self.

13. Peter Temin, The Fall of the Bell System 93–94, 151–2, 329 (1987) (describing the difficulties that Archibald McGill, who had been brought in from IBM as Director of Market Management, encountered in attempting to implement market-based thinking at AT&T).

14. "Managers who had internalized the corporate culture were said to have Bell-shaped heads." *Id.* at 58.

15. As Temin observes, "Leaders of the Bell System often acted as if the regulators were their customers—as if they got revenue from regulators, not customers." *Id.* at 58.

ing Company, one of the first facts you will read is how successful the company was in reducing the percentage of revenues subject to regulation. The transformation of the business culture in the telecommunications industry is all but complete.

In a very real sense, AT&T's fall parallels the error that we ascribe to the centripetal regulator—an inordinate preoccupation with the static rather than the dynamic (or regulating through the rearview mirror). When AT&T Chairman John deButts delivered his famous *cris de cour* against the perils of competition at the 1973 National Association of Regulatory Utility Commissioners (NARUC) meetings,[16] he sought to hold back the competitive forces that technology and liberalized entry rules had unleashed.[17] He succeeded only in strengthening the policymakers' resolve to move forward in opening telecommunications markets to competition.[18] A decade later, AT&T sealed its fate when it elected to retain the "profitable" long-distance business rather than the subsidized ("bottleneck") local exchange business at the divestiture.[19]

---

16. John D. deButts, *An Unusual Obligation*, Speech before The National Association of Regulatory Utility Commissioners (September 20, 1973).

17. In the end, it could be argued that AT&T mismanaged both the regulatory process and the political process. DeButts did not expect his 1973 NARUC speech to have the effect that it did, though other senior managers at AT&T had raised concerns about how it would be received. In addition, AT&T's backing of the Consumer Communications Reform Act of 1976, commonly referred to as the "Bell Bill," had a similar effect in strengthening policymakers' resolve to liberalize entry in telecommunications markets. Peter Temin, *supra* note 13, at 113–133.

18. *Id.* at 96–112.

19. Some industry observers thought that AT&T had pulled off a major coup in jettisoning its local exchange business. See, for example, Paul W. MacAvoy and Kenneth W. Robinson, *Winning by Losing: The AT&T Settlement and Its Impact on Telecommunications*, 1 The Yale Journal on Regulation, 1–42 (1983). Other industry observers were less than convinced that this was a coup on the part of AT&T. See, for example, *Telecommunications In Turmoil* by Gerald R. Faulhaber 5 Yale Journal on Regulation 530–531 (1988). It did not take long for the market to reveal that the "bottleneck" local exchange business was, as Willy Sutton famously quipped when asked why he robbed banks, "where the money is." See, for example, Paul W. MacAvoy and

(AT&T was in essence running backwards at full speed through a minefield.) From this decision there would be no recovery, for AT&T spent the next two decades in countless, futile attempts to re-enter the very markets that it had "voluntarily" exited.[20]

The operational mindset at AT&T that enabled it to excel in keeping the trains running on time never managed to escape the "habitual modes of thought and expression" that were the *sine qua non* for its survival. As Peter Temin observes: "The Bell engineers were not interested in what the salesmen reported that customers wanted ... The two groups were in two different worlds, speaking two different languages. They couldn't (or wouldn't) hear each other."[21], [22]

Thomas McCraw argues that "[a]lmost all businesses, no matter how strong they seem to be at a given moment, ultimately fail—and almost always because they failed to innovate."[23] In this respect, AT&T is a remarkable study in contrasts—AT&T's Bell

---

Kenneth W. Robinson, *Winning By Losing: The First Year of the AT&T Divestiture*, 2 The Yale Journal on Regulation 225–262 (1985) (explaining why the predictions made in their first article, that AT&T had pulled off a major coup in exiting the local exchange business, did not come to pass).

20. Leslie Cauley, End of the Line: The Rise and Fall of AT&T (2005).

21. Peter Temin, The Fall of the Bell System 150–151 (1987).

22. This view contrasts sharply with the perspective of the great industrialist and innovator, Charles Franklin Kettering, who was second only to Thomas Edison in the number of inventions to his credit, and served as head of NCR's inventions department and later served as research chief at General Motors. As reported by Bernstein, Kettering observed that "I didn't hang around much with other inventors or the executive fellows. I lived with the sales gang. They had some real notion of what people wanted." See Mark Bernstein, *A Self-Starter Who Gave Us The Self-Starter*, Smithsonian, July 1988, at 126, 128.

23. Thomas K. McCraw, Prophet of Innovation 495–496 (2007). McCraw observes that, "Only through innovation and entrepreneurship can any business except a government-sponsored monopoly survive over the long term." Ironically, in the case of AT&T, it could be argued that it was the "government-sponsored monopoly" and the centripetal way of thinking that it propagated that was the source of its undoing.

Laboratories, a research and development organization that was second to none, and AT&T's management culture that seemed perennially unable to negotiate the turns in the road.[24] AT&T would ultimately succumb, with a little help from the government,[25] to what Joseph Schumpeter referred to as the "perennial gale of creative destruction."

For all these changes in the technological and economic environment of the telecommunications industry it is remarkable how much of the older regulatory institutions and policies remain in place. To be sure, there have been some regulatory innovations. Incentive regulation, increasingly in the form of price caps,[26] has largely supplanted traditional rate-of-return regulation. And there

---

24. Nothing better illustrates the contrast between Bell Labs' innovation and AT&T's staid management than in how the latter initially regarded the former's cellular technology. As part of the 1984 reorganization plan implementing the antitrust breakup of the Bell System, AT&T agreed to have its newly developed cellular business assigned to the Bell Operating Companies in the belief that cellular telephony would remain a minor supplement to the basic wireline service, growing to no more than a million American users. (Cauley, *supra* at 36–37). The one-million subscriber estimate proved to be short by more than two orders of magnitude. (Today the number of cell phone subscribers in the United States exceeds 240 million.) In time AT&T would recognize its mistake and reenter the wireless business by acquiring McCaw Cellular. Subsequently, the wireless business was spun off as part of a financially induced reorganization. Ultimately the wireless business would return again to AT&T when SBC acquired AT&T and assumed its name.

25. In the interest of fairness, we point out that AT&T was forced to do battle simultaneously with both competitors and competitive-handicapping regulatory policies. It was also hamstrung by antitrust remedies that discounted the importance of economies of scope and failed to fully anticipate the nature of market/technological convergence. On this latter point, see William F. Baxter. *Questions and Answers with the Three Major Figures of Divestiture*, in BARRY G. COLE, ED., AFTER THE BREAK-UP: ASSESSING THE NEW POST-AT&T DIVESTITURE ERA 30 (1991). Hence, if competitive handicapping and antitrust polices did not bring about the demise of AT&T, they were at the very least unindicted co-conspirators.

26. See David E. M. Sappington, *Price Regulation*, in Vol. 1 HANDBOOK OF TELECOMMUNICATIONS ECONOMICS 225–293. (M.E. Caves, S.K. Majumdar and I. Vogelsang eds., 2002)

has been some streamlining of regulation and even forbearance for certain services in selected markets. But the old habits of regulation are still in full display over too much of the domain of regulated communications. Nowhere is this better illustrated than in the recent attempts to implement the Telecommunications Act of 1996,[27] designed to overturn the last vestiges of natural monopoly in telecommunications markets.

The FCC's Tortured Implementation of the 1996 Telecommunications Act

The 1996 Telecommunications Act was a watershed event in the history of telecommunications policy in the United States. While it aspired to reform many different areas of telecommunications, a core concern was the opening of local service markets to competition. In essence, it envisioned substituting a policy of "competition-enabling" for direct regulation as the central constraint on the market power of the incumbent providers. The FCC's journey to implement the 1996 Act in line with congressional intent proved to be both a halting and tortuous one. The basis for the FCC's difficulties was its failure to distinguish clearly and consistently between its traditional regulatory, rate-making role and the "competition-enabling" role with which it had been charged under the Act. As explained by Justice Breyer:

> An agency engaged in traditional ratemaking will seek to protect consumers by mandating low prices as an end result. In doing so, the agency will sometimes try to mimic the prices that it believes (hypothetically) the regulated firm (often a legal monopoly) would have set had it been an unregulated firm in a competitively structured industry ... [28]

---

27. Telecommunications Act of 1996, 110 Stat. 56 (codified in scattered sections of 47 U.S.C.).

28. Verizon Communications v. FCC, 535 U.S. 467, 543 (2002). (Breyer, J. dissenting)

> But that regulatory objective—low, competition-mimicking prices—is not the objective of the relevant statutory provision here. The Telecommunications Act is not a ratemaking statute seeking better regulation. It is a deregulatory statute seeking competition.... It finds the competitive process an indirect but more effective way to bring about the common objectives of competition and regulation alike, namely low prices, better products, and more efficient production methods.[29]

The blurring of these two roles ultimately led the FCC to commit errors reflective of what might be characterized as unprecedented regulatory presumption.[30] The FCC's single-minded pursuit of a "competitive outcome" led it to adopt overly broad network sharing rules that encouraged imitation at the cost of innovation and brought investment in the telecom sector to a virtual halt.[31] We have critiqued the FCC's sharing rules for so-called "unbundled network elements" (UNEs) elsewhere.[32] Here it is enough to note simply that the FCC's policies were largely based on an attempt to ensure certain fixed levels of competition. Such an approach is doomed to disappoint for the simple reason that regulators do not have enough information to define what a satisfactory level will be.[33] Not least of the problems is that changing technology and economic conditions inevitably change the character and

---

29. *Id.* at 543, 544.

30. Alfred E. Kahn, Timothy J. Tardiff and Dennis L. Weisman, *The 1996 Telecommunications Act at Three Years: An Economic Evaluation of Its Implementation by the FCC*, 11 Information Economics and Policy 328–329 (1999).

31. See, for example, Robert W. Crandall, Competition and Chaos: U.S. Telecommunications Since the 1996 Telecom Act (2005); Thomas W. Hazlett, *Rivalrous Telecommunications Networks With and Without Network Sharing*, 58 Fed. Comm. L.J. 477 (2006).

32. Glen O. Robinson and Dennis L. Weisman, *Designing Competition Policy for Telecommunications*, The Rev. of Network Econ. 2008 (forthcoming).

33. Dennis L. Weisman, *The (In)Efficiency of the 'Efficient-Firm' Cost Standard*, The Antitrust Bull., Spring 2000, at 210.

degree of competition. Trying to establish the right competitive outcome is at best an invitation to endless regulatory tinkering to keep pace with changing conditions. The FCC's error was to confuse mandating the competitive outcome with fostering the competitive process,[34] a confusion noted by Justice Breyer when the FCC's first efforts to implement the 1996 Act were reviewed by the Supreme Court.[35]

After being repeatedly rebuked and reversed by the courts, the FCC finally revised its onerous unbundling rules and sought to place increased reliance on market forces. But there is an important difference between finding religion in setting sound competition policy and pinball policymaking in which regulatory agencies change their policies only when they encounter an immovable obstacle in the form of the review courts. And although the FCC has more recently signaled some willingness to be guided by general competitive trends in the industry rather than whether sellers have monopoly power at a specific moment in time,[36] there remain strong inertial tendencies toward traditional market share/market power analysis despite their well-known shortcomings in technologically dynamic industries.[37]

---

34. *Id.* at 197.

35. Iowa Utilities Board v. FCC, 525 U.S. 366, 424 (1999) (concurring in part and dissenting in part).

36. See In the Matter of Petition of AT&T for Forbearance, 22 F.C.C.R. 18,705, ¶¶20, 23, 34–35 (2007).

37. This probably explains why the FCC has approved only two applications (Omaha, Nebraska and Anchorage, Alaska) requesting it to forbear from requiring incumbent providers to share network elements with rivals at regulatorily prescribed rates. Regardless of how competitive these two markets may be, they hardly seem like hotbeds of competitive activity compared to the major metropolitan areas for which a slew of forbearance applications was recently rejected by the FCC. A careful reading of these decisions confirms that the FCC has retreated to the myopic calculus of "market-share-equals-market-power" to inform its decision-making. See, e.g., Petitions of Verizon Telephone Companies for Forbearance, 22 F.C.C.R. 21,293 (2007). It remains to be seen whether the courts will exercise the same level of critical scrutiny of the FCC's forbearance decisions as they have in the case of its unbundling decisions. The *Verizon* case is currently before the court of appeals. Report-

In the end, the implementation of the 1996 Act has suffered from the fact that a centrifugal regulator was required when the FCC was more comfortable in its traditional, centripetal mode. That is to say, the FCC defaulted to its traditional regulatory mode in which it substituted its judgment for the marketplace when its task was to unleash the power of these burgeoning markets in a manner that would enable market forces to provide the requisite discipline. In doing so, it basically ignored the Hippocratic injunction by intervening in markets in a manner that discouraged investments in new facilities that would have put competition on a more secure footing. It could also be fairly described as "contra-Schumpeterian" in failing to think of competition as a dynamic process rather than a static outcome. For Schumpeter, competition was first and foremost a process of discovery and learning played out over time. His great insight was to recognize that while the regulator was fixated on the "snapshot," virtually all of the relevant market information was contained in the "movie."

Kahn has offered the same instruction, cautioning against the regulatory temptation to meddle with the competitive process. Kahn has been particularly outspoken in his criticism of the FCC's pricing policies, but more generally he has criticized the infant industry policy of protecting fledgling firms in the hope that they will grow up to become strong competitors. While the FCC has never explicitly endorsed an infant-industry justification for its policies implementing the 1996 Act, a close examination of those policies—particularly those concerned with unbundled network access—strongly suggests that something like infant-industry protectionism is animating them.[38] The experience with infant-industry protection in the telecommunications industry (and in

edly the court, in oral argument, intimated some dissatisfaction with the FCC's cautiousness on the forbearance petition. See, for example, *Judges Question FCC's Reasoning in Verizon Forbearance Order*, TR DAILY, Nov. 17, 2008.

38. The FCC's past embrace of the stepping stone theory certainly has the flavor of infant-industry protections. For a brief summary of the stepping stone model, see Robinson and Weisman, *Designing Competition*, *supra* note 32.

most other regulated industries, for that matter) confirms that such policies will be abused and ultimately serve to impede rather than promote competition—to the detriment of consumers. Infant-industry protection tends to become a self-fulfilling prophecy because "fledgling firms raised in a protected market environment are often incapable of surviving outside of it."[39] Indeed, as Robert Crandall has observed, "regulators inevitably find themselves hostage to inefficient competitors."[40], [41] Essentially this is a public policy counterpart to the Heisenberg's uncertainty principle in physics: The presence of economic regulation invariably alters the course of the market's competitive transition.[42]

By way of summary, economic regulation of the telecommunications industry has failed to keep up with the technological/market upheavals that have irrevocably transformed the telecommunications marketplace. The traditional "command-and-control" model of regulation must defer to a forward-looking model that focuses less on

---

39. Dennis L. Weisman, *Asymmetrical Regulation*, 18(7) TELECOMMUNICATIONS POLICY 502 (1994).

40. Robert Crandall, *Telecommunications Policy in the Reagan Era*, 3 REGULATION 31 (1988).

41. The problem is exacerbated by the short-term perspective of most regulators. When regulators reduce entry barriers artificially in order to jump-start competition and commoditize the market, they tend to attract an inferior breed of competitor—arbitrageurs rather than innovators. By definition, the type of competitor that enters requires constant nurturing, and regulators comply because they believe that this type of competitor is all they can get. In this manner, the regulator's paternalistic policy becomes a self-fulfilling prophecy. The result is a bad equilibrium in which the weak competitors crowd out the durable competitors. It is in this sense that the centripetal regulator trades off innovation (dynamic efficiency) for imitation (static efficiency).

42. One implication of the uncertainty principle is expressed as follows: "The notion of the observer becoming a part of the observed system is fundamentally new in physics. In quantum physics, the observer is no longer external and neutral, but through the act of measurement he becomes himself a part of observed reality. This marks the end of the neutrality of the experimenter."

Available at http://www.thebigview.com/spacetime/uncertainty.html.

emulating competitive market outcomes and more on enabling the competitive process *a la* Professors Schumpeter and Kahn.[43]

The Internet and "Net Neutrality"

Despite its importance, the business of enabling competition in telecommunications markets after 1996 has been largely invisible to the general public. All told, the number of persons who know anything about the controversies in this field might equal the number of the politically energized party members who attend one of the two national political conventions. It's a number that is non-trivial for some purposes (arranging catering, for example), but it would surely pale beside the number of persons who know "something" about the famous "net neutrality" controversy. Which is ironic, for what there is to know about the net neutrality issue is itself controversial. Among the unknowns is what net neutrality means, whether there is a problem to be addressed, and whether, if there is a problem, the FCC has jurisdiction to address it.[44]

---

43. As Thomas Kuhn observed in his classic study: "Political revolutions are inaugurated by a growing sense, often restricted to a segment of the political community, that existing institutions have ceased adequately to meet the problems posed by an environment that they have in part created.... Their success therefore necessitates the relinquishment of one set of institutions in favor of another...."

THOMAS KUHN, THE STRUCTURE OF SCIENTIFIC REVOLUTIONS 92–93 (1962).

44. The literature on this subject is large and, alas, growing larger by the day. A recent and very helpful overview of net neutrality, what it means and what, if anything, should be done about it is provided by Jonathan E. Nuechterlein, *Antitrust Oversight of an Antitrust Dispute: An Institutional Perspective on the Net Neutrality Debate*, AEI Center for Regulation and Market Studies, Working Paper 08-07, February 2008. Representative of the protagonists in the debate, for and against, neutrality regulation are Tim Wu, *Network Neutrality, Broadband Discrimination*, 2 J. OF TELECOMMUNICATIONS AND HIGH TECH. LAW 141 (2003); and Christopher Yoo, *Would Mandating Broadband Net Neutrality Help or Hurt Competition: A Comment on the End-to-End Debate*, 3 J. OF TELECOMMUNICATIONS AND HIGH TECH. LAW, 23

As to the first unknown, the neutrality issue arose to prominence in the wake of a so-called "open access" rule, which involved a question that somewhat overlapped the telecommunications network sharing issue we discussed earlier. Basically the open access issue was whether cable broadband Internet service providers should be required to lease to independent Internet service providers ("ISPs") access to their networks. In opposition to some local communities that sought to force such access, the FCC took the position that cable operators could not be required to provide access to their "pipes" because the cable operators were not common carriers. The Supreme Court agreed with that position.[45] This produced a somewhat awkward differential treatment between cable service providers and telephone carriers because the latter were, for a time, required to provide such nondiscriminatory access (via DSL facilities) to independent ISPs. The FCC, to its credit, recognized the problem and removed the access obligation from telecom carriers as well.[46]

This disposition of the issue didn't end the controversy over open access. In effect it proved to be just a warm up for a more general type of access question that has emerged under the rubric of network neutrality. This new "access" issue is different from the earlier open access issue in a couple of important respects. The open access debate was driven by independent ISPs such as EarthLink and AOL seeking to use the broadband transport facilities of cable and telephone providers. The net neutrality debate is not about giving independent ISPs a right of access to broadband transport facilities in order to provide a competing Internet access service. Rather, it is about allowing Internet content or applications providers—such as Amazon or Vonage—to reach their cus-

(2004); Tim Wu and Christopher Yoo, *Keeping the Internet Neutral? Tim Wu and Christopher Yoo Debate*, 59 Fed. Comm. L. J.575 (2007).

45. National Cable & Telecommunications Ass'n v. Brand X Internet Services, 545 U.S. 967 (2005).

46. See Time Warner Telecom, Inc. v. FCC, 507 F.3d 205 (3d Cir. 2007), *aff'd*, Appropriate Framework for Broadband Access to the Internet over Wireline Facilities, 20 F.C.C.R.14853 (2005)("Wireline Broadband Order").

tomers without unreasonable restrictions or discrimination by the owners of the broadband facilities. And, at the other end of the line (both figuratively and literally), it is about allowing end subscribers to access the Internet content or applications of their choice without unreasonable restriction. For example, AT&T may have an incentive to make it more difficult for its subscribers to access Vonage, whose VoIP technology makes it a competitor to the voice service that AT&T provides over the public switched telephone network.[47] Or, Comcast might have an incentive to discriminate against use of broadband for video downloads that compete with its cable service.

On the face of it the net neutrality issue seems a legitimate concern. If the providers of broadband service do have dominance, one might be reasonably fearful of their ability to discriminate against certain uses and/or users for strategic, anti-competitive purposes. But even without the aid of a newspaper or a blog to fix one's attention on them, possible problems that need "attention" by regulators/legislators can be imagined without end. From the beginning, the real core of the debate over net neutrality has been over whether the potential problems of discrimination by dominant providers has reached the point where an actual problem can be expected with sufficient probability to justify the cost (including the potential error costs associated with false positives) to warrant regulatory intervention.

For its part the FCC initially took a guarded stance. It announced a set of vague principles of network neutrality,[48] but de-

---

47. By focusing on what happens at the two ends of the network, some forms of the neutrality argument resemble the old controversy about competitive equipment supply and consumer use of "foreign attachments." This latter issue became salient when cell phone customers demanded the right to use their new iPhones with any network service provider. The problem is that Apple designed its phone in a manner that required the network to be configured in a way that apparently only AT&T found suitable for its network.

48. As stated in a recent notice of inquiry, In the Matter of Broadband Industry Practices, 22 F.C.C. R. 7894 (2008), the principles are: (1) To encourage broadband deployment and preserve and promote the open and interconnected nature of the public Internet, consumers are entitled to access the

spite the urging of net neutrality advocates adopted no rules.[49] Its reluctance to go further was based on the fact that, with one widely noted exception—which was quickly remedied by the Commission[50]—there was no evidence that a problem existed in the marketplace that warranted a kind of Rubicon-crossing venture into regulation of Internet services—an area that has been treated as presumptively off limits for (administrative) regulation.[51] For starters there was a question whether any provider really enjoyed such dominance in the market that it could adopt a policy of discriminating against uses or users without effective discipline from disaffected customers. Next there was the vexing problem of how

---

lawful Internet content of their choice; (2) To encourage broadband deployment and preserve and promote the open and interconnected nature of the public Internet, consumers are entitled to run applications and use services of their choice, subject to the needs of law enforcement; (3) To encourage broadband deployment and preserve and promote the open and interconnected nature of the public Internet, consumers are entitled to connect their choice of legal devices that do not harm the network; and (4) To encourage broadband deployment and preserve and promote the open and interconnected nature of the public Internet, consumers are entitled to competition among network providers, application and service providers, and content providers.

49. It did impose de facto rules by making these principles conditions for the mergers involving AT&T and MCI. They were rules in the sense that if the applicants did not follow them the mergers would not be granted. See Nuechterlein *supra* note 44, at 8.

50. In the Matter of Madison River Telephone Co., 20 F.C.C.R.19173 (2005) (a local telephone carrier entered into a consent decree with the FCC after it reportedly blocked the ability of its DSL customers to use an independent VoIP service).

51. Internet services have not hitherto completely escaped FCC regulation. For example VoIP service providers have been subjected to a number of regulatory obligations, such as 911 services, assistance to law enforcement and universal service contributions. See IP-Enabled Services; E11 Requirements for IP-Enabled Service Providers, 20 F.C.C.R.10245 (2005); Communications Assistance for Law Enforcement Act and Broadband Access and Services, 20 F.C.C.R. 149889 (2005); Universal Service Contribution Methodology, 21 F.C.C.R. 7518 (2006). All of these cases dealt with Internet services that are essentially indistinguishable from regulated telecommunications services. The regulatory precedent they provide is thus quite limited.

to identify what practices were engaged in for strategic purposes as opposed to legitimate business purposes of network management (for example routing or caching arrangements or priority of traffic based on time sensitivity). Last, but by no means least, there was a problem of regulatory jurisdiction: Does the FCC have direct jurisdiction over Internet services?

The Commission was suddenly jolted from its cautious, hands-off approach in 2008 when a complaint was filed against Comcast for secretly interfering with its customers' peer-to-peer uploading of high-volume files using BitTorrent and similar technologies. Initially, Comcast denied any such interference.[52] Later it admitted to doing so but claimed that it was only for the purpose of managing traffic to avoid congestion on its network. The FCC found that the intentional downgrading of traffic breached its Internet principles, and that those principles were directly enforceable even in the absence of a set of duly promulgated rules. It did not impose any penalty, but directed Comcast to disclose to the Commission and to the public the contours of its network management practices and to submit a compliance plan showing how it intends to adopt nondiscriminatory management practices.[53]

Does the Comcast episode show that the potential problem of discrimination is now actual? We doubt it. This looks to us like a case for invoking (our version of) the Hippocratic oath: Don't try to solve a problem unless you know there is a problem to solve. It is, admittedly a close call. With a degree of managerial clumsiness that is difficult to explain, Comcast from the beginning gave the appearance of strategic discrimination by hiding what it was doing, then when confronted by evidence of what it was doing,

---

52. For our present purposes the manner of interference is not important, but basically it consisted of falsifying the address of targeted peer-to-peer traffic running through its services in a manner that made it undeliverable, at least until the sender reinitiates the uploading.

53. In the Matters of Formal Complaint of Free Press and Public Knowledge Against Comcast Corporation for Secretly Degrading Peer-to-Peer Applications, 23 F.C.C.R. 13028 (2008). Comcast has appealed the FCC's order to the Court of Appeals for the District of Columbia Circuit.

initially denying it. (History teaches that in cases like this the cover-up is almost always more problematic than the offense itself.) Still, managerial clumsiness is not itself a crime and it ought not to be a regulatory offense either unless it manifests itself in plainly illegal practices.

Although the Commission noted the possibility that Comcast's practices were anticompetitive (in order to protect its own video-on-demand service), it did not find that this was Comcast's purpose, and in fact it cited no evidence to support such a conclusion—as a dissent by Commissioner McDowell emphasized. Rather the Commission concluded that the practices were not narrowly tailored to achieve the claimed purpose of minimizing network congestion since other means are available besides targeting certain applications.[54] No doubt there are; the pertinent question is whether the FCC should decide what is and is not acceptable management, and should decide that on the basis of a thin factual record and tenuous jurisdictional basis.[55]

We see two major harms from FCC intervention here. One is the immediate problem of interfering with private management of Internet traffic without clear standards for doing so. The second is the more long-term harm of establishing a precedent for regulatory intervention in an area that has traditionally been largely outside the regulatory arena. Even the FCC previously has been mindful of the benefits of an unregulated Internet.

Which brings us to the third unknown—regulatory jurisdiction. The jurisdictional issue has been somewhat muddied by a separate question as to whether the FCC's policies of net neutrality were directly enforceable. That involves a complicated question of administrative law that we want to finesse in order to address the more fundamental question of whether the FCC has any jurisdiction at all.

---

54. See Matters of Formal Complaint, *supra* at ¶¶47–51.

55. Arguably, Comcast might be charged with consumer deception. The Commission criticized Comcast for not only failing to disclose but for misleading consumers, *Id.* at ¶53. However, this was not the basis for the Commission's intervention. If consumer deception was the concern a declaratory judgment would be an odd and inappropriate way to address it.

Title VI of the Communications Act gives the FCC jurisdiction over cable "communications."[56] But Internet services are classified as "information services."[57] Information services fall within the purview of the agency only to the extent of an amorphous concept called "ancillary jurisdiction," a concept invented by the Commission itself in the early 1960s as a basis for regulating cable in the absence of express statutory authority.[58] Ancillary jurisdiction has always been a slippery notion to say the least. Comcast argued that for the Commission to exercise this jurisdiction (such as it is), the subject at hand must be ancillary to something that is otherwise squarely within the agency's power. The Commission rejected any such limitation:

> Peer-to-peer TCP connections provided through Comcast's broadband Internet access service are undoubtedly a form of 'communication by wire,' so the subject matter at issue here clearly falls within the Commission's general jurisdictional grant under Title I. And though our exercise of authority must be 'reasonably ancillary to the effective performance' of the Commission's responsibility for 'something,' first and foremost, the 'something' Comcast is looking for is right in the Act itself—it is the national Internet policy enshrined in section 230(b) of the Act... and 'six other separate statutory provisions.'[59]

The FCC's remarkably expansive (and flexible) views of its jurisdiction have always been a matter of concern to those who think that agencies do not possess their own political sovereignty.[60] For twenty years the FCC regulated cable television—under its con-

---

56. See 47 U.S.C. §521 ff.

57. See National Cable & Telecommunications Ass'n v. Brand X Internet Services, 545 U.S. 967 (2005). It upheld the FCC's classification of cable modem Internet service as an information service.

58. Southwestern Cable Co. v. United States, 392 U.S. 157 (1968).

59. Matters of Formal Complaint, *supra* note 53, at paras. 15–16.

60. For a discussion of the proposition regarding the tendency of regulation to spread, see Kahn, *supra* note 8, Vol. 2, pp. 28–32. See also Robinson and Weisman, *Designing Competition Policy*, *supra* note 32.

cept of ancillary jurisdiction—without a shred of guidance from the statute. Eventually Congress caught up with its responsibilities and enacted the Cable Communications Policy Act of 1984, which confirmed that the FCC had the power to do what it had been doing for two decades. In the case of the Internet, section 230(b) does provide some general principles, for example, "promote the continued development of the Internet ... preserve the vibrant and competitive free market that presently exists for the Internet ... encourage the development of technologies which maximize user control over what information is received by individuals...."[61] To derive from these principles authority or meaningful standards for regulating Internet traffic management or Internet service providers generally requires a very creative legal imagination. And no such purpose appears to have been contemplated by the congressional draftsmen, as evinced by the title of section 230: "Protection for private blocking and screening of offensive material." Section 230 was part of an effort to enable private users to control Internet porn, not a grant of general power to the FCC to regulate Internet service in general. Even when coupled with scattered other statutory references to the Internet, this section does not seem to be a sufficient basis for asserting what could be a far-reaching regulatory control over the Internet.[62]

At the very least the absence of a clear expression of statutory authority or formal legislative guidance should be reason to pause before proceeding—particularly when industry participants appear to be actively pursuing resolution of outstanding issues. Due deference to the Hippocratic Oath would suggest that regulation be imposed only in the case of a market failure that poses a risk to consumer welfare that is neither transitory or self-correcting in nature. In our view, that standard has not been met. We noted at the out-

61. 47 U.S.C. §230(b).

62. To the extent Section 230 says anything about regulating the Internet, the most relevant part of the section is this: "It is the policy of the United States—to preserve the vibrant and free market that presently exists for the Internet and other interactive computer services, unfettered by Federal or State regulation." 47 U.S.C. §230(b)(2).

set of this discussion that the term net neutrality is not well-defined. The *Comcast* case involved allegedly inappropriate blocking of traffic, which is high on the list of concerns for which neutrality advocates seek regulation. However, it is not the only concern. Some define neutrality more broadly and seek restrictions on *any* differential treatment of Internet traffic, such as differential pricing of different types of Internet services. We think this is wholly unwarranted. First of all there is nothing discriminatory about different treatment/pricing of different services that impose different costs on the provider.[63] It is not only efficient but entirely equitable that Internet applications should pay according to the marginal costs that they impose on the system—most notably in this case the congestion costs that heavy users impose on other users.

Nor by the same token is it discriminatory to price according to the costs of providing special services. "Access tiering" of Internet services—providing faster or higher quality of service—is no more objectionable here than it is in other markets where it is a ubiquitous practice. Those who object to any such tiering (which is probably a minority of neutrality advocates) seem to do so either from a reflexive concern that it will be used to enhance monopoly rents or that it will handicap some applications/content providers at the expense of others. With respect to the first, even if monopoly power is shown, differential pricing may be socially benign.[64] But even if it is not, the proper remedy is to attack the

---

63. This principle is such a commonplace one that it hardly warrants citing authority, but as is often the case, a cite to Alfred Kahn is appropriate. Alfred E. Kahn, *Telecommunications, the Transition from Regulation to Antitrust*, 18–21 AEI-Brookings Joint Center for Regulatory Studies (2006).

64. As a matter of economic theory the welfare effects of price discrimination are ambiguous depending generally on whether the positive effect on output trumps the maldistribution of resources or, in the case of intermediate purchasers, causes secondary distortion in downstream markets. For a brief summary of the effects of price discrimination see DENNIS W. CARLTON AND JEFFREY M. PERLOFF, MODERN INDUSTRIAL ORGANIZATION 289–91 (Third Ed. 2000). (The maldistribution of resources refers to the possibility that price discrimination through market segmentation can lead to a misallocation of resources – some consumers that purchase the service due to the relatively low

monopoly problem itself.[65] As to the second, the objection to access tiering is tantamount to eliminating competition based on superior services that some firms can afford and others cannot. Alice (of Wonderland fame) had three words for this kind of thinking: "stuff and nonsense."

It is somewhat ironic that two of the leading protagonists in the net neutrality debate, Tim Wu and Christopher Yoo, have each invoked Schumpeterian arguments in support of their respective positions for and against neutrality mandates. Wu argues that net neutrality rules will promote competition among and encourage innovation by *applications* (content) providers.[66] Yoo, on the other hand, worries that such rules will stifle investment in infrastructure development, that is, the development of new competitive *service providers.* Both arguments are Schumpeterian in character, and we would say that both are worth evaluating. However, we do have some evidence of the malign effect of burdensome regulatory mandates on incentives for new investment in network infrastructure that should be the foremost concern,[67] while the benign effect on investment in new applications is a matter of speculation.

Multiple Ownership in Media Markets

Limitations on the number of media that can be held in common ownership (both at the local and at the national level) were

---

price in their submarket value it less than other consumers that do not purchase the service due to the relatively high price in their submarket.)

65. Neuchterlein, *supra* at note 44, argues that if intervention is warranted, it is basically for reasons of antitrust policy and enforcement ought to be assigned exclusively to the antitrust agencies. There is much to be said for an antitrust perspective, but we are agnostic over whether it would necessarily produce results superior to regulation. It very much depends on the specific type of remedy one thinks should be adopted for the problem, if there is a problem.

66. Tim Wu and Christopher Yoo, *supra* note 44.

67. See, for example, Thomas W. Hazlett and Anil Caliskan, *Natural Experiments in U.S. Broadband Regulation,* 7 REVIEW OF NETWORK ECONOMICS 460 (2008) and sources cited in note 31 *supra.*

among the earliest rules adopted by the FCC. As with most FCC rules, the multiple ownership rules are complex and have undergone many changes over the years. In general the changes have been in the numerical limits on ownership (usually, but not invariably, in the direction of liberalizing the limits). In one important instance, however, the change has been in the underlying rationale. This is the case with the so-called "group ownership" or national ownership caps on the number of broadcast stations that can be held, nationwide, in common ownership. The rules have a long history; they were first imposed on FM radio in 1940 and thereafter extended to television and AM radio in 1941 and 1943, respectively. The original limits varied by service, six for FM, seven for AM, three for television, but after a series of adjustments each service received a cap of seven, with the condition that, for television at least, two of the stations had to be UHF. The "seven station" rules remained in effect for twenty years.

After a major review of the rules, the Commission in 1984 decided they were unnecessary and should automatically sunset after six years.[68] As a transitional measure it raised the limit to twelve stations nationwide. The transition proved to be indefinite. Congress expressed its displeasure at the FCC's decision to open up national ownership by declaring a temporary moratorium on implementing the decision. Responding to Congress's disapproval, the FCC reversed its decision eliminating the rule, though it did retain the increased limit of twelve, supplemented by an additional limit that prohibited ownership of television stations reaching more than 25 percent of the country's television households.[69]

Two decades on, congressional opposition to relaxing the multiple ownership rules changed. In 1996, Congress was in a deregulatory mood. While most of that mood concentrated on reforming telecommunications policy, some of it targeted broadcast regulation as well, including several of the broadcast ownership

68. Multiple Ownership of AM, FM and Television Broadcast Stations, 100 F.C.C. 2d 17 (1984).

69. Multiple Ownership of AM, FM and Television Broadcast Stations, 100 F.C.C. 2d 74 (1985).

rules. For radio, Congress eliminated the national ownership limit altogether. With respect to television, Congress directed the Commission to eliminate the numerical limit and to raise the audience percentage cap from 25 percent to 35 percent. It also directed the FCC to conduct a biennial review of all of its broadcast ownership rules, with a view to eliminating any that were deemed unnecessary.[70] In its 2002 Biennial Report (released in 2003) the FCC raised the ownership cap to 45 percent.[71] Congress, which was apparently no longer in the deregulatory mood that it was in 1996, responded with attempts to legislate a return to the old caps. In the face of a threatened presidential veto, it compromised and reduced the cap from 45 percent to 39 percent.[72]

If the number 39 appears arbitrary, it was and it wasn't. It was not based on any obvious economic principle or policy, and even as a compromise figure, it is odd; the conventional heuristic of splitting the difference between the high and low marks would have produced an audience cap of 40 percent not 39 percent. As it happens, however, 39 percent was just enough to allow two networks, Fox and CBS, to avoid divesting stations that they had acquired in contemplation of a new limit. (The FCC had given them a temporary waiver of the old limit pending the outcome of the rulemaking proceeding to reconsider the limit.)

Of course, to ask why Congress did not split the difference between the old and the new is something of a tangent. It explains the politics of the matter, but it doesn't explain anything about the underlying issue. What is the right cap? Why, indeed, is there any cap at all? For most of the history of national ownership rules, the Commission avoided a coherent account of just how the national rules affect diversity.

When it first promulgated group ownership rules, the FCC explained their purpose as being "[t]o obviate possible monopoly,

70. Telecommunications Act of 1996, §202, 110 Stat. at 110–12.

71. 2002 Biennial Regulatory Review—Review of the Commission's Broadcast Ownership Rules, 18 FCC Rcd. 13,620 (2003).

72. Consolidated Appropriations Act, 2004, Pub. L. No. 108–199, §629, 118 Stat. 3, 99 (2004).

and encourage local initiative."[73] In 1953, in the course of raising the limit (from three stations in each service–AM, FM and TV–to seven stations), it elaborated on this rationale slightly by saying that the purpose was to "promote diversification of ownership in order to maximize diversification of program and service viewpoints as well as to prevent any undue concentration of economic power contrary to the public interest."[74] Then, thirty years after its adoption of the "seven stations rule" the Commission concluded that the national ownership caps were irrelevant to the central purpose of ensuring diversity of views—which was a function of ownership in particular markets not ownership of stations in different markets. In short, there was no such thing as a national market for purposes of considering diversity.[75] As we noted, after Congress voiced its displeasure at the FCC's decision, the agency reconsidered, but it offered no explanation for its reversal.[76]

When the FCC next addressed the national ownership rules—as part of its first biennial review mandated by Congress—it declined to make any changes in the rules, but along the way it discovered a new rationale for them: The rules promoted localism by strengthening the bargaining power of independently owned (specifically non-network owned) stations, which in turn promoted local diversity. Neither the diversity or localism arguments convinced the court of appeals, which demanded an explanation for why the Commission had ignored the conclusions it had reached in 1984 about the lack of need for the rules.[77] The remanded proceeding was merged into the next biennial review pro-

73. Federal Communications Commission, Sixth Annual Report 68 (1941).

74. Multiple Ownership of AM, FM and Television Broadcast Stations, 18 F.C.C. 288, 291–92 (1953), *aff'd sub nom.*, United States v. Storer Broadcasting, 351 U.S. 192 (1955).

75. Multiple Ownership of AM, FM and Television Broadcast Stations, 100 F.C.C. 2d 17 (1984).

76. Multiple Ownership of AM, FM and Television Broadcast Stations, 100 F.C.C. 2d 74, 96 (1985).

77. Fox Television Stations, Inc. v. FCC, 280 F.3d 1027, 1044 (D.C. Cir. 2002).

ceeding. As part of that review, the Commission in 2003 still retained the rules but increased the audience cap to 45 percent, which, as we noted, Congress adjusted downward to 39 percent.

So the national ownership rule still stands. But what theory or purpose is it standing on? Congress didn't say what purpose it thought the rules served; it probably didn't know. The FCC's Biennial Report offered an expanded version of the localism *cum* diversity argument that it had earlier offered and that had been rejected by the court. The new purpose of the national ownership cap was not to confine the power of group owners generally, but the power of the *networks.* For most of its history, the national ownership rule was not conceived as a means of containing network power. No such rationale appears in the 1984 report, for example. But when the networks became the chief protagonists for eliminating the rule, it became apparent that one of the primary effects of doing so would be to shift the balance of power of networks *vis a vis* independently owned affiliates. The networks wanted to own more stations in order to lessen their dependence on independently owned affiliates for carrying ("clearing") network programs. The independently owned affiliates opposed for the same reason.[78]

What had originally been a concern about horizontal concentration (albeit an odd one since it dealt with concentration across markets) thus became a concern about vertical integration. This segues into another story, about the FCC's vertical integration policies, specifically the agency's concerns about network dominance of affiliated stations. That story is too complicated to relate here.[79] It is enough to say merely that the FCC has been conflicted between, on the one hand, a regulatory mantra of local station responsibility for (and control of) program choices, and on the other hand, the unavoidable economic reality that the production of high-qual-

78. Interestingly, so did the National Association of Broadcasters. Although the NAB generally purports to represent the entire industry, in this case the industry was divided and the association allied with the stations over the networks.

79. Further detail is provided in GLEN O. ROBINSON AND THOMAS B. NACHBAR, COMMUNICATIONS REGULATION, Chapter 4 (2008).

ity television programming involves costs that can be recouped only by revenues derived from exposure to national audiences, which in turn can only be assured by allowing national networks substantial control over what programs are produced and distributed. Historically, the FCC has tacked back and forth between regulatory aspiration and economic reality, producing a mishmash of regulatory restrictions on network control of program choices that have proved an utter failure, even on the FCC's own terms.[80]

The saga of the national ownership rules is only the latest in this controversy over networks versus stations that originated in the dawn of communications regulations. Of particular interest here is how it illustrates the protean character of FCC regulations: when the original rationale for a rule is found to be wanting, keep the rule and find a different rationale. After all, the FCC in 1984 had found that the national ownership rule was not needed to promote diversity or localism. Somewhere in the new debate over networks versus local affiliates this finding was forgotten or ignored. We cannot know what Hippocrates would say about this regulatory episode, but we think he might be suspicious of a doctor who diagnosed an ailment based on conditions that were discovered not to exist, but who prescribed the same medicine to treat a new set of conditions. For his part Schumpeter would likely have declared the ownership rules generally to be a humbug—a misguided interference with what is by any measure a dynamic and competitive (diversified) market. Even assuming that national ownership does

---

80. The best single example is the FCC's so-called "financial interest and syndication rules" (popularly labeled "fin-syn") that forbade networks from buying secondary distribution rights from program producers, which was coupled with a "prime-time access rule" that gave non-network distributors an exclusive claim on one hour of prime time. Both rules were designed to reduce the networks' control over program choices. The silliness of the rules came to be conceded even by the FCC, but for political reasons it found it difficult to extricate itself from them altogether until a court decision officially declared the fin-syn rules to be arbitrary and capricious. See Schurz Communications, Inc. v. FCC, 982 F.2d 1043 (7th Cir. 1992). The prime time access rules, which were always associated with fin-syn, were subsequently repealed by the FCC in 1995. Prime Time Access Rule, 11 F.C.C.R. 546 (1995).

affect the bargaining relationship between networks and affiliated stations in the manner explained (which is quite plausible), there is no reason to think this adversely affects diversity of viewpoints generally or local content in particular. As to the former, the FCC's own findings in 1984 were that diversity is a function of the number of stations in a local market, which is not affected by national ownership. As to the latter, no evidence in the biennial report rulemaking proceeding showed that network-owned stations offer fewer local programs than non-network stations. Apart from local news, the amount of local programming is trivial in any case, so the only question left would be whether local affiliate choices of *national* programs were more suitable to their local audiences than those that were offered by their networks. As to that, the only evidence the FCC identified could only be described as proof of the well known dictum that in law "data" are the plural form of "anecdote." Absent a more robust concept of evidence that the competitive process is adversely affected to the detriment of the end consumer, regulatory intervention here is simply a matter of adjusting private relationships between the networks and their affiliates. As a matter of regulatory principle, Professor Kahn would counsel that the regulator has no business being in that business.[81]

Recommendations and Conclusion

Given the limited ambition of this essay, our critique of FCC regulation has been necessarily abbreviated, selective, and suggestive. Deriving grand lessons from such a thin selection of regulatory episodes will no doubt seem bold if not foolish. Still, we see some persistent patterns in these cases, repeated in other FCC actions not discussed.

Probably the most obvious pattern is the penchant for detailed controls designed to eliminate any unforeseen contingencies that the play of markets might produce. One sees this most sharply in

81. Alfred E. Kahn, *The Uneasy Marriage of Regulation and Competition*, TELEMATICS, Vol. 1, No. 5, 1984, at 15.

the telecommunications area and the attempts by the FCC to fine tune competition in local service markets. We commented earlier on the FCC's attempts to define competition in those markets by fixed standards rather than seeking to ensure that the dynamic force of competition is not foreclosed by artificial barriers to entry or other market failure considerations. The appropriate recommendation here is simple: Once the minimum conditions for competition are in place, do not attempt to regulate certain outcomes. The Schumpeterian corollary to this is: The conditions for competition should be measured by a long-run perspective. We say this fully mindful of Keynes's famous edict about being dead in the long run.[82] By long run we don't mean a life term. But we do mean a period that may exceed the tenure of the regulator.

Admittedly the long versus short-run problem is not uniquely in control of the regulator. When Congress enacted the 1996 Telecommunications Act, it directed the FCC to adopt regulations to implement its local market competition provisions within six months. Dutifully responding, the FCC fell all over itself to put in place sharing rules and pricing rules that were incompletely considered (to put it charitably). These quickly promulgated rules produced more than a decade of litigation in the courts that defeated Congress' desire for quick action—and also immediate results. The FCC had to respond to the six-month deadline for rules, but it did not need to craft rules with a view to producing immediate, short-run results at the expense of a more sedulous, but ultimately more sustainable set of rules for the long run.

---

82. John Maynard Keynes, A Tract on Monetary Reform 65 (1923). The relevant passage is worthy of quotation in full: "But this *long run* is a misleading guide to current affairs. *In the long run* we are all dead. Economists set themselves too easy, too useless a task if in tempestuous seasons they can only tell us that when the storm is long past the ocean is flat again." (Emphasis supplied). For Keynes, much like Schumpeter, it was the process of disequilibrium in the market rather than equilibrium that should occupy economists' attention. See also P.J. McNulty, *Economic Theory and the Meaning of Competition*, LXXXII Quarterly Journal of Economics 648 (1968) (describing the difference between a condition of equilibrium and the behavioral pattern leading to it).

The disposition to control all contingencies leads naturally to an attempt to develop solutions for problems that have not manifested themselves.[83] A degree of anticipation is not a bad thing. It is one of the advantages of administrative regulation over other forms of government control, such as antitrust or other forms of ad hoc interventions. But this virtue can also be a vice of regulation when it leads to premature action, as we believe to be the case in the net neutrality controversy. Perhaps taking literary liberties with Hippocrates, we described this as a Hippocratic oath problem for the simple reason that premature intervention almost always produces more harm than good. We don't claim that it is wrong to anticipate problems; the harm lies in rules that are so anticipatory that the problems they seek to remedy are not well defined and may even serve unwittingly to produce additional problems.

In the case of net neutrality, admittedly, the FCC has not adopted any specific set of regulations. Indeed, as we saw, that was precisely one of the objections raised to its enforcement action in the *Comcast* case. However, the FCC's demand for accounting from Comcast will have the effect of inviting regulatory surveillance of managerial decisions by service providers without the benefit of any clear engineering or business standards—and all in order to stave off possible strategic behavior that has not been shown to be a significant threat to the normal, expected operation of the market. Again, the FCC was clearly responding to political pressures. There have been proposals for legislation to set standards of net neutrality.[84] In defense of the FCC's action one might

---

83. We do not fault the regulator for this behavior *per se*. It is arguably a rational response to an environment that holds the regulator to account for performance metrics that are easily measured (e.g., prices, blocked Internet applications), but not for performance metrics that are less easily measured (e.g., products and services that do not find their way to market, but would have otherwise.) This explains why regulators are not predisposed to foster the type of dynamic competition that Schumpeter viewed to be the most important for consumer welfare.

84. See, e.g., Internet Freedom Preservation Act, S. 215, 110th Cong. (2007).

argue that its intervention in the *Comcast* case might have the effect of heading off congressional action that would be more mischievous than the FCC's limited actions. Perhaps. However, given the previous history of FCC actions under the claim of "ancillary jurisdiction" (we have in mind the early history of cable television regulation), one must be anxious about entrusting a matter of this potential importance—the regulation of the Internet—to the agency's undefined, standardless discretion.

Choosing between an unfettered agency and an uncontrollable legislator is, we concede, a little like choosing between two equally loose cannons. Congress's action in the case of the broadcast group ownership rules is a case in point. In 1984 when the FCC decided that the rules were irrelevant to the ostensible purpose of promoting diversity, Congress cut off funds to implement the change. Fast forward a little more than a decade, when Congress in 1996 directed the FCC to take a close look at its multiple ownership rules, including the group ownership rules, with a view towards relaxing or removing any that were not shown to be currently needed. Although slow to respond at first, the FCC under prodding from the courts made a number of far-reaching changes in all of its ownership rules in 2003, including raising the cap on the group ownership limits that it had attempted to remove in 1984. Congress immediately responded with what was basically a reprise of 1984: a demand to cease and desist from any changes in the cap, followed by a compromise solution to allow a slight increase in the limit in order to accommodate two of the national networks. Political scientists will no doubt shrug and say, well, Congress is run by politicians not philosophers.

As it happens so is the FCC, and here we suggest is the appropriate place to draw the line between politics and principles. The Communications Act does delegate to the agency a considerable degree of policymaking discretion, but it is not a "home rule" charter conveying independent political sovereignty. The lesson, and the correlative recommendation, is simple: Do not anticipate legislative commands or respond to the wishes of congressional members except where they are clothed in formal legislation. Make Congress do its own work. We cannot say that such a recommendation, if followed, would have changed the outcome of the national ownership rules, but it might have. When Congress in 1984 cut off funds to implement the elimination of the rules, it was only a one-year moratorium. At any time thereafter the agency could have acted on its 1984 judgment. It did not do so. Indeed, it did not do so even after the 1996 Act directed a review of its rules. Its failure to follow through on its 1984 conclusion could not be defended as principled; indeed, it was precisely on that score that the court of appeals reversed the agency in 2002 and forced it to confront the issue.

We began this essay with the idea that the collective wisdom of Hippocrates, Schumpeter, and Kahn could constructively inform the role of regulation in the rapidly evolving telecommunications industry. The objective of regulation in telecommunications, regulating the monopoly prices paid by consumers, is no longer the primary focus of regulation; competition has made that objective largely moot. Today regulators have shifted their focus to regulating that competition in order to ensure its success. While there may be some legitimate role for regulation to play in facilitating the transition from monopoly to competition, we think it is one that poses great risks of undermining the very competition it is supposed to foster. As a result, due deference to the Hippocratic oath calls for a more limited role for *ex ante* regulation going forward. Schumpeter believed that the regulators' efforts to control transitory market power were misguided because they interfered with the competitive process—dynamic efficiency always trumps static efficiency. It would be difficult to point to an industry more technologically dynamic than the telecommunications industry. Kahn recognized that the regulator's penchant for competitive handicapping interfered with market rivalry in a manner that served to harm rather than benefit consumers.[85] And both Schumpeter and Kahn would counsel that regulators should serve to pro-

---

85. Indeed, as FCC staff officials Haring and Levitz long ago observed: "If one of the runners in a race is artificially handicapped, that may make the rivalry less intense and the contest less capable of producing a superior performance." John Haring and Kathy Levitz, *What Makes The Dominant Firm*

tect the integrity of the competitive process rather than protect selected competitors. Their counsel, though often unheeded, is precisely on point.

The collective wisdom of these teachers serves to reinforce the fundamental theme of this essay that in refereeing the struggle between competing firms, the referee's role must be circumscribed. The referee must not be an active party to the contest. Nor should it seek to shape the outcome according to narrowly defined, prefixed outcomes. These ideas are not natural for those steeped in the centrifugal model of traditional regulation. And yet, it is only in escaping these traditional modes of thought and expression that we can complete the transition to the centripetal model of regulation that the times require—a model that is focused less on the control of market power and more on unleashing the power of markets.

Dominant? Office of Plans and Policy, Working Paper Series, No. 25, Federal Communications Commission, April 1989, note 10.

CHAPTER 2

Redefining the Landscape of Internet Regulation

James B. Speta

We are moving, at times steadily and at times in fits and starts, towards a world of big, ubiquitous broadband. Unfortunately, we are moving without any real policy leadership. Although the communications industries of this new world will be even more important than they are now to economic growth, to education, to entertainment, and to politics, we do not yet have a good view of what the regulatory landscape of big, ubiquitous broadband will look like. After consistently declaring that the Internet should remain unregulated, the FCC recently effected an avulsive change in tone—stating that it had the authority to go so far as to set prices and regulate terms of service on the Internet. These claims face a substantial legal challenge: I have previously expressed doubt in their merits,[1] although the Supreme Court has since seemed to endorse them.[2] But those legal issues are not my project here, significant as they are. What is needed now in communications policy is leadership—*strong* leadership, *substantive* leadership. We need a conversation that recognizes the substantial uncertainty present in Internet regulation, that attempts to articulate competing models of Internet regulation in a comprehensive fashion, and that articulates a rational course for Internet policy.

---

1. *See* James B. Speta, *FCC Authority To Regulate the Internet: Creating It and Limiting It*, 35 Loy. U. Chi. L. Rev. 15 (2003).

2. Nat'l Cable & Telecom. Ass'n v. Brand X Internet Servs., 545 U.S. 967, 996 (2005) ("[T]he Commission remains free to impose special regulatory duties on facilities-based ISPs under its Title I ancillary jurisdiction").

This conversation should be much more robust than recent policy pursuits, in which the framing of fundamental questions and the offering of possible answers engages explicitly and broadly. It is hard to overstate how important these questions are or how poorly they have been handled in the recent past. I do not naively assert that answers will be easy, if only parties will engage. Neither do I (even more naively) assert that conversation necessarily leads to agreement. Communications policy is hard—that is, in part, why it is fun[3]—and parties have multi-billion dollar investments and bedrock personal liberty issues to defend.

But leadership, conversation, and comprehensive inquiry have been lacking in recent communications policymaking. Most tellingly, the FCC's recent *Comcast Order*[4] suggests a fundamentally more aggressive regulatory philosophy, one that the FCC has sprung on the country without any substantial inquiry or explanation. In this essay, I argue that one of the most important tasks for the new administration will be to engage industry, public interest groups, and the public at large on Internet policy matters. Good models exist for the sort of conversation that I imagine to address the three most pressing questions: (a) who regulates? (b) what is being regulated? and (c) what is the theory of regulation? First, I describe the significant change in tenor that comes from the FCC's recent foray into Internet regulation. Then, I suggest two models for developing the policy leadership that we need. One of these models is largely internal to the current institutions: It is based on the hope that new leaders of the FCC will take policy more seriously and address Internet regulation systematically (as to which I offer a framework). The second of these models is more exter-

3. *Cf.* Justice Antonin Scalia, *Judicial Deference to Administrative Interpretations of Law*, 1989 Duke L.J. 511, 511 ("Administrative law is not for sissies-so you should lean back, clutch the side of your chairs, and steel yourselves ...").

4. Formal Complaint of Free Press and Public Knowledge Against Comcast Corp. for Secretly Degrading Peer-to-Peer Applications, Memorandum Opinion and Order, FCC 08-183 (Aug. 20, 2008) (hereinafter *Comcast Order*).

nal to the current institutions, but has a precedent in the related field of antitrust. The recent Antitrust Modernization Commission succeeded in marshalling a significant body of evidence and recommendations, consistent with some of the best scholarship and practice. A Communications Policy Modernization Commission might provide a needed jumpstart to thinking at the FCC. I prefer this second model, given both the need to build consensus and the FCC's failings in the *Comcast Order*, but recognize that it would require a greater policy move to form the commission, while the FCC (if new leaders were so inclined) could begin under its current authority.

New Uncertainty for Internet Regulation

In the FCC's recent *Comcast Order*, the FCC articulated a theory of Internet regulation that, on its face, was surprisingly broad. In essence, the Commission asserted that the Communications Act of 1934 gave it as much authority over Internet services as it had exercised over traditional telephone services: the authority to require tariffs, to set prices, even to certificate services. The FCC asserted that it had this power even if Internet services were not "common carrier" services.[5] To be sure, the FCC did not exercise all of this power, for it merely ordered Comcast to cease and desist from blocking certain kinds of Internet traffic. But the FCC described and defended its power in the broadest possible terms.

The FCC's assertion of broad regulatory authority, and the implied assertion that the exercise of such regulatory authority may be justified, marks a severe departure from both the agency's doctrine and tenor for decades. The *Computer II* decisions defined a strategy under which the FCC has consistently treated emerging, data-intensive services only to the lightest regulation. In *Computer II*, the FCC held that data processing services were "enhanced services" and not common carrier services. The FCC made this move,

---

5. *Comcast Order* ¶¶ 16–17.

all concede, in order to keep outside of common carrier regulation a service that was (or at least could be) competitively provided.[6] But the FCC also recognized that pushing "enhanced services" outside of the common carrier definition denied to the agency some regulatory authority, "while those who provide basic services would continue to be regulated, and enhanced service vendors would not be subject to rate and service provisions of Title II of the Communications Act."[7]

Of course, the FCC in *Computer II* did maintain that its ancillary, Title I authority, gave it substantial authority to regulate enhanced services if it so chose.[8] The Commission conceded, however, that defining a service outside of Title II would result in a lighter form of regulation: "Title II and Title III provide the principal regulatory forms of the Communications Act," and "[e]ven though an activity [otherwise] falls within our subject matter jurisdiction, our ability to subject it to regulation is not without constraints."[9]

The FCC's most important (and more recent) Internet decisions reflect a similar set of beliefs: First, that Internet services demanded a different form of regulation from traditional common carriage; and, second, that Title I regulation of Internet services would be, at most, very light. For example, in the IP-enabled services rulemaking notice, which formed the basis of many subsequent opinions, the FCC noted "its established policy of minimal regulation of the Internet and the services provided over it."[10] Similarly, the Commission noted the difference between common car-

---

6. *See, e.g.*, Robert Cannon, *The Legacy of the FCC's Computer Inquiries*, 55 Fed. Comm. L.J. 167, 169 (2003) ("In addition, this is not a history of technologically based regulation, segregating one computer from another based on the technology employed. Rather, this is a market policy, segregating competitive markets from noncompetitive markets.").

7. Amendment of Section 64.702 of the Commission's Rules and Regulations (Second Computer Inquiry), 77 F.C.C. 2d 384, 430 (1980).

8. *E.g.*, *id.* at 432.

9. *Id.* at 432–33.

10. IP-Enabled Services, *Notice of Proposed Rulemaking*, 19 F.C.C.R. 4863, 4865 (2004).

rier regulation and the alternative of ancillary regulation: "Various regulatory obligations and entitlements set forth in the Act—including a prohibition on unjust or unreasonable discrimination among similarly situated customers and the requirement that all charges, practices, and classifications, and regulations applied to common carrier service by 'just and reasonable'—attach *only* to entities meeting this [common carrier] definition."[11]

In the *Vonage* order, in which the FCC preempted state regulation of VoIP services, the FCC noted that its deregulatory policies applied whether VoIP was a traditional telecommunications service or an information service. If it was a telecommunications service, then it was subject to the Commission's prior deregulation of nondominant carriers and its findings that "prohibiting tariffs would promote competition and the public interest, and that tariffs for these services *may actually harm consumers* by impeding the development of vigorous competition."[12] If Vonage's service were an information service, the same policies would apply, for "it would be subject to the Commission's long-standing national policy of nonregulation of information services, particularly regarding economic regulation."[13] The Commission there recalled its history: "In a series of proceedings beginning in the 1960s, the Commission issued orders finding that economic regulation of information services would disserve the public interest because those services lacked the monopoly characteristics that led to such regulation of common carrier services historically."[14]

These themes were echoed when the FCC classified all Internet access services as "information services," which the agency said "es-

---

11. *Id.* at 4879 (emphasis added); *see also id.* at 4892. ("The Act distinguishes between 'telecommunications service[s]' and 'information service[s],' and applies particularly regulatory entitlements and obligations to the former class but not the latter.")

12. Vonage Holding Corp. Petition for Declaratory Ruling Concerning an Order of the Minnesota Public Utilities Commission, 19 F.C.C.R. 22,404, 22,416 (2004), *aff'd*, 483 F.3d 570 (8th Cir. 2005).

13. *Id.* at 22,416–17.

14. *Id.* at 22,417.

tablishes a minimal regulatory environment for wireline broadband Internet access services to benefit American consumers and promote innovative and efficient communications."[15] In so doing, the FCC noted that "a wide variety of competitive and potentially competitive providers and offerings are emerging in this marketplace."[16] Finally, the FCC thought that Congress itself was pushing policy in the direction of "light" regulation: "[W]e must consider the broadband objectives Congress established in section 706. Those objectives make clear that the Commission must encourage the deployment of advanced telecommunications capability to all Americans by removing barriers to infrastructure development."[17]

I do not wish to exaggerate matters. In both *Computer II* and since, the FCC has maintained that it has significant regulatory authority under Title I, should it choose to use it—although it has tended both not to use it and to state that its Title I authority is more limited than its common carrier authority. And, at the same time that it was issuing the order deregulating wireline Internet access services, the FCC issued the Policy Statement that urged the "four Internet freedoms."[18] The Commission there stated that it had "jurisdiction necessary to ensure that providers of telecommunications for Internet access or Internet-Protocol-enabled (IP-enabled) services are operated in a neutral manner."[19] Indeed, this Policy Statement provided much of the basis for the FCC's recent action.

Nevertheless, one fundamental limit has always been maintained: that ancillary regulation under Title I is something *less* than the full panoply of economic regulation available to the Commission under Title II. As the D.C. Circuit said in a typical case (in

---

15. Appropriate Framework for Broadband Access to the Internet over Wireline Facilities, 20 F.C.C.R. 14,853, 14,855 (2005).

16. *Id.* at 14,880; *see also id.* at 14,865 ("[B]roadband Internet access services in most parts of the country are offered by two established platforms, which continue to expand rapidly, and by several existing and emerging platforms and providers, intermodal and intramodal alike.")

17. *Id.* at 14,894–95.

18. Appropriate Framework for Broadband Access to the Internet over Wireline Facilities, *Policy Statement*, 20 F.C.C.R. 14,986 (2005).

19. *Id.* at 14,988.

which the Court denied the FCC authority to control the rates of a private dark-fiber service, even though the service was offered by a company that also provided other common carrier services), "the specific regulation of rates under title II of the Act and the requirement to obtain permission prior to withdrawal of service pursuant to section 214 do not, without more, apply to the private service offered by a sometime common carrier."[20]

This is why the FCC's *Comcast Order* is so jarring. The *Order* alters the FCC's more-or-less consistent tone of nonregulation of Internet services in three important ways. First, the FCC's action implicitly questions the degree of competition in Internet access services. While the FCC has previously avoided taking a strong position on whether such services were competitively provided or not, it has always maintained that its decisions should be driven by long-term view of the market possibilities and not by a current assessment of the state of competition.[21] The *Comcast Order*, by contrast, advances the theory that Comcast's actions "pose significant risks of anticompetitive abuse."[22] The core of that theory is that Comcast was blocking BitTorrent video traffic in order to protect revenues that it was earning from traditional cable television

20. Southwestern Bell Tel. Co. v. FCC, 19 F.3d 1475, 1482 (D.C. Cir. 1994).

21. *E.g.*, Appropriate Framework for Broadband Access to the Internet over Wireline Facilities, 20 F.C.C.R. at 14,881 ("We find that the parties' competing analyses, though useful, fail to recognize all of the forces that influence broadband Internet access service deployment and competition, so we adopt neither. The parties' arguments are premised on data that are both limited and static. Most importantly, the competing analyses fail to recognize the dynamic nature of the marketplace forces.... We find that an emerging market, like the one for broadband Internet access, is more appropriately analyzed in view of larger trends in the marketplace, rather than exclusively through the snapshot data that may quickly and predictably be rendered obsolete as this market continues to evolve.")

22. *Comcast Order* ¶ 47; *see also id.* at ¶ 50. ("To the extent, however, that providers choose to utilize practices that are not application or content neutral, the risk to the open nature of the Internet is particularly acute and the danger of network management practices being used to further anticompetitive ends is strong.")

services.[23] But this theory makes sense only if Comcast has a monopoly position to defend in video (a position the FCC has not been willing to take in previous proceedings[24]) and enough market power in the Internet access service to prevent customers from switching to DSL.[25] While the core of the FCC's order was based on Comcast's failure to disclose its particular practices, the Commission's relief went beyond disclosure to mandating "application neutral" network management practices.

Second, the FCC advanced a very broad theory of its regulatory authority over Internet services. Most notably, the FCC asserted that its Title I ancillary authority allowed it to impose exactly the same form of economic regulation that characterized common carrier regulation. Looking to Section 1 of the Act, the FCC said it had authority to adopt any rule to ensure that wireline communications were "rapid" and "efficient" and provided "at reasonable charges."[26] Coming quite close to endorsing price regulation, the Commission found "that exercising jurisdiction over the complaint would promote the goal of achieving 'reasonable charges'" by allowing cable customers to download Internet video, "much of it free."[27] The FCC echoed this theme when it said that its action was ancillary to its authority under Section 201 of the Act to ensure reasonable charges and asserted that it was adjusting economic burdens between Comcast and other Internet companies.[28] Although the FCC did not subject Comcast to any price regulation,

---

23. *Id* ¶ 5.

24. *Annual Assessment of the Status of Competition in the Market for the Delivery of Video Programming*, Twelfth Annual Report, 21 F.C.C.R. 2503, 2506 (2006) (stating that competition to cable is helping consumers, without directly stating that the market is, or is not, competitive).

25. Carl Kaysen and Donald F. Turner, Antitrust Policy 157 (1959) ("[T]ying implies some market power on the part of the seller practicing it.... The power frequently arises because of legal monopoly enjoyed by the seller in the tying good—a patent or a copyright—but it need not. Some power in the market for the tying product will suffice, whatever its basis.")

26. *Id.* ¶ 16.

27. *Id.*

28. *Id.* ¶ 17.

its jurisdictional theory completely eliminates the distinction that it previously recognized—that ancillary regulation, no matter how broad, stopped short of including traditional economic regulation.

Third, the *Comcast Order* has the tone of an invigorated FCC supervision of Internet services, and particularly of an FCC imposing broad and specific rules of practice. Of course, as the FCC itself noted, it has frequently said that it would monitor the market to ensure that carriers did not overstep their bounds. But each of these prior statements (with one exception[29]) came in an order or decision in which the agency was generally deregulating or was refusing to impose a condition sought by an opponent to a merger.[30] Moreover, the FCC has usually said that it will proceed on a case-by-case basis to address concerns. In the *Comcast Order* itself, the FCC hailed the value of adjudication in responding to criticism that it was acting in an area where it had not previously adopted rules.[31] But the irony is palpable, for the FCC adopted a rule of practice much broader than was required by the case. The FCC did not simply order *Comcast* to stop sending "reset" packets to interrupt peer-to-peer communications. The FCC instead articulated a very strong presumption against any network management techniques that discriminated between applications as well as those that discriminated on the basis of content: "To the extent, however, that providers choose to utilize practices that are not application or content-neutral, the risk to the open nature of the Internet is particularly acute and the danger of network management practices being used to further anticompetitive ends is strong. As a result, it is incumbent on the Commission to be vigilant and subject such practices to a searching inquiry...."[32]

---

29. The exception is the *Madison River Consent Decree*, in which the FCC and a local telephone company entered a consent order under which the telephone company agreed to stop blocking VoIP ports on its Internet service. *See Madison River Commun.*, Order, 20 F.C.C.R. 4295 (EB 2005).

30. *See Comcast Order* ¶39 (citing *Wireline Broadband Order*, *Cable Modem Declaratory Ruling*); *see also id.* ¶27 (discussing Comcast/Adelphia/Time Warner Merger Order).

31. *See id.* ¶¶29–33.

32. *Id.* ¶50.

In sum, the FCC's more or less consistent approach to enhanced (then information, then Internet) services has been to leave them unregulated and to maintain that its own authority over them had important limits. The *Comcast Order*, while only one decision, may herald a significant change in course. In all events, it introduces both uncertainty and opportunity for the next administration.

Rebuilding a Way Forward

What I believe is needed now is discussion and analysis of the possibilities of Internet access and the shape of possible Internet regulation to respond to the seeming shift in course that the *Comcast Order* signals. That order may or may not be correct (I think its broader aspects are almost surely incorrect), but its premises merit much more extended analysis. The market for usefully high-speed Internet access may (or may not) be relatively concentrated. That concentration may (or may not) create incentives for the providers to interfere with applications and content innovation. And the appropriate response to any such interference may (or may not) be broad restrictions on the access providers. But—remarkably—one cannot look to FCC research or decisions for answers to these fundamental questions, or even much engagement with them in the past five years.

Leadership on these issues could take two forms. In the first, the FCC's new leadership could systematically attempt to define the challenges and models of Internet regulation, gathering data, and holding serious public workshops to refine strategy. Alternatively, Congress or the administration could create a body similar to the Antitrust Modernization Commission,[33] populated with academic and industry experts. This body would be given a period of time (the AMC had 3 years) to define a series of issues, take

33. *See* Antitrust Modernization Commission Act of 2002, §11054(h), 116 Stat. 1856, 1857.

comments and develop evidence, and issue recommendations. Congress appropriated $4 million for the work of the AMC, and some similar resources would be necessary.

Each of these models has advantages (to which I will turn shortly), but either commission must grapple with three fundamental issues in short order: better marketplace data, better economics, and better articulation of regulatory models.

1. *Technical Feasibility.* The commission should first convene a series of workshops on the state of the broadband market, including both current deployment statistics and discussion of future scenarios. The first step in developing a regulatory strategy is a better sense of the current market and the possible technological futures. The FCC last year did announce significant improvements in the collection of broadband services data to reflect both the evolving definition of broadband and the means of broadband deployment, but the degree to which this was overdue cannot be exaggerated. The FCC's broadband statistics defined "broadband" at an unreasonably slow speed given consumer demands, and the data collected on deployment were hardly detailed enough to provide an accurate picture of the market. The commission should build on this with technical roundtables discussing evolving technologies and the prospects for their commercial deployment. In the first few years after the Telecommunications Act of 1996, the FCC organized a series of such technical roundtables, which framed the agency's reports to Congress and its evolving IP strategies.[34]

2. *Economics.* A second series of workshops should build on this technical information, both concerning the current market and reasonably possible futures, to discuss the extent to which various market segments are (or are likely to be) competitive. In these workshops, the questions would be familiar: What are the various segments of the Internet market; how many players are in the market; what are the competitive dimensions of those markets; how

---

34. *See* http://www.fcc.gov/Bureaus/Common_Carrier/Public_Notices/1998/da982004.html.

do the markets intersect with one another? Much useful work has been done and is being done in the academy on these questions, but express engagement by and with policymakers on these questions would be useful.

Again, it is hard to exaggerate the absence of this engagement in the current policy process. Although the seeming heart of its *Comcast Order* is an economic argument (that Comcast interrupted peer-to-peer sessions in order to protect its own video products), the *Order* does not cite a single economist, economics article, or any economics theory that supports its view. Only two economists testified at the public hearings that the FCC held, and neither of them advanced the FCC's theory (one of them strongly argued that any FCC action against Comcast would not be supported by economic theory). A majority staff report of the House Committee on Energy and Commerce has also just concluded that the FCC (generally through the person of the Chairman) had suppressed important data necessary for regulatory decisionmaking.[35]

If the FCC-led option were chosen, the need for transparency and open participation would be especially great. I think that the FCC ought to hold the workshops in conjunction with other government agencies. In particular, the Federal Trade Commission can contribute additional economics expertise. The FTC has already held useful hearings on some Internet competition issues,[36] and, given that agency's assertion of overlapping jurisdiction over the Internet, a joint workshop would be part of a useful, public dialogue over the respective roles of the two agencies. In this re-

35. Subcommittee on Oversight and Investigations of the House Energy and Commerce Committee, Deception and Distrust: The Federal Communications Commission under Chairman Kevin J. Martin, at 2–3 (Dec. 2008) *available at* http://energycommerce.house.gov/images/stories/Documents/PDF/Newsroom/fcc_majority_staff_report_081209.pdf.

36. *E.g.*, FTC Public Workshop: Possible Anticompetitive Efforts to Restrict Competition on the Internet (2002), *available at* http://www.ftc.gov/opp/ecommerce/anticompetitive/index.shtm; FTC Workshop To Examine Broadband Connectivity, including Net Neutrality (2007), *available at* http://www.ftc.gov/opa/2007/01/broadbandwrkshp.shtm.

gard, the extraordinarily productive joint hearings on IP and competition issues held by the FTC and the Department of Justice could provide a useful model.

Second, FCC commissioners, FTC commissioners, and members of the executive branch (the assistant secretary of commerce for communications and information) should convene and participate in any hearings jointly, together with key staff members. Although the agencies speak through their decisions and all of these officials participate in conferences and give speeches, sustained joint participation would enable the public and the regulated community to observe the agencies' engagement and working views.

Third, commission hearings ought to be rigorous. The FCC's most recent, high-profile public hearings—the media concentration field hearings and the public hearings on the *Comcast Order* —simply were not designed for the rigorous development and examination of facts. Substantial portions of these hearings were given over to floor statements by those with no particular expertise in the subject matter and with no particular access to the facts. The structure of the hearings did not allow the actual discussion of important ideas. In the media concentration hearings, the Commissioners said very little, and academics and industry members were restricted to very short speeches, with no interaction. Public participation is, of course, important, especially in contested areas such as these. In its media concentration proceedings, the FCC did develop a significant number of studies, although the process of evaluating those studies could have been more rigorous. But in the *Comcast* proceedings, the Commission did nothing that resembled fact-finding—either in an adjudicatory or rulemaking sense. The parties did not call witnesses themselves; there was no testimony or cross-examination on the basis of admissible evidence; and many of the technical experts called admitted to speculating about the underlying practices. We will have to see whether the FCC developed a record that the D.C. Circuit will call adequate for the very limited remedy the FCC actually ordered. But the FCC did nothing to develop a record adequate for the bigger policy questions raised by the proceeding.

3. *Regulatory Models.* The commission, on its own or in conjunction with the other regulators, should also, as a third step, convene a series of workshops and discussions of different regulatory models. This was the point of the IP-enabled services notice —to consider whether the nonregulation model that had previously dominated was still in the public interest. But the question of regulatory models is, of course, much broader. At one extreme, one could consider reimposing common-carrier regulation on all Internet services. There is, after all, a substantial argument that the classification of Internet transit as an information service has no true technical basis: Internet services are as much transport services as traditional telephony. I do not view this as a good idea, and I do not think that any other commentator seriously wishes for an unyielding common carrier system applicable to all services. But given the *Comcast Order*, it would be useful to develop a consensus recommendation (and to hear the FCC Commissioners say so). At the other end of the spectrum, Professor Philip Weiser, through his Silicon Flatirons project, has recently proposed a model of self-regulation for the Internet, prompted in part by the need for closer engagement on the "reasonable network management issues" raised by the *Comcast Order*.[37]

When he was FCC Chairman, Michael Powell frequently spoke on the meta-structures of regulation. In recent years, the discussion has moved back to specific regulatory issues and away from self-conscious contemplation of regulatory models. This is understandable, especially given the failure of the attempt to "rewrite the Communications Act" that so many (myself included) thought would succeed in 2005–2006. Nevertheless, the need is great.

I think that these three steps provide a framework for leadership on Internet policy. I would like to believe that a new Chairman of the FCC could lead that agency forward through these issues. The FCC has a degree of institutional and industry expertise

37. Philip J. Weiser, Exploring Self-Regulatory Strategies for Network Management, Aug. 25, 2008, *available at* http://www.silicon-flatirons.org/documents/publications/summits/WeiserNetworkManagement.pdf.

that it would be difficult to duplicate, and it has in the past been able to broadly and deeply address important policy issues. (I am here thinking, most recently, of its work on spectrum policy, culminating in the Spectrum Policy Task Force Report.[38]) Additionally, if the FCC were able to lead the way, it would save the time that an external commission would take. On the other hand, an external commission could garner a degree of credibility that the FCC, unfortunately, is currently lacking. The external commission could also work more broadly, recommending statutory changes that, perhaps, the FCC could not.

Recommendation and Conclusion

I recommend that the new administration order systematic, substantive inquiry into Internet policy. New leadership is needed at and from the FCC, and, if that agency cannot be relied upon to provide it, then the administration must appoint a new commission to do so, perhaps along the lines of the recent Antitrust Modernization Commission that was charged with making recommendations to update our antitrust laws. New leadership on Internet policy is especially needed, given the significant uncertainties created by the FCC's recent *Comcast Order*. That *Order* suggests a fundamental and ill-conceived departure from the "non-regulation" of the Internet that the FCC has long practiced and that many experts regard as having been successful.

Indeed, the FCC articulated a vision of its regulatory authority over the Internet as broad as its authority over traditional common carrier services, going so far as to suggest that economic regulation of Internet services could be part of the agency's agenda. This new theory and the agency's new tone were hardly based on a substantial inquiry into the state of Internet competition. Even the agency's proceedings concerning Comcast's specific practices were more theater than fact-finding, and its order created a far

38. *See generally* James B. Speta, *Spectrum Policy Experiments: What's Next?*, 2008 U. Chi. Legal F. 389.

broader limit on network management than was necessary to decide the case (a limit that was, of course, not specifically noticed or substantially evaluated).

Given the importance of communications to our economy and our polity—and given that communications is increasingly dominated by Internet communications—we need a vigorous and rigorous investigation of Internet markets, Internet economics, and Internet regulatory possibilities, and a clearly articulated set of policies.

CHAPTER 3

Network Neutrality after *Comcast*: Toward a Case-by-Case Approach to Reasonable Network Management

Christopher S. Yoo

Introduction

Over the past few years, network neutrality has emerged as perhaps the most contentious issue in communications policy. The issue has been the focus of numerous congressional hearings[1] and played a pivotal role during the consideration of comprehensive reform legislation in 2006.[2] Network neutrality also drew substantial attention from the Federal Trade Commission, which conducted two days of hearings and authored a lengthy report on the

1. *See, e.g., The Internet Freedom Preservation Act of 2008: Hearing on H.R. 5353 Before the Subcommittee on Telecommunications and the Internet, H. Comm. on Energy and Commerce*, 110th Cong. (May 6, 2008); *Net Neutrality and Free Speech on the Internet: Hearing Before the Task Force on Competition Policy and Antitrust Laws, House Committee on the Judiciary*, 110th Cong. (March 11, 2008); *Communications Reform Bill Hearing II: Hearing on S. 286 Before the S. Comm. on Commerce, Science & Transportation*, 109th Cong. (2006); *Network Neutrality: Competition, Innovation, and Nondiscriminatory Access: Hearing Before the Telecom and Antitrust Task Force of the H. Comm. on the Judiciary*, 109th Cong. 4 (2006); *Net Neutrality: Hearing Before the S. Comm. on Commerce, Science & Transportation*, 109th Cong. (2006).

2. *See* Christopher S. Yoo, *Network Neutrality and the Economics of Congestion*, 94 Geo. L.J. 1847, 1859–60 (2006).

subject.[3] Most importantly, it has been a recurrent issue before the Federal Communications Commission (FCC), having influenced the clearance of numerous mergers[4] and prompted a recent notice of inquiry.[5] Network neutrality even emerged as a point of contention during the presidential campaign.[6] Given Barack Obama's support for network neutrality both as a U.S. Senator and as a presidential candidate,[7] pressure for the adoption of network neutrality regulation will likely intensify in the near future.

I have long argued for a middle course in network neutrality. Rather than regulating network management practices through categorical, *ex ante* restrictions, I have advocated an *ex post*, case-by-case approach that imposes liability when and only when a particular practice is shown to give rise to harm competition.[8] Such a

---

3. *See* FED. TRADE COMM'N, STAFF REPORT ON BROADBAND CONNECTIVITY COMPETITION POLICY (June 2007), *available at* http://www.ftc.gov/reports/broadband/v070000report.pdf.

4. *See* Daniel F. Spulber and Christopher S. Yoo, *Mandating Access to Telecom and the Internet: The Hidden Side of Trinko*, 107 COLUM. L. REV. 1822, 1873–74 (2007) (discussing the role network neutrality played in the SBC-AT&T, Verizon-MCI, Adelphia-Time Warner, and AT&T-BellSouth mergers); Sprint Nextel Corp. and Clearwire Corp., Applications for Consent to Transfer Control of Licenses, Leases, and Authorizations, FCC 08-259, at 41 ¶99 (Nov. 7, 2008), *available at* http://hraunfoss.fcc.gov/edocs_public/attachmatch/FCC-08-259A1.pdf; Applications of Cellco Partnership d/b/a Verizon Wireless and Atlantis Holdings LLC for Consent to Transfer Control of Licenses, Authorizations, and Spectrum Manager and *De Facto* Transfer Leasing Arrangements, Memorandum Opinion and Order and Declaratory Ruling, FCC 08-258, at 88 ¶191 (Nov. 10, 2008), *available at* http://hraunfoss.fcc.gov/edocs_public/attachmatch/FCC-08-258A1.pdf.

5. Broadband Industry Practices, Notice of Inquiry, 22 F.C.C.R. 7894 (2007).

6. *See* Lee Gomes, *Debugging Obama-McCain*, FORBES, Oct. 13, 2008, at 72.

7. *See* Obama '08, *Barack Obama: Connecting and Empowering All Americans, Through Technology and Innovation*, http://www.barackobama.com/pdf/issues/technology/Fact_Sheet_Innovation_and_Technology.pdf; Barack Obama, *Net Neutrality* (June 8, 2006), http://obama.senate.gov/podcast/060608-network_neutral/.

8. Christopher S. Yoo, *Would Mandating Broadband Network Neutrality Help or Hurt Competition?: A Comment on the End-to-End Debate*, 3 J. ON

case-by-case approach would strike a balance between two opposing considerations. On the one hand, economic theories exist that demonstrate circumstances under which vertical integration and exclusivity arrangements can harm consumers. On the other hand, the scholarly consensus recognizes that those circumstances are quite limited and that vertical integration and exclusivity arrangements often benefit consumers. A case-by-case approach offers the promise of allowing regulatory authorities to redress the potential anticompetitive harms without preventing the realization of the potential benefits.

The FCC's recent order sanctioning Comcast for its network management practices embraced the type of *ex post*, case-by-case approach described above.[9] That said, the ultimate impact of the order remains unclear. As an initial matter, Comcast is currently challenging the legality of that order in the courts. Congress is poised to consider network neutrality legislation that would change the regulatory landscape considerably if Comcast should prevail in its challenge. Even if the *Comcast* order is upheld and serves as the foundation for a regime of network neutrality, by its nature the FCC's decision was limited to the particular fact pattern that was before the agency, which inevitably left the vast majority of the substantive content of the resulting case-by-case approach to future cases. Thus, the precise manner in which network neutrality regulation will be implemented remains an open question.

In this chapter, I discuss the type of considerations that a case-by-case approach should take into account. In particular, I address

---

TELECOMM. & HIGH TECH. L. 23, 43–46, 58–59 (2004) [hereinafter Yoo, *Comment on End-to-End*]; Christopher S. Yoo, *Beyond Network Neutrality*, 19 HARV. J.L. & TECH. 1, 7–8, 24, 75–76 (2005) [hereinafter Yoo, *Beyond Network Neutrality*]; Yoo, *supra* note 2, at 1854–55, 1900, 1908; Christopher S. Yoo, *Network Neutrality, Consumers, and Innovation*, 2008 U. CHI. LEGAL F. 179, 186–87, 212, 227, 238, 246–47, 257, 261 [hereinafter Yoo, *Consumers, and Innovation*].

9. Formal Complaint of Free Press and Public Knowledge Against Comcast Corporation for Secretly Degrading Peer-to-Peer Applications, Memorandum Opinion and Order, 23 F.C.C.R. 13028 ¶¶28–40 (2008).

claims that network neutrality is needed to preserve innovation, protect consumers, and promote competition on the Internet, showing that on closer inspection the issues are not as clear as network neutrality proponents suggest. On the contrary, the ambiguousness of network neutrality's policy implications make it ideally suited to a case-by-case approach instead of *ex ante* prohibitions. Moreover, the potential benefits from deviating from network neutrality provide important considerations that a well designed case-by-case approach should take into account.

Network Neutrality and Innovation

When the Internet first arose, it was designed around a protocol known as TCP/IP. One of TCP/IP's distinguishing features is that it routes traffic without any awareness of the source of the traffic or the application with which it is associated.[10] Since those early days, network providers have begun to experiment with different network architectures. Some are prioritizing traffic associated with certain applications over other traffic. Others are charging higher prices to content and application providers who use higher bandwidth services.

According to network neutrality proponents, these changes threaten innovation in Internet content and applications in two ways. First, content and application providers' successes depend in no small part on the number of customers they can reach. Allowing network providers to exercise greater control over the traffic flowing through their networks would enable those network providers to restrict the number of end users that any particular content or application provider could reach, either by blocking them entirely or by charging content and application providers more in order to reach them.[11]

---

10. TCP/IP stands for transmission control protocol/Internet protocol.

11. Mark A. Lemley & Lawrence Lessig, *The End of End-to-End: Preserving the Architecture of the Internet in the Broadband Era*, 48 UCLA L. Rev. 925, 932 (2001) ("Because it does not discriminate in favor of certain uses of the

Second, TCP/IP fosters a particular type of innovation. Network neutrality proponents argue that one key to the Internet revolution is the commitment to an architecture in which the pipes through which the data flows are as simple and general as possible and in which all of the intelligence is concentrated in the computers operating at the edge of the network. This architecture frees content and application providers from the need to obtain permission from network providers before deploying their innovations. In other words, TCP/IP promotes innovation by decoupling content and application providers from the network through which that content and those applications travel. Any deviation that creates a tighter integration between the network and the content/applications that the network is carrying would chill innovation by raising the danger that part of the value of any innovations might be captured by the network provider.[12]

Although there is certainly considerable truth to both of these claims, important cases exist in which deviations from network neutrality would actually prove more effective in promoting innovation. The possibility that innovation might benefit from allowing network providers to experiment with different architectures suggests that *ex ante* network neutrality restrictions would probably be a policy mistake and provides an important consideration that any case-by-case approach must take into account.

Changes in the Optimal Level of Standardization

Consider first the claim that standardization and interoperability facilitate innovation by guaranteeing that content and application providers will be able to reach the broadest possible range of

---

network and against others, the Internet has provided a competitive environment in which innovators know that their inventions will be used if useful.").

12. *Id.* at 930–33, 939–46; LAWRENCE LESSIG, THE FUTURE OF IDEAS 34–37, 40–41, 162 (2002); Tim Wu, *The Broadband Debate, A User's Guide*, 3 J. ON TELECOMM. & HIGH TECH. L. 69, 73–74 (2004).

potential customers.[13] There is no question that standardization provides many benefits. Being able to offer products that are interoperable with as many other products as possible lowers the risks of innovation. Standardization also benefits consumers by maximizing price competition among those products.

Despite these benefits, not all products are standardized, nor should they be. Economic theorists have long recognized that one of the inevitable costs of standardization is the loss of product variety that must be traded off against the benefits of standardization. Such losses are trivial if customer preferences are homogeneous and, in effect, everyone wants the same thing. In those cases, the optimal solution is to standardize the network in accordance with what consumers desire most. A different situation exists when end users' preferences vary widely. As customer preferences become increasingly heterogeneous, eventually the optimal solution is to establish multiple standards, with each tailored toward a different subsegment of end users.

The shifts in the population of end users have changed in ways that make moves toward a more diverse, nonstandardized Internet more likely. What began as a medium through which a small number of academics sent e-mail and shared files has evolved into a mass market phenomenon. A rapidly growing number of end users are using the network in an ever increasing variety of ways.

Viewed from this perspective, the deployment of protocols optimized to perform different tasks may represent nothing more than the response of an industry attempting to meet consumer demand. As what consumers want becomes increasingly varied, it is natural and inevitable that the network will evolve to meet those demands. In other words, the shift away from the one-size-fits all Internet may actually represent nothing more than the natural byproduct of network providers' attempts to satisfy what consumers want.

---

13. For a more technical discussion of the ideas that follow, see Yoo, *Beyond Network Neutrality*, *supra* note 8, at 33–37; Yoo, *Consumers, and Innovation*, *supra* note 8, at 212–14, 243–45; Yoo, *Comment on End-to-End*, *supra* note 8, at 56–59.

I advance this argument without taking anything away from the benefits that standardization and interoperability can provide. In fact, a network firm faces powerful incentives to adhere to the existing standard. Moreover, the emergence of sufficient competition among last-mile providers should be sufficient to protect against anticompetitive outcomes without any need for governmental intervention.

Suppose, for example, that there are three network providers that all interconnect through the same protocol. How should policymakers respond should one of those providers wish to deviate from that protocol in a way that renders it noninteroperable with the other providers? Three outcomes are possible.

- First, the new standard may provide significant benefits to all consumers, in which case the provider that changed standards will increase its customer base until the other network providers follow suit. If so, the optimal result emerges without government intervention, and the last thing that policymakers should do is step in to compel adherence to the old standard.
- Second, the new standard may hold no appeal for consumers, in which case the network provider that changed standards will hemorrhage customers to its competitors until it returns to the fold. Once again, the optimal solution will occur without the need for governmental intervention to mandate the old standard.
- Third, the new standard may appeal to some consumers, but not to others. If there are a sufficient number of customers that prefer the new standard, the result may well be that the provider that shifted to the new standard will continue to employ it, while the other providers continue to adhere to the old standard. In this case, nonstandardization yields benefits, and it would be a mistake for policymakers to intervene to mandate adherence to the old standard.

This simple example illustrates the economic insight that any firm seeking to differentiate its services does so in the face of powerful incentives to remain standardized and will only do so if it believes that the new standard will provide sufficient benefits to offset the reduction in the value of the network caused by the reduction in the number of other end users that its customers could reach through its network. In fact, this effect is so strong that the traditional concern in the economic literature is that network firms will be too unwilling to deviate from the existing standard and will adhere to established technologies even after they have become obsolete.[14] Even these concerns are dissipated if there is sufficient competition among network providers. Although the last-mile broadband market has not to date been highly competitive, in the last three years mobile wireless broadband networks have emerged as an increasingly viable broadband alternative. Furthermore, as I discuss in greater detail below, additional increases in competition among last-mile broadband depends in no small part on network providers' ability to prioritize traffic on the basis of applications and content.

Note also that this hypothetical is framed as a polar choice between complete interoperability and complete noninteroperability. As network neutrality proponents acknowledge, complete noninteroperability is rarely a problem. Consumers can easily detect any attempt to completely block access to particular content and applications and are likely to force network providers to desist from any such practice.

The real issue lies in the spectrum of partial interoperability lying between these two extremes. In this space, prioritizing one set of applications does not preclude subscribers from running other applications. Instead, it represents a form of partial interoperability, in which all applications run on all networks, but some applications run better on some networks than others. One aspect of the economic literature on standardization that has been largely overlooked shows that the presence of perfect, low-cost adapters that can serve as a gateway between two technologies essentially

---

14. Yoo, *Beyond Network Neutrality*, *supra* note 8, at 73. For a review of the literature on tipping and lock-in in the context of broadband, see Christopher S. Yoo, *Vertical Integration and Media Regulation in the New Economy*, 19 Yale J. on Reg. 171, 278–82 (2002).

eliminates any anticompetitive concerns associated with nonstandardization.[15] When adapters are imperfect, the welfare implications are ambiguous.[16]

Circumstances thus exist where permitting network providers to deviate from the current network architecture may actually enhance rather than inhibit innovation on the Internet. Whether that is the case depends largely on the underlying heterogeneity of demand. And the presence of adapters might in some (but not all) cases ameliorate any welfare losses caused by nonstandardization. The complexity and the fact-intensiveness of the analysis offers strong support for a case-by-case approach that carefully examines each set of circumstances before intervening in order to make sure that the preconditions for harming innovation are met. The failure to undertake such nuanced assessments creates the real danger that mandating network neutrality may actually harm the innovation that network neutrality proponents seek to promote.

Changes in the Optimal Level of Integration Between Networks and Applications

As noted earlier, network neutrality proponents also contend that innovation is best promoted when there is minimal integration between the traffic riding on the network and the network itself. The claim is that decoupling content and applications from the network frees content and application providers to pursue

---

15. Michael L. Katz & Carl Shapiro, *Network Externalities, Competition, and Compatibility*, 75 Am. Econ. Rev. 424, 439 (1985) ("[I]f the costs of adapting are negligible, and there are no other entry barriers, the market will be perfectly competitive.").

16. Joseph Farrell & Garth Saloner, *Converters, Compatibility, and the Control of Interfaces*, 40 J. Indus. Econ. 9, 32 (1992) ("[C]onverters might seem to promise the benefits of compatibility without the loss of variety due to standardization. Indeed, when converters are costless and perfect, this is true; but that is rare. In general, the welfare impact of the availability of converters is ambiguous.")

whatever innovation they would like without having to seek permission from the network owner. The problem with this argument is that no protocol is optimized for every application. Thus the commitment to any particular architecture inevitably favors certain types of innovation over others, which suggests that the term "network neutrality" represents something of a misnomer.

The way that the current network architecture is skewing innovation can most easily be understood by focusing on two principles around which the current network is designed.[17] First, TCP/IP routes traffic on a "best efforts" basis, that is, it routes traffic without providing any guarantees that any particular packet will actually arrive at its destination. If the network becomes congested, some packets will be dropped and will have to be resent. Second, TCP/IP routes traffic on a "first come, first served" basis without giving priority to content associated with any particular application.

This approach to routing worked well for traditional early Internet applications, such as traditional e-mail and web browsing. Both primarily conveyed text and as a result were not particularly bandwidth intensive. For these applications, delays of a fraction of a second were almost imperceptible, and consumers were not adversely affected if any particular packet was dropped and had to be resent.

Many contemporary Internet applications—such as streaming video, telemedicine, and online video games—are less tolerant of delay.[18] The problem is that TCP/IP cannot guarantee the quality

---

17. For a more technical discussion of the ideas that follow, see Yoo, *Beyond Network Neutrality*, *supra* note 8, at 8, 20–23.

18. Another oft-cited example is Internet telephony, also known as Voice over Internet Protocol (VoIP). Indeed, telephony is one of the examples that the scientists who laid out the Internet's original architecture said would be an exception to the system of end-to-end rechecking that characterized TCP/IP. *See* J.H. Saltzer et al., *End-to-End Arguments in System Design*, 2 ACM Transactions on Computer Sys. 277, 285 (1984). Somewhat ironically, modern VoIP services do not even use TCP/IP, opting instead for a protocol known as UDP. Moreover, even though voice is relatively sensitive to delay, its bandwidth requirements are so low that it can be carried effectively through the bandwidth that exists today. *See* Edward W. Felten, *Nuts and Bolts*

of service that these applications need to survive. Although network neutrality proponents have suggested that the better solution would be for network providers to build more bandwidth,[19] the bandwidth limitations of some modes of transmission (such as wireless) are so severe that deploying more bandwidth is not a realistic solution under any time frame. Even when adding bandwidth is feasible, maintaining sufficient capacity is quite a challenge when conservative estimates project that network demand is growing at 50 percent each year and might double in the near future. The unpredictability of geographic shifts in population further complicates bandwidth planning, as do the unexpected surges in demand caused by the emergence of new services like YouTube. Bandwidth, moreover, cannot be expanded instantaneously. Unless network providers are expected to be perfectly prescient, situations will exist in which expanding bandwidth is simply not available as an option. In those circumstances, a simple solution would be to prioritize traffic associated with applications that are less tolerant of delay over traffic associated with applications that are more tolerant of delay.[20]

Network providers confronted with these constraints have no choice but to turn to some form of network management. Consider AT&T's U-verse offering. Rather than undertaking the expense of rewiring its entire service area for fiber, AT&T is attempting to deploy a triple play of voice, data, and multichannel video through a VDSL platform traveling over the existing network of telephone wires. To do so, AT&T must deploy a wide variety of techniques to conserve bandwidth. For example, instead of following cable television's practice of transmitting all of the avail-

---

of Network Neutrality 9 (July 6, 2006), *available at* http://itpolicy.princeton.edu/pub/neutrality.pdf.

19. Lessig, *supra* note 12, at 47; *Net Neutrality: Hearing Before the S. Comm. on Commerce, Science, and Transportation*, 109th Cong. 3–4 (2006) (statement of Gary R. Bachula, Vice President, Internet2), *available at* http://commerce.senate.gov/pdf/bachula-020706.pdf.

20. Yoo, *Beyond Network Neutrality*, *supra* note 8, at 22–23, 70–71; Yoo, *Consumers, and Innovation*, *supra* note 8, at 187–90, 228–32.

able channels regardless of whether the subscriber is watching them, AT&T employs a switched digital video technology that only transmits those channels that customers are actually viewing. In addition, AT&T violates network neutrality by prioritizing its own IP video traffic over other traffic, a practice that was explicitly condoned by the network neutrality commitment included in the order approving AT&T's acquisition of BellSouth.[21]

Mobile wireless broadband providers face similar problems. Many of them throttle video for the simple reason that unless they do so, the decision by a small number of end users to download video would render the service unusable for every other customer. Other mobile wireless providers are experimenting with a wide range of alternative solutions. Some are employing increasingly intelligent networks that can detect whether a particular mobile device is located in a high-bandwidth or low-bandwidth area. When in a low-bandwidth location, the network holds back traffic associated with applications such as e-mail, which are not particularly sensitive to delay, and gives priority to traffic associated with applications such as voice that are very sensitive to delay. Many of these solutions are quite innovative. The problem is that they require a greater degree of prioritization and integration between networks, applications, and devices than permitted by most forms of network neutrality. Barring prioritization and restricting intelligence to the edges of the network would foreclose these solutions from being implemented, which in turn would place a burden that would fall particularly disproportionately hard on those applications that are sensitive to latency.

TCP/IP's inability to support the new demands that end users are placing on the network has led many of the leading figures in the establishment of the Internet to suggest that the existing network architecture may be becoming obsolete.[22] It also explains why

---

21. AT&T Inc. and BellSouth Corp. Application for Transfer of Control, Memorandum Opinion and Order, 22 F.C.C.R. 5662, 5814 (2007).

22. Andrew Orlowski, *Father of Internet Warns Against Net Neutrality*, The Register, Jan. 18, 2007, http://www.theregister.co.uk/2007/01/18/kahn_net_neutrality_warning/ (quoting TCP/IP co-author Robert Kahn);

the National Science Foundation has begun a project known as the Global Environment for Network Innovations, which is dedicated to providing a new platform to avoid the limitations built into the Internet's current design that inhibit emerging applications and technologies.[23]

These examples illustrate that government-mandated adherence to the Internet's current design would be anything but neutral. Contrary to the claims of network neutrality proponents, the Internet's current architecture only fosters competition among a particular subset of Internet content and applications, i.e., those content and applications optimized for the network as it exists today. It effectively discriminates against innovations that depend on a different network design.

This in turn suggests that allowing network providers to experiment with architectures that prioritize particular applications and permit a closer integration of network, applications, and devices would foster a different and perhaps deeper kind of innovation. If so, mandating that the Internet remain seamlessly interoperable with the intelligence residing solely at the edges of the network might have the perverse effect of inhibiting the very innovation that network neutrality proponents seek to promote. The possibility that innovation might well be better promoted by allowing greater integration between the network and the applications and devices running on it is thus an important consideration that should be taken into account in any case-by-case approach to network neutrality.

David Talbot, *The Internet Is Broken*, MIT TECH. REV., Dec. 2005/Jan. 2006, at 63, *available at* http://www.technologyreview.com/article/16356/ (quoting Internet elder statesman and onetime chief protocol architect David D. Clark); Carol Wilson, *Point of No Return*, TELEPHONY, Apr. 3, 2006, *available at* http://voip-blog.tmcnet.com/blog/rich-tehrani/voip/point-of-no-return.html (quoting former FCC Chief Technologist and so-called "grandfather of the Internet" David Farber).

23. GENI: Global Environment for Network Innovations, Conceptual Design Project Execution Plan, GDD-06-07, at 7 (Jan. 10, 2006), *available at* http://www.geni.net/GDD/GDD-06-07.pdf.

Network Neutrality and Consumers

Network neutrality proponents often frame their arguments in terms of consumers as well as innovation. One argument is that network neutrality would maximize consumer choice by allowing end users to assert complete control over the content and applications they access. For the reasons laid out above, it would only maximize choice among a constrained set of options, i.e., content and applications optimized for the existing set of protocols. At the same time, it would limit consumer choice by forestalling the emergence of innovations based on architectures that allow a tighter integration of the network and applications. This loss is often hard to discern, as it is difficult to determine the value of an opportunity that never appeared. But the loss to consumers is quite real, nonetheless.

I would like to focus the rest of this section on the two other claims about how network neutrality would affect consumers. The first is that allowing network providers to offer prioritized service would create a two-tiered Internet in which only the rich would get the fast lane, while those unable or unwilling to pay would be consigned to the slow lane.[24] The second is that allowing network providers to charge content and application providers more for premium services would force consumers to pay twice.[25]

Closer analysis reveals that these claims are more complicated and controversial than network neutrality proponents suggest. In many cases, permitting network providers to offer multiple classes of services may actually lower the prices that consumers pay. Any attempt to mandate network neutrality must take into account the possibility that doing so may end up harming as well as benefiting consumers.

---

24. Lawrence Lessig & Robert W. McChesney, *No Tolls on the Internet*, Wash. Post, June 8, 2006, at A23; 152 Cong. Rec. S8367–68 (daily ed. July 27, 2006) (statement of Sen. Ron Wyden).

25. *Net Neutrality: Hearing Before the S. Comm. on Commerce, Science, and Transportation*, 109th Cong. 6 (2006) (statement of Vinton G. Cerf, Vice President and Chief Internet Evangelist, Google, Inc.), *available at* http://commerce.senate.gov/pdf/cerf-020706.pdf [hereinafter Cerf testimony].

The Potential Consumer Benefits from Tiered Services

The error in the claim that only deep-pocketed consumers and corporations would be able to gain access to the fast lane is well illustrated through an analogy to postal services.[26] It is simply false that only the rich and the well heeled use overnight mail and that small companies and consumers of moderate means are consigned to using first class mail. Instead, customers choose their service based on how much they need a given level of service. Customers who do not mind if a particular letter takes as many as three days to travel from coast to coast will continue to use first class mail regardless of their ability to pay. Conversely, companies with business models that depend on overnight delivery recognize that overnight service requires greater costs. They willingly and gladly pay more for faster services for the simple reason that without premium prices, the overnight services on which their business models depend would not exist. This is true whether the firm is a Fortune 500 with enormous reserves or a startup that is working hard to conserve its cash. Similarly, consumers who absolutely, positively need a letter delivered overnight are similarly grateful for the existence of carriers able to provide those services. Although they would no doubt wish to pay the lowest price possible, they recognize that the price for an overnight letter will inevitably exceed the 44 cents needed for a first-class stamp.

Consider further what would happen if the postal authorities forbade carriers from differentiating between overnight mail and regular first class mail and instead required them to offer a single class of service. The postal service would face three choices. It could require that all mail travel as first class mail, in which case all letters would take three days to travel coast to coast and cost 44 cents. Unifying service in this manner would frustrate the interests of businesses and consumers who need overnight delivery but can no longer obtain it no matter how much they might be willing to pay for it. Alternatively, the postal service could require that

26. Yoo, *Consumers, and Innovation*, *supra* note 8, at 232–33.

all mail travel as express mail, in which case all letters would travel coast to coast overnight and would cost more than $15. This would force all mailers to pay higher prices even though many of them would not need speedy delivery. Lastly, the postal service could split the difference, such as by delivering coast-to-coast mail in two days for a cost of approximately $5 in a manner similar to priority mail. Although this service would be well suited to some customers, it would simultaneously increase the prices for those who were perfectly happy with the level of service provided by first class mail and deny service to those who need overnight delivery. The more straightforward solution is to allow the postal service to offer multiple classes of service. That way, each customer can obtain the services they need while only paying for the levels of service that they actually need.

How does this play out in the context of the Internet? The fact that traffic is growing at a rate of 50 percent per year or more means that network providers must invest heavily to increase the bandwidth capacity of their networks. Verizon has committed to invest $24 billion to deploy its fiber-based FiOS network. Other providers have chosen less costly solutions, such as AT&T's deployment of its VDSL U-verse network and the cable industry's upgrade to DOCSIS 3.0. But even in those cases, the capital expenditures are substantial.

In an ideal consumer world, network providers would provide these bandwidth enhancements without raising prices. The reality is that network providers must have some reasonable prospect of recovering these capital expenditures if they are expected to undertake them. Thus, absent the unlikely event of direct government subsidies, a network provider that was unable to offer different classes of service would have to raise the prices for all consumers to the price needed to support the higher level of service. This would have the unfortunate effect of raising prices for end users who only use the Internet for low bandwidth applications such as e-mail and are perfectly happy with the service they were receiving previously. Moreover, unless some form of metered pricing is imposed, the price would be set equal to the usage levels of the average consumer. This would overcharge below-average users while simultaneously undercharging above-average users, in effect forcing low-bandwidth users to cross-subsidize high-bandwidth users.[27]

Moreover, a network provider that is only allowed to offer a single class of service will choose the bandwidth level that appeals to the largest number of customers possible. Limiting network providers to offering a single class of service thus makes it unlikely that those consumers who do want the highest level of bandwidth possible will be able to get it.

The situation is quite different if you allow differential pricing. Rather than raise prices on everyone, network providers have the ability to charge higher prices to those who need the enhanced services without raising the prices for those who were happy with the prior levels of service. Such a solution would accord with economic efficiency and general ideas of fairness, in that it would require those who need and benefit from the improved service to pay for those improvements without placing additional burdens on those who do not benefit from the service enhancement.

On a broader level, these insights about the benefits of differential pricing for enhanced services provide another example of how the Internet is evolving away from one-size-fits-all solutions. By focusing exclusively on the consumer benefits from nondiscrimination among the content and applications that exist today, network neutrality proponents overlook the benefits arising from the ability to tailor pricing and services to individual consumers' needs.

The Economics of Two-Sided Markets

At a somewhat more technical level, economic theory not only justifies allowing network owners to charge differential prices to consumers. The economics of two-sided markets also identify potential consumer benefits from allowing network operators to im-

---

27. Yoo, *supra* note 2, at 1853–54.

pose differential prices on content and application providers as well.[28]

The economics of two-sided markets are somewhat complex. Conventional economics has long recognized the existence of "network economic effects," which cause a network to increase in value as the number of users connected to it increases. To use a classic example, the value of a telephone network to consumers is thus determined by more than just the price charged and the services provided, as is the case with most goods. It also depends on the number of other subscribers connected to the network. The more people you can reach through the network, the more valuable it becomes.

The telephone system is an example of a one-sided market, in that the value to any particular caller is determined in no small part by the number of similarly situated callers. When a market is two-sided, instead of bringing together a single class of similarly situated users, networks bring together two completely different classes of users. In those cases, the value is determined not by the number of users of the same class, but rather the number of users of the other class. To put it in terms of a concrete example, consider the economics of broadcast television, which generates revenue from advertisers based on the number of viewers the industry can deliver. The value of the network for advertisers is not determined by the number of other advertisers. Instead, the value of the network increases with the number of a different class of network participants (i.e., television viewers).

The economics of two-sided markets indicate that it may be socially beneficial for content and application providers to subsidize the prices paid by end users. The fact that the Internet has become increasingly dominated by advertising revenue paid to content and application providers rather than network providers makes this particularly likely to be true. An advertiser's willingness to pay for

---

28. For a more extended discussion of the implications of the economics of two-sided markets for network neutrality, see Yoo, *Consumers and Innovation*, *supra* note 8, at 222–27.

an ad on any particular website depends on the number of end users viewing that website. Under these circumstances, the optimal solution may be for the website owner to subsidize the total number of end users by making payments to the network provider to help defray their costs of connection. The costs of subsidizing more users would be more than offset by the additional revenue generated by the fact that advertisers can now reach more potential customers.[29]

These revenue-side pressures are reinforced by cost-side considerations. The cost of connecting content and application providers to the Internet is quite low, typically only requiring a single high-speed line to a small number of business locations. The cost of connecting end users to the Internet is much higher, requiring the wiring and upgrading of equipment in entire neighborhoods. In an industry in which the primary revenue is flowing to content and application providers and the costs involved in connecting content and application providers are much smaller than the costs of connecting end users, one would expect some cash to flow from content and application providers to those who are providing connections to end users.[30]

These dynamics are again well illustrated by broadcast television. In many ways, broadcast television and the Internet are analogous. The movie studios that create television programs play a similar role to content and application providers. Television networks aggregate programs and deliver them nationally in much the same manner as server-side network providers and backbone providers. Local broadcast stations provide last-mile connectivity that is quite similar to the role played by DSL and cable modem providers. In addition, the revenue structure is quite comparable, in that television networks receive advertising revenue in much the

---

29. *Id.* at 225–26.

30. P. Faratin et al., *Complexity of Internet Interconnections: Technology Incentives and Implications for Policy* 13 (Sept. 30, 2007) (paper presented at the 35th Annual Telecommunications Policy Research Conference), *available at* http://web.si.umich.edu/tprc/papers/2007/797/Clark%20Lehr%20Faratin%20Complexity%20Interconnection%20TPRC%202007.pdf.

same manner as content and application providers. Furthermore, the cost structure is somewhat similar in that connecting individual homes is much more costly than distributing programming nationally.

For decades, the standard business arrangement has been for television networks to subsidize the operations of local broadcast stations by paying them to be members of their television networks. The industry's revenue and cost structure make such arrangements quite logical. The cost of paying these broadcast stations to affiliate with a network is more than offset by the increase in advertising revenue made possible by the fact that the network is now able to reach a larger audience. Broadcast television thus represents a prime example of when firms operating on one side of the market find it economically beneficial to subsidize end users on the other side of the market.

Furthermore, the magnitude of the affiliation fees that the networks pay to broadcast stations is anything but uniform. The precise amount paid varies with the relative strength of the network and the relative strength of the broadcast station. Stronger broadcast stations receive more, while weaker ones receive less. Equally interesting is the fact that in recent years, the cash flow has begun to vary in its direction as well as magnitude, with weaker stations having to pay rather than be paid to be part of the television network. The dynamic nature of this pricing regime benefits consumers by providing incentives for networks to invest in better quality programming and by providing an incentive for stations to provide better carriage.

Pricing flexibility is the standard mechanism by which our society rewards socially beneficial behavior and reallocates resources. This process of equilibration works well so long as entry barriers are relatively low and inputs are relatively mobile. These conditions are easily met with respect to content and applications, which are already very competitive and unprotected by entry barriers (and therefore likely to remain that way). The upsurge of mobile wireless as a last-mile platform has made these conditions easier to satisfy on the network provider side as well. The impending emergence of new broadband platforms made possible by the 700

MHz auction and other technologies promises to open the last mile to competition still further in the future.

The two-sided market analysis reveals the problems with the claim that allowing network providers to charge content and application providers for premium services would force consumers to pay twice. As a general matter, pricing flexibility makes it easier for network providers to recover the costs of building additional bandwidth. Left to their own devices, network providers would set prices designed to maximize the revenue generated by each side of the market. So long as competitive entry is sufficiently feasible to prevent network providers from simply pocketing the extra returns, facilitating network providers' ability to generate revenue from one side of the market will reduce the proportion of the fixed costs that the network provider will have to recover from the other side of the market. Thus, granting network providers pricing flexibility with respect to content and application providers should reduce the economic burden borne by end users.

Conversely, preventing network providers from exercising pricing flexibility with respect to content and application providers while permitting them to exercise pricing flexibility against end users simply increases the proportion of the cost network providers must recover directly from end users. This simultaneously raises the prices paid by consumers and decreases the likelihood that the capital improvements will ever be built.[31] Conversely, enhancing pricing flexibility on both sides of the market increases the likelihood that network providers will recover a greater proportion of the costs of upgrading the network from content and application providers. Charging content and application providers premium prices for premium services is thus a way to reduce, not increase, the burden borne by consumers.

This is not to say that allowing network providers to offer multiple classes of services would always be economically beneficial. If

31. *Wall Street's Perspective on Telecommunications: Hearing Before the S. Comm. on Commerce, Science, and Transportation*, 109th Cong. 3–4 (2006) (testimony of Craig E. Moffett, Vice President and Senior Analyst, Sanford C. Bernstein & Co.), *available at* http://commerce.senate.gov/pdf/moffett-031406.pdf.

perfect price discrimination were feasible, differential pricing schemes would invariably benefit society. Perfect price discrimination is impossible, however, and to the extent that price discrimination is imperfect, the practice might reduce as well as increase economic welfare. That said, economic textbooks generally conclude that imperfect price discrimination is more likely to be beneficial than not.[32] In any event, the real possibility that price discrimination may benefit—and not just harm—consumers counsels strongly against erecting a categorical ban against the practice and provides an important consideration that a well designed case-by-case approach should take into account.

Network Neutrality and Last-Mile Competition

Perhaps the most important consideration that should be incorporated into a case-by-case analysis is the impact that any network neutrality mandate would have on competition in the last mile. It is often overlooked that mandating access to the existing network represents only one of two ways to promote competition in content and applications. The other is to promote entry by new last-mile providers.[33] Once a sufficient number of last-mile providers exists, any content or application provider unable to obtain access from one last-mile provider will simply turn to one of its competitors. Indeed, most network neutrality proponents agree that the emergence of competition in the last mile would render network neutrality regulation unnecessary.[34]

There are a number of important considerations that should inform the choice between these two approaches. As an initial matter, experience has shown that mandated access regimes are ex-

---

32. Richard G. Lipsey et al., Economics 241 (8th ed. 1987); F.M. Scherer & David Ross, Industrial Market Structure and Economic Performance 495 (3d ed. 1990).

33. Yoo, *Comment on End-to-End*, *supra* note 8, at 67–68.

34. Cerf testimony, *supra* note 25, at 7.

tremely difficult to implement.[35] For example, if the network provider offers its own content and applications, a simple nondiscrimination mandate will simply lead the network provider to charge a nondiscriminatory price that is so exorbitant that independent providers of content and applications will not be able to pay it. The fact that the vertically integrated content and applications will also have to pay the higher price is of little consequence, because any losses suffered by the content and application division will be offset by gains enjoyed by the networking division. Thus, absent rate regulation, the network provider can continue to exclude unaffiliated content and applications simply by transferring profits from one division to another. In addition, without rate regulation, access rules simply require the network owner to share its monopoly while continuing to allow it to charge the monopoly price. The lack of any price decrease means that consumers do not benefit at all.[36]

Any access regime must thus necessarily be accompanied by rate regulation. As I have argued at greater length elsewhere, rate regulation is particularly likely to fail when the commodity being regulated varies in quality. For example, research has shown that cable operators were able to deflect the impact of regulation by degrading the quality of their programming. Thus, regulators seeking to impose rate regulation over such providers must undertake the difficult job of regulating quality as well as price. Furthermore, the implementation of rate regulation is particularly ineffective in industries undergoing rapid technological change.[37]

The fact that compelled access forces two unwilling business partners to do business with one another means that the network provider will do no more than the minimum necessary to comply

35. Yoo, *Beyond Network Neutrality*, *supra* note 8, at 37–48; Yoo, *supra* note 2, at 1896–97; Yoo, *supra* note 14, at 244–46, 268–69.

36. Yoo, *Beyond Network Neutrality*, *supra* note 8, at 15; Yoo, *Comment on End-to-End*, *supra* note 8, at 56.

37. Christopher S. Yoo, *Architectural Censorship and the FCC*, 78 S. Cal. L. Rev. 669, 685–87 (2005); Yoo, *Beyond Network Neutrality*, *supra* note 8, at 42–43.

with its legal obligations. The parties can be expected to argue over a wide range of nonprice issues. As the Supreme Court has recognized, such negotiations are likely to be extremely protracted and difficult to police when the interface is complex and multifaceted, given that the network owner will have an almost limitless number of ways to degrade service at its disposal.[38] Thus, in order to succeed, access requires nearly comprehensive regulation of the business relationship between the two parties. It is for these reasons that the FCC's experience policing access regimes has not been a happy one. The agency's attempts to implement such varied regimes as leased access, video dialtone, and open video services have largely failed. Equally troubling is the difficulties the agency has encountered implementing the access provisions of the Telecommunications Act of 1996, which has engendered a decade of litigation and few real benefits.[39]

Perhaps most troubling is that the mandatory access approach contains no exit plan. When competitive entry is possible, short-run supracompetitive returns are not only unproblematic, they are essential to the proper functioning of the economic system. It is the desire to share in these supracompetitive returns that stimulates others to reallocate resources and sell a competing product. This entry will occur until all supracompetitive returns are dissipated. The imposition of rate regulation as part of access regulation short circuits this mechanism, because limiting the network provider's ability to earn supracompetitive returns reduces the incentive for others to enter the market. This dynamic is again nicely illustrated by the broadcast television industry. The longstanding triopoly of television networks led the FCC to impose a wide variety of measures to limit broadcast networks' profitability. Because these rules limited the profitability of new networks as well as incumbents, they actually became an entry barrier, as demonstrated by the fact that the Fox network needed to be exempted from these

38. Verizon Commc'ns Inc. v. Law Offices of Curtis V. Trinko, LLP, 540 U.S. 411, 414 (2004).

39. Yoo, *Beyond Network Neutrality*, *supra* note 8, at 39–42; Yoo, *supra* note 14, at 244–46, 268–69.

rules before it became viable.[40] Access regulation is thus best understood as surrender to the putative monopoly and presumes that regulation will be indefinite.[41] Such an approach might be defensible if entry by competitors is impossible. As noted above, that precondition becomes less true with every passing year.

Consider the alternative, which is promoting innovation and consumer benefits by promoting competition in the last mile. Even network neutrality proponents concede that the need for regulation disappears once sufficient last-mile competition has emerged. As it turns out, there is a deep connection between setting priorities for applications and promoting last-mile competition. The connection is illustrated by the problems faced by companies using white spaces in the spectrum to provide wireless broadband in rural areas. Given the limited amount of bandwidth they are permitted to use, these companies must prioritize time-sensitive applications (such as voice) over less time-sensitive applications (such as file downloading) if they are to provide adequate service. In addition, they completely bar certain high-bandwidth applications altogether, as a single user employing them would prevent any other user from obtaining service. Such prioritization is an integral part of their survival as a last-mile competitor.

Another example is AT&T's U-verse network, which uses the limited bandwidth previously deployed for voice communications to offer video as well. Because video is one of those applications that is very sensitive to delay, the only way AT&T can offer an acceptable video service is by giving video traffic priority over other traffic. The resulting competition with cable for multichannel video helps satisfy one of our nation's longest standing goals in communications policy. Certain technologies simply cannot provide the guaranteed quality of service needed to support high-bandwidth applications such as video unless video traffic is given priority.

As noted earlier, mobile broadband providers are similarly experimenting with different solutions to solve the strict bandwidth

---

40. Yoo, *Beyond Network Neutrality*, *supra* note 8, at 49 n.188.
41. *Id.* at 11, 51, 76; Yoo, *Comment on End-to-End*, *supra* note 8, at 56.

limitations that they face. Many throttle video for the simple reason that if they did not do so, video downloading would render the service unusable by other customers. Others prioritize traffic associated with latency-sensitive applications over other traffic. Others are transferring functions into the computing power contained in handheld devices. Still others are transferring functions into the network itself.

I have shown elsewhere how allowing network providers greater flexibility in managing congestion on the Internet can provide real benefits to consumers.[42] Indeed, it is possible to analyze the engineering tradeoff between building additional bandwidth and permitting network providers to prioritize traffic. If network providers are not allowed to use prioritization to guarantee throughput rates, they must maintain additional bandwidth to ensure that sufficient excess capacity exists to carry that traffic without delay. A recent study estimated that a network without prioritization might have to maintain up to 60 percent more capacity than a network offering prioritized service.[43] The need to maintain excess capacity will deter the buildout of broadband networks by raising the density of customers needed for the service to break even. The failure to prioritize thus threatens to worsen the digital divide by making it more difficult to serve rural areas.

These examples underscore the incredible variation in technical challenges confronting different transmission technologies and how innovative the industry has been in meeting those challenges. Without the ability to prioritize traffic on the basis of the underlying application, many of these providers could not survive as last-mile competitors. It is difficult to predict which, if any, of these strategies will prove successful. Indeed, it is quite likely that different portions of the industry may adopt different solutions dictated by their underlying technology.

---

42. Yoo, *supra* note 2, at 1863–85.

43. Joseph D. Houle et al., *The Evolving Internet—Traffic, Engineering, and Roles* 5 (paper presented at the 35th Annual Telecommunications Policy Research Conference, Sept. 30, 2007), *available at* http://web.si.umich.edu/tprc/papers/2007/786/Evolving%20Internet.pdf.

Any case-by-case approach must be careful to take these considerations into account and to leave network providers with enough flexibility to experiment with different strategies. Too strict an approach would forestall innovative solutions to address bandwidth limitations.

Recommendations and Conclusions

To date, the debate over network neutrality has been framed in largely categorical terms, with both sides trying to claim the virtues of freedom, innovation, consumer welfare, and competition. A closer analysis of the issue reveals that it is more complex and variegated than the terms of the existing debate suggest. The economic literature does acknowledge the existence of circumstances under which deviations from network neutrality might give rise to anticompetitive harms. At the same time, the literature shows that those harms can only arise under limited circumstances and that deviations from network neutrality may actually create substantial benefits.

The ambiguity of network neutrality's policy implications underscores the propriety of adopting a case-by-case approach. As the Supreme Court has long recognized, *ex ante* categorical rules are blunt instruments that do not permit fine distinctions. This is why the Supreme Court has reserved them for things that are so clearly detrimental that little would be lost if the practice were to be banned altogether. And even then, the Supreme Court has long recognized that such *ex ante* approaches should not be applied when a practice is so new that the Court does not have sufficient experience to predict the likely economic impact of prohibiting it. When a practice is either new or when its economic impact is unclear, as seems to be the case with deviations from network neutrality, the better approach is to take an *ex post*, case-by-case approach.[44]

44. For classic statements, see Northern Pacific Railway Co. v. United States, 356 U.S. 1, 5 (1957); Continental T.V., Inc. v. GTE Sylvania Inc., 433 U.S. 36, 49–51 (1977); Broadcast Music, Inc. v. Columbia Broadcasting Sys-

The bigger question is how that case-by-case approach should be applied. The foregoing analysis identifies numerous considerations that policymakers should take into account. In most cases, these considerations require a close examination of the facts of each particular case. Eventually, enough precedents will exist to permit those planning in the shadow of network neutrality rules to discern the principles being applied. The problem is that considerable uncertainty will exist until a sufficient critical mass of decisions is reached.

The FCC would thus be well advised to offer more details about the approach it will apply in future cases. The most logical approach would be to use the basic principles animating antitrust law to fill in the content of the case-by-case analysis.[45] Antitrust jurisprudence represents perhaps the most systematic and comprehensive body of law designed to evaluate practices to make sure that they promote the interests of consumers and innovation. Equally important, by placing the burden of proof on the party challenging a particular practice, antitrust law is designed to ensure every economic actor has enough breathing room to experiment with different approaches. Although it is tempting to place the burden of proof on those who wish to deviate from the status quo, there are risks in adhering to, as well as deviating from, the status quo. That is why leading theorists have concluded that prophylactic regulation in favor of the status quo is justified only when the potential adverse consequences are truly catastrophic and irreversible.[46] Any other rule would prevent society from finding which, if any, alternative states of the world might be socially beneficial.[47]

---

tem, Inc., 441 U.S. 1, 8–9 (1979); Business Electronics Corp. v. Sharp Electronics Corp., 485 U.S. 717, 723 (1988). For the Court's most recent statements, see State Oil Co. v. Khan, 522 U.S. 3, 10 (1997); Texaco Inc. v. Dagher, 547 U.S. 1, 5 (2006); Leegin Creative Leather Products, Inc. v. PSKS, Inc., 127 S. Ct. 2705, 2712–13 (2007).

45. Christopher S. Yoo, *What Can Antitrust Contribute to the Net Neutrality Debate?* 1 INT'L J. COMM. 493 (2007).

46. *See* CASS R. SUNSTEIN, LAWS OF FEAR: BEYOND THE PRECAUTIONARY PRINCIPLE 26–34 (2005).

47. *See* Yoo, *Beyond Network Neutrality*, *supra* note 8, at 12, 74; Yoo, *supra* note 2, at 1852, 1855, 1899, 1908.

In addition, antitrust law teaches that any case-by-case approach must also be careful to protect consumers, not competitors. Every change inevitably creates winners and losers, and deviations from the status quo are often opposed by the players dominating the current market, as they are the ones with the most invested in the network as it exists today and thus are the ones with the most to lose. The success that the Internet has enjoyed under its current architecture should not blind policymakers to the fact that the world is constantly changing. They should instead take care to remain open to the possibility that abandoning the one-size-fits-all solution that has long characterized the Internet may be the best way to promote innovation and to benefit consumers.

CHAPTER 4

What Broadcast Licenses Tell Us about Net Neutrality: *Cosmopolitan Broadcasting Corporation v. FCC*

Richard A. Epstein

Licensing Then and Now

For the past several years, we have witnessed a nonstop intellectual debate over the merits of net neutrality as a guiding principle for organizing the broadband capacity within the United States. At its heart the dispute over net neutrality deals with the question of who controls the various pipes that control transmission over the Internet. As with physical systems, the options here are two. The first model creates a system of public regulation of private pipes that gives the state an active role in determining the composition of the traffic. Accordingly, one common variation on net neutrality is that the government should play the same role with communications, by directing the traffic in accordance with its own prior beliefs about the just mix of broadband users. Thus the government could seek to create parity across different user classes by prohibiting a broadband provider from imposing any heavier charges, or even any charges, against any particular class of users.[1]

1. For a critique of that position, see C. Scott Hemphill, *Network Neutrality and the False Promise of Zero-Price Regulation*, Colum. L. & Econ. Working Paper No. 331, (April 2008), *available at* SSRN: http://ssrn.com/abstract=1119982.

The second model is that of a closed system of real property, exemplified by private roads in planned unit developments. In this situation, the major function of the state is to police the boundary lines that demarcate the territory of one property owner from the rest of the world. Except in conditions of extreme necessity, the owner has the right to exclude all others, and thus to set the terms and conditions on which selected individuals may enter the property. Accordingly, the prosaic action for trespass gives an owner relief against unwanted entrants. This legal regime gives the owner space to create institutions of private self-governance that include the right to issue licenses to others on whatever terms and conditions he sees fit. The major function of private property is to set up a world where gains from trade can be realized through voluntary exchanges.

To be sure, under classical legal theory the right to exclude is denied to firms that hold a monopoly position, whether acquired by state grant or natural condition, for supplying certain services. In those situations, the relevant norm calls for the provision of service on reasonable and nondiscriminatory terms. Yet owners that do face competitive pressures are not subject to these service obligations, for now Adam Smith's invisible hand will happily align private self-interest with the public good. The threat that other actors have to go elsewhere provides all the discipline that is needed against market abuses. This distinction has been long understood in both England and the United States.[2]

One of the major disputes in the current net neutrality debate is over which of these two models should govern. Do the major broadband carriers enjoy monopoly power, or even market dom-

---

2. See, e.g., Allnut v. Inglis, 104 Eng. Rep. 206 (K.B. 1810), which in turn rests on Sir Matthew Hale's treatise, *De Portibus Maris* ("Of the Gates of the Sea"). Hale lived from 1609 to 1676. His treatise was published posthumously in the 1780s. For the incorporation of these principles into American Law, see Munn v. Illinois, 94 U.S. 113 (1876), where the English authorities are discussed extensively at 94 U.S. at 126–29. For a discussion, see Richard A. Epstein, Principles for a Free Society: Reconciling Individual Liberty with the Common Good 282–285 (1998).

inance in the broadband business that might justify the imposition of some service obligations? Without question, many locations are served by relatively few providers. But it does not follow that they enjoy a monopoly position worthy of state regulation. To take a leaf from Harold Demsetz, in doubtful cases a static analysis of market structure should yield to a dynamic one.[3] I have recently harped on just this theme in my own writings that caution against the invocation of antitrust monopolization theories under Section 2 of the Sherman Act.[4] Thus, the prospect of future competition from new technologies or distant rivals will discipline incumbent firms even before the new rivals appear on the scene. Accordingly, the wise course of action is to classify the doubtful cases as competitive, in order to avoid introducing regulation that could easily prolong an incumbent's monopoly position.

For the moment, however, I shall bracket that difficult question in order to comment on a second issue of great import: Why in general is it always inappropriate to regulate business operations that work in competitive markets? This problem has dogged the Federal Communications Commission since the dawn of modern communications. My contribution addresses how just this dynamic played out with broadcast licenses in connection with a once well-known case, *Cosmopolitan Broadcasting Corp. v. Federal Communications Commission*.[5] In that case, the court affirmed the FCC's revocation of the company's broadcast license for WHDI on the ground that it had improperly delegated its oversight authority to its sublicensees who determined the content of their own broadcasts. Today this case, like broadcast licenses in general, gives rise to little litigation, let alone discussion. The important broadcast licenses have all been allocated, and their renewal is regarded in some sense a foregone conclusion. But in the formative era of

3. See Harold Demsetz, *Why Regulate Utilities?*, 11 J. L. Econ. 55 (1968)

4. Richard A. Epstein, *Monopolization Follies: The Dangers of Structural Remedies under Section 2 of the Sherman Act*, forthcoming Antitrust L. J. (2009); Richard A. Epstein, *Monopoly Dominance or Level Playing Field: The New Antitrust Paradox*, 72 U. Chi. L. Rev. 49 (2005).

5. 581 F.2d 917 (D.C. Cir. 1978) (Bazelon, J.).

communications law and policy, the initial allocation of frequencies was one of the most hotly disputed issues of the time. That issue, and the *Cosmopolitan* case, deserve to be raised from their long-time neglect because they supply us with much insight as to the merits of public control over broadband content.

My thesis here is simple: The analysis that works for broadcast works for broadband. In order to show how this thesis plays out, I first examine the coincidental debate between Friedrich Hayek and Felix Frankfurter over the proper analysis of highways, be they for automobiles or information. I next look at how these principles play out in connection with the issue of government control over broadcast licenses as presented in *Cosmopolitan Broadcasting*, where intrusive regulation threatened effective entrepreneurial solutions that the FCC itself had failed to adopt. And last I draw out the implications of this historical experience for the debate over network neutrality.

Hayek vs. Frankfurter

The early 1940s were a period that was marked by two trends. The first of these was the consolidation of the New Deal state through the expansion of the modern administrative state, whose work is often represented by Felix Frankfurter, one of its tireless champions. The second was the counterrevolution against central planning that was led by Friedrich Hayek, most notably in his classic, *The Road to Serfdom*. Ironically, there was an odd pairing of these intellectual giants over the role of highways in the organization and distribution of traffic.

In one famous passage, F.A. Hayek observed that the genius of the highway system was that the government only had the power to set the rules of the road, but did not have any power to determine the composition of the traffic.[6] The point here is that this system of open access avoids the endless struggles to see whose use of property is more important than anyone else's. In truth, the

6. Friedrich A. Hayek, The Road To Serfdom 74 (1944).

daily operation of any highway system is more complex than Hayek's simple, if profound, observation about open access suggests. In practice state control and ownership of the highways has resulted in just the kinds of (misguided) regulatory practices that one associates with industrial policy more generally. Thus it is commonplace that state and city governments are prone to exclude from the roads those firms that wish to run, for example, private jitney services in competition with state-run bus companies.[7] The Interstate Commerce Commission used to give trucks licenses to carry loads from California to New York, only to drive back empty because they were denied a license to go from New York to California. From time to time, courts intervene to make sure that selective regulations do not impose undue restrictions on competition. One famous example is *Frost v. Railroad Commission of State of California*,[8] when Justice Sutherland struck down a condition whereby California sought to make all private carriers (who carried only their own goods) into common carriers (who had to service all comers). In his view, the state could not alter the natural balance between the two kinds of carriers. But that constitutional boomlet was short lived, for only six years later, Sutherland upheld regulations that were indistinguishable from those in *Frost*.[9] In effect, any effort to apply the doctrine of unconstitutional conditions was in the end shipwrecked by the use of the rational basis doctrine to sustain what was in the end yet another disguised, but indefensible form of economic protectionism.

Yet notwithstanding the historical practices, Hayek's basic insight could be recast in normative terms. Highways operate best when the regulations are used to govern those activities that increase the value of a common resource, which include the maintenance of infrastructure through appropriate user charges, a set of traffic rules to prevent accidents, a system of licensing to keep dangerous drivers off the road, and a set of tort and criminal sanc-

---

7. Ross D. Eckert & George W. Hilton, *The Jitneys*, 15 J. Law & Econ. 293 (1972).

8. 271 U.S. 583 (1926).

9. Stephenson v. Binford, 287 U.S. 251 (1932) (Sutherland J.).

tions to deal with dangerous drivers. To put the point in its simplest form, the presence of these regulations should pass without complaint because they are in general consistent with the plan that seeks to run an open-access competitive system on top of a state-owned monopoly. Hayek's insight is not inconsistent with these common and sensible forms of regulation.

The situation with the spectrum raises many of the same issues posed by highways. Here again we face the question of whether the state should confine its operations to setting the rules of the road or to determining the composition of the traffic. The key point to note here is that the former task is far *easier* for the spectrum than it is for roads. System design is far easier, for all that is required is a collective determination to prevent interference between users on neighboring frequencies. There are no potholes to fix or tickets to issue. The allocation task gets easier with time, moreover, because better technology allows the transmission of tighter signals within any given bandwidth, which in the absence of government licensing restrictions, would allow broadcasters to increase the number of stations on less bandwidth, thereby releasing space for other high intensity uses such as data transmission. (We have just this problem today with the underutilized TV band, which, given the license restrictions, cannot be redeployed for more valuable uses.[10]) In addition, the state need not incur any front-end costs to create or maintain infrastructure. Nor does spectrum utilization pose the risk of any serious physical damage. Drunk drivers do not roam the airwaves. So we learn once again the size of the state should shrink, not expand, as we move from physical to intangible networks.

It never worked out that way, however, for in contrast to Hayek's (oversimplified) vision of a highway system stands Felix Frankfurter's famous declaration about the spectrum. This matter arose under the 1934 Communications Act, which decrees that the FCC should award its broadcast licenses under a standard that

10. See Thomas W. Hazlett & Vernon L. Smith, *Don't Let Google Freeze the Airwaves*, Wall St. J., Oct. 3, 2008, at A 21.

turns on the "public interest, convenience and necessity."[11] One possible approach to this is to allocate frequencies by bid, at which point the key issue becomes the design of an auction that yields the greatest revenues from the sale of licenses. That auction could also contain various measures to prevent, if such were thought desirable, excessive concentration in any given industry. Or it could leave the issues of collusion and monopolization to the antitrust laws. Either way, the government role would be to first define and then enforce the property rights. The utilization of broadcast spectrum would be a private matter, just as such utilization of resources is with newspapers and other print media.[12]

This slimmed-down account of a way to view the FCC's powers was gratuitously rejected in *National Broadcasting Company v. United States*.[13] At issue in that case was a challenge to the FCC's planned breakup of NBC's Blue and Red Radio Networks into two separate companies, NBC and ABC. The "chain regulations" at issue in that case raised a vintage antitrust inquiry that asked about excessive concentration within the industry. Given that NBC had a dominant market position, the only issues raised in *NBC* concerned industrial concentration, which, ironically enough, is a proper topic of government control under the test set out above.[14] But Justice Frankfurter was never one to praise libertarian institutions. Rather, he went out of his way to reject them when he upheld the FCC regulations on "chain" radio stations. For him both history and logic supported a far larger role for government action. He offered an extensive account of how the rapid introduction of new stations in the 1920s led to massive signal interference that degraded the effectiveness of transmission and cried out for government regulation. Once again he was right, after a fashion. Interference is a common tort that undermines clear property rights in frequencies. The only question that remains is whether

11. 47 U.S.C. §307(a).

12. See, e.g., Associated Press v. United States, 326 U.S. 1 (1945). (First Amendment does not insulate press from antitrust claims.)

13. National Broadcasting Co. v. United States, 319 U.S. 190 (1943).

14. *Id.* 194–196.

to adopt a bottom-up rule that awards a frequency to its first user,[15] or a top-down rule that allows the government through the Department of Commerce to allocate frequencies through some method of its own choosing.[16]

The key question in *NBC* was whether the FCC had the power to regulate the contracts between the networks and the individual stations. In attacking this question, Justice Frankfurter took a standard progressive tack, by showing his exuberant preference for judicial deference to administrative action. In so doing, he argued, over a dissent by Justice Murphy,[17] that the statutory standard of "public interest, convenience and necessity," was sufficient to cover the case:

> The Act itself establishes that the Commission's powers are not limited to the engineering and technical aspects of regulation of radio communication. Yet we are asked to regard the Commission as a kind of traffic officer, policing the wave lengths to prevent stations from interfering with each other. But the Act does not restrict the Commission merely to supervision of the traffic. It puts upon the Commission the burden of determining the composition of that traffic. The facilities of radio are not large enough to accommodate all who wish to use them. Methods must be devised for choosing from among the many who apply. And since Congress itself could not do this, it committed the task to the Commission.
>
> The Commission was, however, not left at large in performing this duty. The touchstone provided by Congress was the "public interest, convenience, or necessity," a criterion which "is as concrete as the complicated factors for judgment in such a field of delegated authority permit."[18]

---

15. Chicago Tribune Co. v. Oak Leaves Broadcasting Station, Ill. Circuit Ct., Cook County, Nov. 17, 1926, reprinted in 68 Cong. Rec. 215–19 (1926).

16. National Broadcasting Co. v. U. S., 319 U.S. at. 210–212.

17. *Id.* at 228 ("The Communications Act of 1934 does not in terms give the Commission power to regulate the contractual relations between the stations and the networks.")

18. *Id.* at 215–16.

The deep intellectual confusions in his overconfident opinion have long been exposed.[19] The scarcity of which Justice Frankfurter spoke is a condition of all human relations, not just the spectrum. An auction that requires bids at a positive price can eliminate any imbalance between supply and demand. The ostensible scarcity, leading up to queues and interference, was a necessary consequence of the disequilibrium that arises whenever legislation limits price to zero: Demand will always exceed supply. That will result in shortages when parties must obtain the goods and services from others. And it will generate signal interference if each is permitted to take to the airwaves with impunity: The tumults on land without property rights also take place in the airwaves without property rights. Even if we suppose that the FCC's power goes to offering an enforcement of the antitrust law, the truly dangerous assertion is that the FCC "merely" can supervise the traffic to avoid interference, when the proper conception supposedly gives it the power to determine the "composition of the traffic."

When that phrase is taken literally, we have switched from a system in which government creates and enforces property rights into one in which it engages in full scale administrative planning of the sort that Progressives long supported in every area from land planning, through zoning, to agricultural cartels and mandatory collective bargaining in labor cases. The disdain for competitive solutions dependent on the ability to trade through strong property rights permeates Frankfurter's opinion. He much preferred the government to engage in active administration of the public trust that Congress conferred upon it.

Spectrum Allocation, Done Badly

The ensuing concentration of power in state hands creates the genuine risk of state monopolies that could skew news coverage and political debate in the United States. But the risks of that were

19. Ronald H. Coase, *The Federal Communications Commission*, 2 J. L. & Econ. 1 (1959).

smaller than in the United Kingdom because state regulation of private networks poses less of a threat than the state operation of the only radio stations, as was the case in Great Britain with the BBC.[20]

Yet even if we put aside the political question, the central issue is this: Just how does the government determine the composition of the traffic. That inquiry did not have to be faced head on in *NBC* because its antitrust focus did not involve the issuing of new licenses or the revocation of old ones. But once it came to the fore, it can be said with complete confidence that the FCC, under the constant supervision of the courts, has not in the sixty-five years since *NBC* been able to develop a coherent test to decide just how much weight, and why, to afford such factors as local ownership, program diversity, technical competence, and the like.

Indeed, a moment's reflection should indicate that virtually none of the supposed relevant factors makes the slightest bit of difference. The simple point is that issues such as technical competence are self-correcting unless they cause interference, at which point the usual trespass remedies are available. But on such matters as program diversity, the proper unit of analysis is not the individual station but the local market. Any given station could have a heavy concentration by format or political view, so long as the necessary corrective is supplied by other broadcasters with different views. Nor need we fear that these will not emerge. The second broadcaster will have strong incentives to serve those pockets of demand that are not served by the first, and so on down the line.

There is, moreover, a clear way in which each station could increase its own diversity in programming. The secret here, which is what sent the *Cosmopolitan Broadcasting* licensee down for the count, is the ability of any property owner to issue licenses to multiple third parties for all or part of its property by turning itself into a time broker who is indifferent to how the licensed spectrum is used. The term "license" takes on different meaning as we move

---

20. For a discussion of some of these issues, see RONALD H. COASE, BRITISH BROADCASTING: A STUDY IN MONOPOLY (1950).

from public licenses with no clear social objective to private licenses with clear profit-making intentions. The licensing agreements for land, for patented technology, and artistic work are limited only by the ingenuity of the parties to wring out the last element of value from the asset by apportioning it among the largest number of users. There are always situations where the activities of one licensee could clash with those of another, but not to worry, because the licensor will resolve those conflicts unless he is asleep at an expensive switch. He will internalize those externalities when he issues the full set of licenses: The only way to maximize licensing revenues, and through that profits, is to find those configurations that maximize value to users, which take into account not only matters of interference but also the competitive interactions that could take place among various licensees. (Think here of a shopping center that restricts the number of big-box stores on the premises.)

The set of licenses that are issued by the government are in form similar to private licenses, but the incentive structures are not. What is at stake here is a bureaucratic beauty contest in which bidding is not used to sort out the strength of the competing applicants. Cheap talk becomes the order of the day. That system, moreover, has serious limitations when the number of licenses is small relative to the huge demand. In connection with broadcast licenses, the concern is that the winning bidders will appeal to dominant market segments so that fringe groups will not be able to participate fully in the marketplace. Indeed, one object of the FCC regulations is to preserve those interests by forcing its licensees to take those voices into account in determining programming. Fat chance.

It is here that the *Cosmopolitan* time brokerage approach shows the bankruptcy of the present licensing system. Instead of designing and implementing a broadcast strategy that reflected its own uniform vision of programming, what *Cosmopolitan* did was to decide to introduce the bidding system for all of its own programming time. In effect it became a market entrepreneur that did what the FCC refused to do: It created a set of time slots on its station and sold them off to the highest bidders to be used as they saw fit. The results were a veritable bazaar of programming in multiple languages, all done by WHBI's licensees.[21] The virtues of this system should be apparent. By converting itself into a greedy cash licensor, the substantive decisions for each hour of programming were decentralized, which gave more organizations as licensees a voice in the kinds of viewpoints and topics that could reach the air. The decisions on content were thus made by individuals who had the greatest knowledge of the desires of their potential audiences. It also allowed the individual sublicensees to sell advertisements that matched their intended audience. And it used an aggressive program of diversification to reduce the risk of systemic bias in the selection of program content. Best of all, the superior allocation of resources came at a far lower cost because no administrative agency was required to pass on the suitability of the various programmers.

It may well be that the First Amendment arguments have never carried much weight in the broadcast area because the licensees were subject to control that the government exerted as an owner rather than as a regulator. Thus, as Justice White intoned in the *Red Lion* case:

> Thirty years of consistent administrative construction left undisturbed by Congress until 1959, when that construction was expressly accepted, reinforce the natural conclusion that the public interest language of the Act authorized the Commission to require licensees to use their stations for discussion of public issues, and that the FCC

---

21. "The following is a breakdown of WHBI's weekly foreign language programming in 1969: Spanish (45.5 hours); Italian (35.5 hours); Greek (10 hours); Hungarian (4 hours); Arabic (2.5 hours); Polish (2.75 hours); Brazilian (2.05 hours); Portuguese (2 hours); Lithuanian (1 hour); Slovakian (55 minutes); Croatian (.5 hours); Albanian (.5 hours); Ukrainian (.5 hours); Romanian (.5 hours); Armenian (.5 hours); Yugoslavian (.5 hours); Bulgarian (.5 hours); Norwegian (.5 hours). Reply brief for appellant, Appendix A at Exhibit # 6. By 1972, WHBI also broadcast in Korean, Macedonian, Urdu, Hindi, Bengali, Japanese, and Russian." *Cosmopolitan*, 581 F.2d at 919 n. 2.

> is free to implement this requirement by reasonable rules and regulations which fall short of abridgment of the freedom of speech and press, and of the censorship proscribed by § 326 of the Act.[22]

Yet it quickly became equally clear that the imposition of a similar obligation on newspapers, without the state ownership of radio frequencies, *did* run into serious constitutional issues, where it constitutes an "intrusion into the function of editors."[23]

But put aside the constitutional question, and ask whether, as a matter of first principle, the public licensee process works better than an ownership model whereby the spectrum is auctioned off on a once-and-for-all basis, whereby each owner then can do with it what it will. The actual litigation in *Cosmopolitan* lent no confidence to the sunny view that administrative control can get things right. As a general matter, government licenses are for short periods, and the renewal often is a costly and ponderous proceeding that allows interlopers to hold up the licensee for collateral concession—free ads for me—that could not happen if property rights were perpetual and transferable.

The fragility of the present FCC licenses became evident in the ease with which the FCC made out its case that Cosmopolitan breached its statutory obligation, which imposed on it a "nondelegable" duty to exercise "adequate control and supervision over the

---

22. Red Lion Broadcasting Co. v. FCC, 395 U.S. 367, 382 (1969), where the scarcity in frequencies was used as a justification for upholding the Fairness Doctrine whereby those who were personally attacked were given equal time to speak. Justice White traced the justification for regulation to the need to prevent the "chaos" of interference, id. at 375 n. 4. Early on the Commission had expressed its view that the "public interest requires ample play for the free and fair competition of opposing views, and the commission believes that the principle applies ... to all discussions of issues of importance to the public." Great Lakes Broadcasting Co., 3 F.R.C. Ann. Rep. 32, 33 (1929). The claim for fair competition is a dead giveaway that the competition will not be "free."

23. See Miami Herald Publishing Co. v. Tornillo, 418 U.S. 241, 257–258 (1974).

programming and other operations of Station WHBI consistent with licensee responsibility."[24] The lame defense that *Cosmopolitan* offered played within the established rules of the FCC. It did not therefore say that the tests were ill-conceived. Rather it argued that it was in compliance with the statutory standard because it exercised sufficient control through the selection of its sublicensees even though it did not examine the content of their broadcasts.[25]

The inadequacy of Cosmopolitan's defense under the Federal Communications Act should be regarded as a condemnation of the statute, not of Cosmopolitan's practices. It is only if one has the administrative conceit that direct oversight adds social value to the content of the programming that the case presents an interesting challenge. But *Cosmopolitan* is devoid of any explanation of the source of the supposed comparative advantage that one licensee has over its sublicensees for divining the "tastes and ascertained needs of the community," as if that task could be done in any holistic way.[26] The imperatives of the administrative state thus take on a life of their own and become the impregnable starting points for the entire discussion. At no point does any issue of first principle disrupt the closed order. Cosmopolitan's bold business plan was undone by its tepid legal defense.

Recommendation and Conclusion

The lessons of the *Cosmopolitan* case for the current net neutrality debate should now be self-evident. The sorry, if foreordained, performance of the D.C. Circuit in dealing with the broadcast licensees and the use of time brokers should give a strong warning to those who think that Congress or the FCC should exert any direct control over the broadband providers. The proper limits of government action in this area should be defined by the an-

24. *Cosmopolitan*, 581 F.2d at 920.

25. *Id.* at 922–23.

26. See *Cosmopolitan* 581 F.2d at 921, quoting Network Broadcasting by Standard (AM) and FM Broadcast Stations, 63 F.C.C. 2d 674, 680 (1977).

titrust laws. Efforts to impose additional restrictions often turn out to be far more anticompetitive than the practices they displace. The larger danger lies with government actions to expand its own authority by the repetitive use of one intellectual trick. Treat the rules that are necessary for the definition, creation, and enforcement of property rights as though they are indistinguishable from all other forms of regulation. Then conclude that those who accept the one system of regulation are helpless to resist on principle the full range of government controls that go far beyond the classical liberal definition of property rights. Laissez-faire, we are told, is doomed by self-contradiction because its opponents find it literally impossible to imagine how the law of property, contract, and tort can intelligently govern any substantive area. The claim is that so long as regulation is inevitable, the choice among forms of regulation cannot be governed by any intelligible principle.[27]

The claim that laissez-faire falls of its own weight is not confined to telecommunications but arises in other areas. Someone announces that so long as one accepts the Statute of Frauds or the standard recordation principle, there suddenly are no principled grounds to reject the minimum wage, the antidiscrimination laws or mandatory collective bargaining. After all, these too are all government regulations of freedom of contract. But such arguments are untenable because they ignore any connection between the chosen regulation and its effects on overall social welfare. A writing requirement and a recordation statute are intended to strengthen the system of voluntary exchange by reducing the uncertainties of transactions and giving notice to the world of the state of the title in question. The other regulations all restrict the voluntary exchange in ways that destroy potential gains from trade. So long as we understand the difference between positive and negative sum games, we should be able to assess which forms of regulation strengthen markets, and which undermine it.

---

27. For an early defense of this position, see Robert L. Hale, *Coercion and Distribution in a Supposedly Non-Coercive State*, 38 POL. SCI. Q. 470 (1923), as defended in BARBARA FRIED, THE PROGRESSIVE ASSAULT ON LAISSEZ-FAIRE: ROBERT HALE AND THE FIRST LAW AND ECONOMICS MOVEMENT (1998).

A similar pattern is at work in the modern debates over net neutrality. The defense of that position starts out as a plea to end discrimination. Yet there is little evidence that the new dose of regulation will produce any gains in the short run. In the long run, we can expect a repetition of the sorry performance of the FCC (or, for that matter, Congress) with respect to broadcast rights to work its way through the law of net neutrality. The sad truth is that the parties who seek to develop sophisticated and sensible schemes for state control quickly lose control over the administrative process to persons whose ambitions for state control are not bound by any fine-grained rationale. The dangers for this predictable drift usually suffice to err on the side of caution. Stated otherwise, the expected rate of depreciation of sound public norms that rely on administrative discretion is high. There are too many pressure points to keep the rascals at bay. So the recommendation here is to follow classical liberal principles that treat all state intervention as a mistake until it is shown to be a good. More practically, and much to the point of the current public policy debate: Keep private control over broadband pipes by abandoning the siren call for net neutrality.

CHAPTER 5

Universal Service: Can We Do More with Less?

John W. Mayo

"Yes, we can." In fact, from the historic beginning of our nation's focus on universal service until the present, our well-intentioned public policy to promote universal telephone service has violated virtually every economic principle that would allow us, as a nation, to do more, with less. And while many policy issues create a range of opinions within the economics community, this is one of the most widely agreed to conclusions in the realm of microeconomic policies today.

Moreover, concerns over our current universal service policy are far more than the obsessions of academic economists bent on criticism of policymakers' failures to adopt "optimal" policies. The $7 billion dollars spent on universal service in 2007 is both a large absolute number and large relative to other important policy initiatives. To put this cost in perspective, federal outlays for trade adjustment assistance (arguably our nation's front line policy instrument to retool our workforce in the face of globalization) are less than $900 million, and funding for the Job Corps (our principal program to ensure the employability of young, disadvantaged members of the labor force) is approximately $1.5 billion. Indeed, funding for the Centers for Disease Control and Prevention has hovered only a bit higher at around $8 billion for the last few years.

While few would question whether universal service is worthy of some support, the relative expenditures on universal service are likely to strike many as patently unreasonable. Indeed, one study indicates that "[t]he welfare losses endured in the name of universal service have undoubtedly totaled in the tens of billions of dollars over the years."[1] Yet another calculates the annual welfare loss from current universal service policies to be between $2.4 and $7.0 billion dollars annually.[2] And as we look toward the future, our long-standing policy pursuit of universal service for telephony is increasingly being augmented with discussions of a large-scale universal service policy for broadband. Consequently, the articulation of economically efficient principles and policies are not only relevant for reforming the current set of universal service policies but also for shaping the future.

The goal of this chapter is to lay out the basis for the conclusion that "yes we can … do more with less." To do so, I first lay out the economic principles that underpin the need for a universal service policy. As we shall see, the primary economic rationale for a policy of promoting universal service for traditional telephone service has been the prospect that subscription to telephony is characterized by a network externality that may create a systematic under-subscription to the public switched network. In light of the increasing focus on broadband, I also compare the traditional economic rationale with those being offered for the universal provision of broadband in the United States. I then benchmark existing universal service policies against these economic principles.

With these principles in hand, I then turn to an overview of the current system. As we shall see, the contrast between the economic principles that should guide universal service and those in place is striking. The chapter then examines the forward-looking lessons to be learned from our nation's experience with universal service policies to date. The chapter concludes with a discussion of the policy opportunities facing the Federal Communications Commission (FCC) and Congress.

---

1. A.H. Barnett and David L. Kaserman, *The Simple Welfare Economics of Network Externalities and the Uneasy Case for Subscribership Subsidies*, 13 J. of Regulatory Econ. 245–246 (1998).

2. Robert W. Crandall and Leonard Waverman, Who Pays for Universal Service? Table 8.6 (2000).

Economic Principles to Guide Universal Service Policy

The economic principles to guide universal service policy bifurcate into two general questions. First, is there an economic rationale for a universal service policy? Second, if a universal service policy is to be pursued, what economic guideposts should shape the policy?

It is tempting to skip the first question. As a practical mater, the pursuit of universal telephone service is well-entrenched and continues to have robust support in policy circles. Why, one may reasonably ask, should we consider the rationale for a policy that has enjoyed support for nearly a century? Two answers seem to emerge. First, while the theoretical rationale may have remained the same, the evolution of the industry may now provide a different—more or less—compelling rationale for a universal service policy today than existed 50, 20 or even 10 years ago. Second, the prospect of the policy pursuit of broadband universal service compels that we consider the policy rationale for universal service afresh.

The economic rationale for a universal service policy stems from the widely observed prospect for telephony to exhibit network externality characteristics.[3] Such network externality characteristics arise because subscription to the public switched telephone network is determined by households individually comparing the *private* benefits they individually receive from such subscription with the price of subscription. Because other households (society) value the ability to speak on the telephone with the potentially subscribing household, however, the *social* benefits from subscription exceed the private benefits of subscription. The potential exists in this circumstance for an under-subscribed public switched network.

---

3. A potentially important distinction for policy purposes arises when individual-level network externalities are internalized by a network provider. For a discussion, see Stanley J. Liebowitz and Stephen E. Margolis, *Network Effects*, in Vol. 1 Handbook of Telecommunications Economics 76–97. (M.E. Caves, S.K. Majumdar and I. Vogelsang eds., 2002)

Two features of the present telecommunications landscape are especially relevant when considering the foundational rationale for a universal service policy provided by the presence of network externalities. First, one may reasonably distinguish between the aggregate presence of network externalities in traditional telephony, which provides a rationale for a universal service policy, and the magnitude of such externalities on the margin, which should guide policymakers regarding the size of such a policy.[4] With respect to the latter, roughly 95 percent of American households have telephone access, and it is estimated that there are now over 260 million wireless telephone subscribers.[5] Consequently, it is likely that the magnitude of the marginal network externality is exceedingly small for traditional voice telephony today.

Second, given the forward-looking focus on broadband universal service, it is perhaps important to note that network effects from broadband are more likely to be indirect than direct.[6] Direct externalities, which are quite relevant in the case of traditional voice telephony, arise when the utility of the service to consumers depends directly on the number of total subscribers to the service in question. Indirect externalities arise when the utility of the service to purchasers is not directly affected by the number of other subscribers to the network but rather only indirectly as the size of the network affects the pricing or availability of complementary goods or services. Such indirect externalities are likely to be more prevalent in the case of broadband than traditional voice telephony. For example, as the size of the base of broadband consumers grows, the business case for developing and offering increasingly attractive and sophisticated broadband-based content increases. Thus, while a broadband customer may benefit directly from the speed and facility with which

---

4. Barnett and Kaserman, *supra* note 1.

5. CTIA Mid-Year Semi-Annual Wireless Industry Survey (2008), *available at* http://files.ctia.org/pdf/CTIA_Survey_Mid_Year_2008_Graphics.pdf.

6. For a more detailed discussion of direct and indirect externalities, see Michael L. Katz and Carl Shapiro, *Network Externalities, Competition, and Compatibility*, 75 The Am. Econ. Rev., 424–440 (1985) and Liebowitz and Margolis, *supra* note 3.

she may reach other broadband providers, a potentially larger external value may derive from the larger and more sophisticated set of services that content providers offer with a larger broadband base.

While the presence of direct and indirect network effects may provide a *bona fide* economic rationale for a broadband universal service policy, one cannot help but observe that this seems not to be the rationale offered by policymakers for what appears, increasingly, to be universal support for a universal broadband service policy. Instead, policymakers most often couch their support for the rapid deployment and adoption of broadband in economic development terms. While such a rationale may prove to be well-founded, economic research on the economic development consequences of broadband deployment and adoption is limited.[7]

The second critical question that must be addressed in shaping an efficient universal service policy is what economic guideposts should shape such a policy. Because network externalities create the potential for an under-subscribed network, subsidies are likely to be the policy instrument of choice to elicit a larger network base. This immediately begs the question: Are there economic principles that should guide the collection and distribution of universal service subsidies? In this regard the following economic principles of efficient subsidization are essential:

Table 1 Economic Principles of Subsidization

- Establish clear goals to be accomplished by the subsidization program
- Make subsidies explicit and transparent
- Collect subsidies from the widest possible funding base
- Target subsidies to those in need of subsidies
- Design subsidies to relax complementary binding constraints to the achievement of the goal

7. See Sharon Gillette, William Lehr, Carlos A. Osorio and Marvin T. Sirbu, Measuring the Economic Impact of Broadband Deployment, Final Report, National Technical Assistance, Training, Research, and Evaluation Project #99-07-13829, submitted to Economic Development Administration, February 28, 2006, and the literature cited therein.

While each of these guiding principles may appear straightforward and noncontroversial, a look at the evolution of traditional narrowband universal service policy reveals that each of these principles has been egregiously violated. It is to that evolution that we now turn.

The Evolution of Universal Service Policy in the United States

Legislative Milestones

Attention to the prospect of providing "universal" telephone service throughout the United States is often attributed to Theodore Vail, who as president of AT&T in 1907 articulated a vision of "one system, one policy, universal service."[8] Subsequent to this call from the private sector for universal service, three significant changes to the universal service goals of the nation occurred. First, the passage of the Federal Communications Act in 1934 established the national goal "to make available, so far as possible, to all the people of the United States, a rapid, efficient, Nationwide, and world-wide wire and radio communication service with adequate facilities at reasonable charges."[9]

Second, Congress passed the Telecommunications Act of 1996, which calls upon the FCC and the states to "encourage the deployment on a reasonable and timely basis of advanced telecommunications capability to all Americans." [10]

And, third, the most recent legislative measure to guide the nation's universal service policy came in late 2008 with the passage of the Broadband Data Improvement Act.[11] While this Act was

---

8. For a detailed discussion of Vail's vision of universal service, see Milton Mueller, Jr., Universal Service: Competition, Interconnection and Monopoly in the Making of the American Telephone System 92–103 (1997).

9. Communications Act of 1934, 47 U.S.C. § 1.

10. Telecommunications Act of 1996, 47 U.S.C. § 157nt.

11. Broadband Data Improvement Act, 47 U.S.C. § 1301 nt.

principally designed to modernize the record-keeping and accounting of the deployment of broadband services, the preamble to the Act states that "continued progress in the deployment and adoption of broadband technology is vital to ensuring that our Nation remains competitive and continues to create business and job growth."[12]

The evolution of universal service policy as articulated through these various legislative milestones has significantly altered the nation's universal service goals over time. In particular, note that early legislation emphasized the *availability* of telephony while the most recent legislation has indicated that "deployment and adoption" are relevant targets. This evolution rather substantively alters the appropriate economic policy tools and methods for those responsible for implementing universal service policy. Additionally, early legislation focused on narrowband voice telephony, while the most recent legislation has targeted advances in "broadband technology" as "vital to ensuring that our nation remains competitive." Thus, policymakers have significantly expanded the target for universal service on a going-forward basis.

A final, potentially significant, observation emerges from the combination of economic principles and the understanding of the evolution of advocacy for universal service in telephony. Specifically, it is noteworthy that the earliest calls for universal service were by the private sector. Similarly, private firms today have championed the deployment of modern broadband infrastructure. Indeed, only a moment's reflection is necessary to conclude that, as a general matter, the value of a private firm's network is enhanced by deepening the deployment and utilization of that network. This is, of course, not to say that the deployment of a network to 100 percent of the population will inherently result as a consequence of purely private decisionmaking. To the extent that firms have private incentives for network expansion, however, it is likely to be possible to fashion going-forward universal service policies that harness the private sector's inherent incentives for net-

12. *Id.*, at Preamble.

work expansion through complementary private sector-public sector partnerships.

Regulatory Implementation

However well-meaning regulators may have been in their pursuit of universal service goals over the years, the actual policies that have been implemented under this epithet have violated virtually every one of the economic principles identified above. For over half a century, the primary vehicles for advancing universal service have been implicit rather than explicit policies that, at least nominally, might appear to support the goal of universal service. Specifically, through a complex system of allocating local exchange network costs between the federal and state jurisdictions, and between residential and business consumers, regulators have been able to effectively establish a system of "residual pricing" whereby maximum "contributions" have been extracted from a host of telecommunications services while only collecting the minimal, residual revenues from basic local exchange services that make the local exchange telephone companies financially whole.[13] This system has resulted in residential local rates that have historically been held below the incremental cost of providing local residential service and has created a complex web of internal cross-subsidies.[14] Specifically, cross-subsidies from long-distance to local services, from business customers to residential customers, and from urban to rural areas have been used to maintain these artificially low residential rates. Because of these cross-subsidies, the prices of long-distance services, local rates to business customers, and even local rates to residential customers in densely populated urban areas

13. For a more complete discussion, see David L. Kaserman, John W. Mayo, and Joseph Flynn, *Cross-Subsidization: Beyond the Universal Service Fairy Tale*, 2 J. of Regulatory Econ., 231–251 (1990).

14. For a more detailed discussion, see David L. Kaserman, and John W. Mayo, *Cross-Subsidies in Telecommunications: Roadblocks on the Road to More Intelligent Telephone Pricing*, 11 Yale J. on Reg., 119–147 (1994).

have tended to exceed their marginal costs, often by a considerable amount.[15] This implicit system of cross-subsidization has been roundly criticized as economically inefficient, inequitable, unsustainable, and ineffective.[16]

While the implicit system of subsidies within the telecommunications industry has evoked economic criticism, two explicit universal service programs have also been the subject of scrutiny. An untargeted program known as the High Cost Support Fund was established to enable areas with high costs to recover some of these costs from a federal universal service fund, leaving a smaller remainder of the costs to be recovered through end-user rates or state universal service support mechanisms. The stated intention is to "hold down rates and thereby further one of the most important goals of federal and state regulation—the preservation and advancement of universal telephone service."[17]

The High Cost Support Fund payments are not targeted to individuals that may be in need of a subsidy in order to subscribe to the pubic switched network, but rather are simply funds transferred to local exchange carriers in the hope that the funds will result in lower telephone rates for their customers and the promotion of universal telephone service. Importantly, it is not only the incumbent local exchange carrier within an area that may receive high cost support. Other eligible telephone companies that service the area (either wireline or wireless) can also receive high cost support, the amount of which is tied to the high cost support per line received by the incumbent local exchange carrier in the area and the number of lines served. The initial amount of funding per

15. See, for example, Karen Palmer, *A Test for Cross-Subsidies in Local Telephone Rates: Do Business Customers Subsidize Residential Customers?*, 23 Rand J. of Econ., 415–433 (1992).

16. See, for example, Kaserman, Mayo and Flynn, *supra* note 13; Kaserman and Mayo, *supra* note 14; Robert W. Crandall and Leonard Waverman, Who Pays for Universal Service? (2000); and Alfred E. Kahn, *The Road to More Intelligent Telephone Pricing*, 1 Yale J. on Reg. 139–158 (1984).

17. Federal Communications Commission, Universal Service Monitoring Report, CC Docket No. 98–202, at 3-1 (2008).

line for the incumbent carrier is set based upon the firm's embedded (historical accounting) cost of providing service.

Unfortunately, the High Cost Support Program fares very poorly when judged by the economic principles of subsidization described in Table 1. The goal of the program "to hold down rates" is neither clear (as to when the goal has been accomplished) nor congruent with the specific mission of promoting universal deployment or subscription to telephony. While the program is "explicit," the mechanisms by which it is intended to promote universal service are anything but transparent. Specifically, eligible companies receive funds with no accountability for how these funds explicitly promote universal service. For rate-of-return regulated companies, the receipt of these funds may be used to reduce the revenue requirement for the company, but this reduced revenue requirement may be implemented by the company in any number of ways including the possibility of reduced charges to customers that will subscribe whether or not they enjoy a subsidized price.

While the link between the receipt of payments from the High Cost Support Fund and subscription is tenuous for rate-of-return firms, it is all but absent for price-cap-regulated firms.[18] Specifically, price-cap-regulated firms are under no obligation to alter rates based upon the receipt of payments from the High Cost Support Fund. A detailed econometric study of the relationship of payments from the High Cost Support Fund (these payments were previously referred to as the High Cost Assistance or the HCA program) received by rural telephone companies and households' subscription to the telephone network found that "we cannot reject

18. Regulators have increasingly replaced traditional rate-of-return regulation with price cap regulation. Under price cap regulation, the prices of telephone services are capped (generally allowing for formulaic adjustments upward with inflation and downward with productivity enhancements) with no explicit tie to a firm's cost. Absent the tie to the realized costs of the firm, price cap regulation is often championed as creating improved incentives for firm efficiency. For a more detailed discussion, see David E.M. Sappington, *Price Regulation*, HANDBOOK OF TELECOMMUNICATIONS ECONOMICS, Vol. 1 227–296. (M.E. Caves, S.K. Majumdar and I. Vogelsang eds., 2002)

the null hypothesis that the untargeted HCA subsidy scheme has had no direct impact whatsoever" on telephone subscription.[19] Thus, in the absence of a specific mechanism by which the High Cost Support mechanism will promote telephone subscription, it appears that billions of dollars are being provided to telephone companies with little or no discernible impact on the actual achievement of universal service.

The High Cost support mechanism also fares badly relative to the economic principles regarding the financing and targeting of the funds. As the principles in Table 1 indicate, to be efficient, subsidies should be collected from the widest base possible and targeted narrowly. The High Cost Support mechanism, however, employs exactly the opposite strategy, collecting subsidies from a subset of telecommunications users (long-distance consumers) and providing those funds to companies (rather than people who are making subscription decisions).

A final troubling aspect of the High Cost Support Program centers on the moral hazard issues raised by the program. Specifically, under the High Cost Support Program, the magnitude of subsidy funding is determined by the magnitude of the costs that the firm can demonstrate that it has incurred. While the High Cost Support mechanism has certainly been motivated by the desire to defray the economic costs (i.e., the minimal costs necessary to provide service of a particular quality), the structure of the program creates incentives for rural telecommunications firms to incur costs that exceed those that are, economically speaking, necessary.

Finally, the program is presumably motivated by the desire to increase subscription rates in rural areas. Yet, the program targets the goal simply to "hold down rates." Many rural residents can, however, fully afford to pay for the costs that their subscription imposes on the public switched network. Surely residents of the rural resorts such as Vail, Colorado, Deer Valley, Utah, and Sun

19. Eriksson, Kaserman and Mayo, *Targeted and Untargeted Subsidy Schemes: Evidence from Postdivestiture Efforts to Promote Universal Telephone Service*, 41 J.L. AND ECON. 477, 495 (1998).

Figure 1

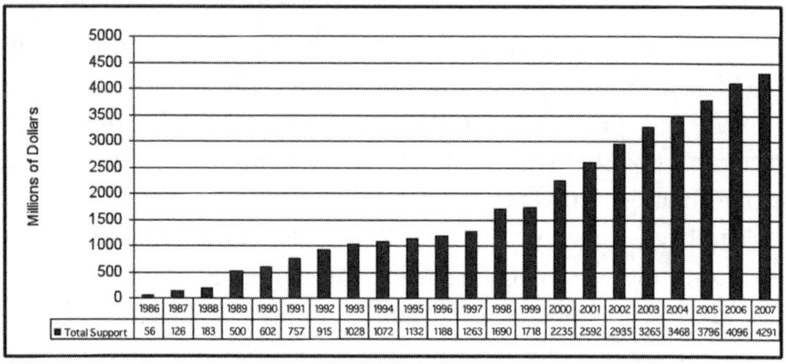

Source: Federal Communications Commission, Universal Service Monitoring Report, CC Docket No. 98-202, 2008, Chart 3-1.

Valley, Idaho can afford to pay for the costs that their subscription causes society to incur as a result of their subscription.

The combined result of these program attributes is that the costs of the High Cost Support Program have grown dramatically over time. As seen in Figure 1, High Cost Support now exceeds $4 billion annually.

A second explicit program designed to promote universal service is known as the Low Income Program. Within the Low Income Program are two specific programs that are designed to promote universal service. The Lifeline Program was established in 1984 to provide eligible low-income households with a monthly subsidy for subscribing to the public switched telephone network. Because the program is administered at the state level, the amount of benefits and eligibility criteria vary from state to state. Eligibility is most often determined by participation in one of the following seven federal "portal" programs: Medicaid, Food Stamps, Supplemental Security Income (SSI), Federal Public Housing Assistance (Section 8), the Low-Income Home Energy Assistance Program (LIHEAP), the National School Lunch Program's free lunch program, or Temporary Assistance for Needy Families (TANF). Benefits, too, vary with an average of state and federal monthly support per household ranging from $7.53 in Indiana to $13.50 in

Alaska, Florida, and Guam.[20] After a modest start, the Lifeline Program has now grown to over three-quarters of a billion dollars annually.

A companion program to Lifeline, known as Link-Up, provides a one-time subsidy to low-income households at the time that they initiate telephone service. In 2006, over 1.6 million households received Link-Up support, with benefits averaging $19.25 per household.[21]

The Low Income Programs fare significantly better in their consistency with the economic principles discussed above. Specifically, they are explicit and targeted. The funding for these programs is designed to target those individuals who, in the absence of a subsidy, would not subscribe. An econometric assessment of the effectiveness of the Lifeline program determined that the program has, indeed, increased subscription to the public switched telephone network.[22] As such, Lifeline and Link-Up represent the success stories of policy efforts to promote universal service. Even here, however, there is significant room for reform. The estimates to date indicate that the cost of adding a subscriber through the low-income subsidy program is quite high.[23] One reason for the high cost of adding subscribers via the Lifeline program has been the low rate at which even eligible households avail themselves of the Lifeline program. A recent study of the determinants of participation of low-income households in the Lifeline program found that participation rates are negatively influenced by limitations that some states place on the ability of Lifeline households to utilize optional calling features such as call forwarding or three-way calling.[24] The study also determined that: (1) the larger the number of public policy "portals" the greater the likelihood of participa-

---

20. Federal Communications Commission, *supra* Table 2.3.

21. *Id.*, Table 2.12 (non-tribal beneficiaries).

22. Eriksson, Kaserman and Mayo, *supra* note 19.

23. *Id.*

24. Mark Burton, Jeffrey Macher, and John W. Mayo, *Understanding Participation in Social Programs: Why Don't Households Pick Up the Lifeline?* 7 The B.E. Journal of Econ. Analysis and Policy, 1–26 (2007).

tion; and (2) higher financial benefits of these portal programs attracts greater participation in the Lifeline program. So, for instance, higher Food Stamp benefits enhance the likelihood of participation in the Lifeline program.

Broadband Universal Service: Lessons Learned From Narrowband

While the economic principles to guide policymakers that seek to subsidize an activity in pursuit of a goal such as such as universal service are clear [see Table 1], our examination of the evolution of universal service policies suggests that these principles have uniformly been violated in the pursuit of narrowband universal service for voice telephony. Recall, for instance, the first principle: "Establish clear goals to be accomplished by the subsidization program." Unfortunately, the goals of narrowband universal service have morphed significantly over time, making it difficult to identify a point in time in which we might "declare victory." As described in a recent review of the economic literature on universal service, "[u]niversal service is a chameleon-like phrase."[25]

What began as a policy designed to promote "availability" morphed into one in which the goal by some, but not all, policymakers seemed to be to charge the lowest possible subscription rates for telephone service consistent with the survival of the telephone company. A second economic principle, to make subsidies explicit and transparent, has also been violated. Implicit subsidies brought about by excessively pricing some services (for example, access services and long distance) to promote low prices on other services (for example, basic local service) have significantly distorted

25. Michael H. Riordan, *Universal Residential Telephone Service*, in Vol. 1 HANDBOOK OF TELECOMMUNICATIONS ECONOMICS 423, 424. (M.E. Caves, S.K. Majumdar and I. Vogelsang eds., 2002)

economic efficiency and have arguably failed to advance the cause of increasing subscription.[26]

Perhaps the most egregious violations to economic principles have come in the manner of financing universal service subsidies and in directing the use of these funds. Recall from Table 1 that economic principles dictate that universal service subsidies should be collected from the widest possible base. The rationale for this is straightforward; by broadening the base, the distortion from the subsidies is minimized on a per-capita basis. The flip side of this principle is that subsidies should be targeted narrowly to those economic agents (generally, households) that will alter their behavior in a manner consistent with accomplishing the universal service goal. Subsidies to households that would, absent the subsidy, continue to subscribe to the public switched telephone network are economically wasteful. No behavior is changed, with the only result being that these households receive a wealth transfer. In the case of universal service policy for narrowband telephony, the funding and targeting economic principles, sadly, have been stood on their heads. That is, instead of funding the subsidy broadly and targeting the subsidy narrowly, policymakers have done exactly the opposite. Funds for the subsidy have been raised from a set of "access charges" that have been imposed on long-distance calling (users), while the benefits from this subsidy have generally flowed through to all subscribers to the telephone networks in the form of lower local monthly telephone rates.

The final principle mentioned in Table 1 also provides a benchmark for universal service policies to date. The principle calls upon policymakers to design subsidy mechanisms to recognize the potentially retarding effects of complementary goods and services prices. In the case of narrowband telephony, for example, the targeted Lifeline Program, which is administered at the state level, has different requirements that vary by state. These state-level eligibility requirements include varying degrees of bureaucratic controls and different restrictions on the ability of households to use "vertical features" such as three-way-calling and call forwarding. Such

---

26. Kaserman and Mayo, *supra* note 14.

restrictions on complementary services to the basic subscription created a significant deterrent to the willingness of households to avail themselves of the subsidy.[27] In the case of broadband service, subsidies for subscription to broadband are likely to be undermined absent a policy that recognizes the effects of less than universal computer ownership by households. That is, absent computer ownership, significant broadband subsidies are likely to be impotent in accelerating broadband subscription.

Recommendations and Conclusion

During the second presidential debate of 2008, there was considerable discussion of the financial crisis. At one point in the debate, then Senator Obama argued that a key component of the financial crisis has been our nation's attempt to solve a twenty-first century problem with twentieth-century regulation. Almost everyone, of all political stripes, would agree as the phrase is applied to the financial sector.

President Obama's description, in general, would not seem to apply to modern telecommunications markets. In particular, a number of dimensions of the telecommunications industry and policy have been resoundingly successful. Policy developments have enabled long-distance prices to fall from $.70 cents per minute in 1983 to roughly $.07 per minute today.[28] Similarly, the opening of wireless markets to competition and the auctioning of spectrum have enabled prices for wireless services to decline substantially from $.47 cents per minute in the mid-1990s to roughly $.05 per minute today.[29] With the evolution of telecommunications

---

27. Burton, Macher, and Mayo, *supra* note 24.

28. Federal Communications Commission, Trends in Telephone Service, Table 13.4 (2008). Prices are inflation-adjusted and stated in 2006 dollars.

29. John W. Mayo, *It's No Time to Regulate Wireless Telephony*, 5 The Economists' Voice, 2 (2008).

policy, telecommunications services, as well as goods and services that rely on telecommunications, have become both inexpensive and ubiquitous. For instance, there are now over 260 million wireless subscribers in the United States. Moreover, broadband telecommunications infrastructure grew from only 4 million lines in 2000 to at least 120 million lines in late 2007.[30] In general, the commitment by policymakers to enable competition and establish policies to promote investment in telecommunications infrastructure has been laudable.

At the same time, however, President Obama's phrase does not completely miss the mark in the realm of telecommunications policy. In particular, the now century-old effort to promote universal service remains woefully antiquated, misdirected, and, from an economic perspective, massively bloated. The Broadband Data Improvement Act, signed into law at the end of 2007, points toward the future. It indicates that, "[c]ontinued progress in the deployment and adoption of broadband technology is vital to ensuring that our Nation remains competitive and continues to create business and job growth."[31]

In light of this clearly articulated goal, there should be little doubt that we should no longer linger on narrowband issues, but rather turn directly to the task of reforming and retooling universal service policy. Today, with roughly 95 percent of all households reporting availability of telephone service and some 260 million wireless subscribers, it is time, perhaps well past time, to declare victory in the quest to provide twentieth-century narrowband universal service and to turn to the twenty-first century challenge of broadband deployment and adoption.

In the face of a costly and backward-looking universal service policy and a clear, twenty-first century challenge of broadband deployment and adoption, the FCC has recently begun substantive efforts to reform universal service. It is essential that these reform

---

30. Federal Communications Commission, High-Speed Services for Internet Access: Status as of December 31, 2007, at 1(2009).

31. Broadband Data Improvement Act, *supra*, § 102 (1).

efforts move forward in the Obama administration. While the details of an FCC reform plan can and should receive considerable discussion, the fundamental need for reform is, and has been, well known and long overdue. Given the clarity of economic principles and the possibility for improvements based on the lessons learned from narrowband universal service policy, a significant opportunity for the nation to "do more with less" presents itself as we turn to broadband universal service policies.

As clear as the path may seem, the path forward will certainly face challenges. Given the overwhelming *prima facie* case for universal service reform, however, opponents to such reform have increasing adopted a "yes, but ..." defense which essentially concedes that reform is necessary but argues that such reform is either: (a) in need of more discussion; or (b) properly done at the state rather than federal level. While surely the process of reform should permit all parties to proffer their perspectives, it simply must be emphasized that *discussion* of reform has been going on for roughly twenty years.[32] The positions and perspectives of virtually every industry player are well known and have been for a very long time. The call for further discussion should not be allowed to derail the critical need for tangible universal service policy reform.

It is also important not to allow the discussions of the appropriate venue (federal or state) to derail the move to universal service policy reform. Indeed, opponents of universal service reform have previously argued that state-level reforms must await the articulation of a retooled federal universal service policy. These same players now argue that FCC reform should defer to the leadership of the states. To accept this "dog-chasing-its-own-tail" argument will simply prolong the perpetuation of the massively costly and misdirected universal service subsidy mechanism. Moreover, a mechanism for the proper balancing and coordination of federal and state policy already exists in the form of the Federal-State Joint Board.

In conclusion, we stand at a moment that is ripe for substantively turning the corner on an antiquated, costly and "so-last-cen-

---

32. David. L. Kaserman, John W. Mayo and Joseph Flynn, *supra* note 13.

tury" universal service system. We can, indeed, do more with less, and the administration and Congress should encourage efforts by the FCC to streamline and refocus this twentieth-century policy to the challenges of the twenty-first century.

CHAPTER 6

Unifying the Intercarrier Compensation Regime

Gerald W. Brock

Introduction

Intercarrier compensation is the payment that one telecommunications carrier makes to another when a customer pays one carrier for a message that is transmitted across the facilities of both carriers. A wide variety of intercarrier compensation methods have been voluntarily negotiated by carriers or mandated by regulators to meet specific circumstances. While each method has some merit for satisfying the particular technology, price structure, and service configuration of the situation for which it was designed, the combination of possible methods has created numerous opportunities for arbitrage and creates pernicious incentives to inefficiently route and classify traffic to take advantage of particular intercarrier compensation rates. The Federal Communications Commission initiated a proceeding in 2001 to replace the variety of intercarrier compensation methods with a single unified method.[1]

This paper argues that the current combination of intercarrier compensation methods should be replaced by a single unified framework, but that it is not possible to prescribe a specific rate that is feasible for the wide variety of intercarrier arrangements.

1. Developing a Unified Intercarrier Compensation, Notice of Proposed Rulemaking, 16 F.C.C.R. 9610 (2001) (hereinafter "Unified Intercarrier Compensation").

The goal is to be neutral with regard to technology, industry structure, and pricing plans so that the intercarrier compensation structure does not limit the ability to experiment with new approaches. The new system should consist of voluntary bargaining, guided by regulatory-determined presumptions rather than prescriptions, and supported by the decisions of industry arbitrators when voluntary negotiations fail. The proposed system builds on the existing structure of reciprocal compensation agreements for traffic flowing between local exchange telephone companies. It expands the reciprocal compensation structure across broad geographical areas in recognition of the fact that technological changes have greatly reduced the distance sensitivity of the cost of transmitting communications. When private bargaining fails to reach a solution, the proposed system uses industry arbitrators rather than the reciprocal compensation system of state regulatory commission arbitration to produce a result.

Existing Intercarrier Compensation Systems

There are three major types of "intercarrier" compensation: access charges, reciprocal compensation agreements, and customer-to-carrier payments. Access charges are payments from a long-distance company to a local exchange telephone company for the origination or termination of long-distance traffic. Access charges are regulated and the structure is prescribed in detail, with intrastate access regulated by state regulatory commissions and interstate access regulated by the FCC. The access charge structure was implemented in 1984 after the divestiture of AT&T's local exchange companies from the long-distance company.[2] Access charges were initially designed to reproduce the revenue flows that resulted from pre-divestiture politically determined formulas for the sharing of long-distance revenue between AT&T's long-distance division and local telephone companies. Those formulas in-

---

2. See United States v. Am. Tel. & Tel., 552 F. Supp. 131 (D.D.C. 1982), *aff'd sub .nom.* Maryland v. United States, 460 U.S. 1001 (1983).

cluded particularly favorable arrangements for independent rural telephone companies. The initial access charges required high payments to local carriers per minute of long-distance traffic originated or terminated, and while subsequent revisions greatly reduced the rates, access charges continue the pattern of providing a combination of actual cost recovery and subsidy. The access charge structure was designed for separate local and long-distance companies with long-distance toll rates paid to the long-distance company which then shares some of the revenue with local telephone companies. It has survived the mergers that have recreated integrated local and long-distance telephone companies.

Reciprocal compensation agreements govern the payments between two local telephone companies serving the same geographic area, such as a Competitive Local Exchange Carrier (CLEC) and an Incumbent Local Exchange Carrier (ILEC). The assumption behind reciprocal compensation is that each company charges its own customers for originating calls but that some of its customers want to call customers of the other network. Each network gains from interconnection and the right of its customers to call the other network.

Reciprocal compensation normally requires equal payments in each direction so that if the traffic flow is balanced between the networks, then there is no payment in either direction. If traffic is unbalanced, the sending network makes a payment to the receiving network.[3] If traffic between the two networks is expected to be reasonably balanced, the companies may agree to exchange traffic on a "bill-and-keep" basis. That is, they agree to exchange communications bound for customers of the other company without payment in either direction. Because communication costs are primarily determined by the network costs of connecting each customer and only change slightly with the number of minutes trans-

3. For example, if company A originates 100 minutes of traffic to customers of company B while company B originates 50 minutes of traffic to customers of company A, and the reciprocal compensation rate is $.01 per minute, then company A would pay $.50 to company B. (A pays B $1.00 for traffic it sends while B pays A $.50 for traffic that it sends.)

ported, companies may find it desirable to use bill-and-keep even with unbalanced traffic in order to avoid the transaction costs of measuring and billing for traffic flows.

Reciprocal compensation agreements are governed by provisions adopted in the Telecommunications Act of 1996[4] and the associated rules.[5] Generally, those provisions encourage private negotiation as the preferred method of determining intercarrier compensation. When private negotiations fail to reach an agreement, the parties may request binding arbitration from the state public utility commission that has jurisdiction in the geographic area covered by the agreement.

As a regulatory matter, customer-to-carrier payments are not technically classified as intercarrier compensation because one of the parties is a "customer" instead of a "carrier." However, there is no set of characteristics that clearly distinguishes customers from carriers. When the customer is a residential subscriber with a single telephone line, there is no question that the subscriber is a customer who obtains service from a carrier and pays for that service. However, when the customer is a large corporate network, the transaction could be described as a customer obtaining service from a carrier or as the interconnection of two networks that are exchanging traffic. The classification matters for regulatory purposes because a customer pays a carrier for service while two local carriers are assumed to provide mutual benefits to each other by exchanging traffic. The FCC has made specific determinations in particular cases where the classification is unclear. For example, dial-up Internet Service Providers ("ISPs") are considered customers. Paging networks are considered carriers. Payphone companies are considered customers.[6]

In the unregulated world, there is no clear distinction between carriers and customers. A facilities-based Internet access provider (such as a cable television company) is conceptually similar to a local telephone company in terms of the transmission of traffic.

---

4. Telecommunications Act of 1996, 110 Stat. 56 (codified in scattered sections of 47 U.S.C.)

5. 47 U.S.C. §251 and §252; 47 C.F.R. §51.

6. Unified Intercarrier Compensation, 16 F.C.C.R. at 9615 (2001).

But it is normally considered a customer of an Internet backbone provider (that pays the backbone provider for service) rather than a carrier that exchanges traffic according to intercarrier compensation arrangements. Whether one company pays another as a customer for traffic passed across the network boundary, or whether the companies exchange traffic on a peering basis without payments in either direction, depends on how both companies evaluate the mutual benefits of the traffic exchange and not on the classification of the companies as customers or carriers.

The murky boundary between customers and carriers creates a complication for any scheme of intercarrier compensation that provides either special regulatory burdens or privileges to companies classified as carriers. In the early controversies over switched long-distance competition and bypass of access charges (1975–1985), the fundamental problem was the ability of companies to take advantage of favorable customer arrangements instead of the less favorable intercarrier arrangements. As online services and the Internet developed, the regulatory classification of Internet Service Providers as customers of the local telephone company was a key component in promoting the spread of online services. That classification entitled ISPs to receive service at standard local business line monthly rates instead of paying the high usage-sensitive access rates for traffic exchanged with the local telephone company that would have been required had they been classified as long-distance carriers.

In the late 1990s, the favorable treatment of interconnection among Local Exchange Companies (LECs) created a form of arbitrage in which companies attempted to transform themselves from customers into LECs instead of the earlier arbitrage form in which companies attempted to transform themselves from carriers into customers. If a dial-up ISP could create a CLEC "front" so that the traffic coming to it was treated as incoming reciprocal compensation traffic, then the ILEC would make net payments to the ISP instead of the ISP paying the ILEC. These cases are examples of the general economic finding that in any situation of price discrimination, companies will find innovative ways to qualify for the favored price and avoid the disfavored price.

A Proposal for Intercarrier Compensation Reform

The most straightforward method of intercarrier compensation reform is to abolish all of the current mandates regarding intercarrier compensation and rely entirely on individual bargaining to reach mutually acceptable agreements. However, there are two major problems with relying entirely on bargaining: (1) individual bargains require time and effort and the necessity to reach individual bargains among large numbers of interconnecting carriers will create high transaction costs; (2) continued market power in segments of the telecommunications market and potential market power from the strategic use of network effects limit the effectiveness of free bargaining.

As has been extensively discussed, terminating monopoly remains a problem even when there is considerable competition. The FCC has described the problem as follows:

> This problem [terminating access monopoly] results from the fact that an end user typically subscribes to only one LEC. Hence, other carriers seeking to deliver calls to that end user have no choice but to purchase terminating access from the called party's LEC. These originating carriers generally have little practical means of affecting the called party's choice of access provider.... a number of CLECs, whose terminating access charges are not regulated, have taken advantage of this situation by charging terminating access rates that significantly exceed those charged by rate-regulated ILECs.[7]

Terminating monopoly power even with competition provides a reason to place some limits on free bargaining solutions. A second reason for some limits is to prevent the use of interconnection and compensation as a method of exploiting network effects in

7. *Id.* at 9616 (2001).

order to exercise monopoly power. The entire history of competition in telecommunications has included controversies over interconnection and compensation rates because a new carrier cannot normally gain customers without interconnection and an established monopolist has no incentive voluntarily to grant that interconnection.

Changes in technology, industry structure, and pricing patterns have made the access charge structure poorly suited to providing a framework for current and future intercarrier compensation. Access charges assume that the end user pays separate long-distance and local telephone charges, but most wireless pricing plans and some wireline pricing plans do not distinguish charges for local calls from long-distance calls. Access charges were designed for a technology in which significant costs were incurred to carry telephone calls over long distances, but the costs of bulk transmission have declined so significantly that the cost of transmitting telephone calls may be considered largely distance insensitive.

And access charges were designed for separate local and long-distance telephone companies, but mergers between local and long-distance companies have significantly changed the post-divestiture industry structure. Access charges were designed to keep long-distance charges to the consumer above the cost of providing service and to use the excess revenue to subsidize local exchange carriers through high charges for originating or terminating long-distance calls. But those implicit subsidies have been gradually replaced by explicit subsidies paid through the Universal Service Fund.[8] Now, access charges should be abolished and subsidies for universal service should be separated from intercarrier compensation.

The existing reciprocal compensation structure of private bargaining supported by specified obligations and an arbitration pro-

---

8. The FCC's access charge reform issued order after the 1996 Act observed: "The existing system of implicit subsidies and support flows is sustainable only in a monopoly environment" and "access charges should ultimately reflect rates that would exist in a competitive market." Access Charge Reform, First Report and Order, 12 F.C.C.R. 15,982, at 15,996, 16,001 (1997).

cedure is the foundation for this proposal. The general principles used in the 1996 Act for CLEC to ILEC interconnection are broadly applicable to all services. That is, interconnection provides mutual benefits to the carriers and intercarrier compensation should be based on reciprocal compensation. Furthermore, the basic structure of deference to privately negotiated agreements supported by binding arbitration has proved useful. The framework developed for local telephone interconnection can be expanded into a framework of unified intercarrier compensation that can be applied to the wide range of existing services and to future services without regard to specific technology or jurisdictional status.

The distinction between long-distance and local service has been effectively erased in wireless communications pricing plans and is disappearing in wireline pricing plans. Thus, it is reasonable to extend the local interconnection approach more broadly and to think of carriers that provide service over different geographical areas as providing mutually beneficial services to each other, rather than the divestiture model of a long-distance carrier charging customers for the long-distance service and purchasing access from local carriers. Consider the case of a large integrated carrier such as Verizon or AT&T connecting with an independent rural LEC. In the current structure, the integrated company pays terminating access charges to the LEC for long-distance traffic delivered to the customers of that LEC, and the customers of the LEC pay long-distance charges to their chosen long-distance provider in addition to their payments for local service to the LEC. However, with the very low cost of transmitting communications over long distances, there is no necessity to clearly distinguish the distance. The integrated company and the rural local company see mutual benefits from interconnection and that interconnection could be treated as analogous to local interconnection: The rural company accepts incoming traffic from the integrated company and distributes it to its customers and the integrated company accepts traffic from the rural company and distributes it to its customers.

While the integrated company distributes traffic over a much wider geographical area and the rural company distributes it over relatively high cost sparsely used facilities, neither incurs significant costs per minute, and it is not clear that either would be disadvantaged by a bill-and-keep arrangement (though that would be a legitimate question for an arbitration panel to consider if the companies could not reach a voluntary agreement). In other words, under this proposal it is likely that rural companies would give up their current substantial terminating access charges but would gain free long-distance service for their customers in exchange. That would allow adoption of the distance insensitive pricing model used by wireless carriers and Internet providers.

In addition to expanding the geographical reach of reciprocal compensation, this proposal would replace the existing use of state regulatory commission arbitration with arbitration by panels of industry experts on interconnection and compensation agreements. While binding arbitration by state regulatory commissions has been useful in solving private bargaining impasses, it has also created high transaction costs as parties attempt to convince the regulators of the merits of their position. Economic theory suggests that contracts that more accurately reflect the goals of the parties are more likely to be developed with expert arbitrators than with more generalist arbitrators because of the more detailed and precise information that can be utilized in the contract.[9]

That literature distinguishes three categories of information: private, observable, and verifiable. Private information is known only to one party. That party may choose to disclose the private information to another party, but there is no automatic assurance that such disclosure is done in a truthful way.[10] Observable information is known to both parties to a transaction, but observing it

---

9. The literature on the economics of contracts is extensive, but one relevant contribution is AVINASH DIXIT, LAWLESSNESS AND ECONOMICS: ALTERNATIVE MODES OF PRIVATE GOVERNANCE (2004), and especially the second chapter of that book, *Private Ordering in the Shadow of the Law.*

10. The contracting problems that arise under asymmetric information when one party has relevant private information that may not be disclosed at all or disclosed accurately has been extensively developed, beginning with George Akerlof's famous example of the lack of credibility carried by a used car salesman's mere assertion that he is selling a high-quality used car. See

may be a function of the parties' ongoing relationship, informal understandings, and detailed knowledge of the relevant standard industry practices. Observable information cannot necessarily be proved to a third party. Verifiable information can be proved to a third party such as a court. Contract terms that are designed for court enforcement must be based on verifiable information even though that information is only a proxy for what the parties really care about, while contracts without court enforcement may be based on observable but non-verifiable information. Such contracts can provide superior performance if there is some non-court method of enforcement.

Professor Dixit summarizes the difference as follows:

> Contracts that are intended to be enforced in a court of law can only stipulate actions that are conditioned on verifiable information; courts cannot judge whether a breach of the contractual terms has occurred if they cannot verify whether the circumstances that call for an action have actually transpired. However, observable information can be the basis for contracts that are enforced by extralegal or private methods, because the two parties can know fully well whether a breach has occurred. Such extralegal methods of enforcement come in two broad types. One is enforcement by insider third parties with specialized knowledge that enables them to verify information that outsider general courts of law cannot; arbitrators in industry associations are the most prominent enforcers of this kind. The second is based on a relationship or ongoing interaction between the parties; a breakup of this relationship constitutes the punishment that may deter one of the parties from breaching.[11]

In the Dixit framework, a contract that is enforced by arbitration can be superior to one enforced by the courts because it can

---

George Akerlof, *The Market for 'Lemons': Quality Uncertainty and the Market Mechanism*, 84 Q. J. of Econ. 488–500 (1970).

11. Dixit, *supra* note 9, at 27.

take account of information more closely related to the actual goals of the contracting parties. The benefit arises from the superior ability of an expert arbitrator compared to a non-expert to judge the significance of information. While the formal model is based on resolving disputes over the interpretation of an existing agreement, the same reasoning suggests that expert arbitrators will be able to use their detailed knowledge to devise arbitrated agreements that are more closely related to the goals of the parties than non-expert arbitrators would be able to do.

Even without knowledge of the formal economic models, it is easy to believe that expert arbitration is superior to non-expert arbitration if the experts are unbiased. However, use of industry experts as arbitrators risks either actual or perceived bias that could lead to an outcome favorable to the company or industry segment represented by the arbitrator. There is some unavoidable trade-off between expertise and neutrality, but methods can be devised to reduce the likelihood of bias. The problem of getting an industry expert to use the expertise to create good arbitration outcomes instead of biasing the outcome toward the interests of the arbitrator is analogous to the problem of inducing individuals to contribute to a public good, and the literature related to contributions to public goods can provide insights on designing the arbitration. The public goods problem arises because it is normally socially beneficial for all members of a defined group to cooperate in contributing to the public good, but it is in the interest of any single individual to free-ride on the efforts of others and to defect from cooperation. Robert Axelrod's classic study of such problems concluded that a key component in inducing the cooperative solution was to "enlarge the shadow of the future" with a second useful component as "the players' ability to recognize each other from the past, and to be confident about the prior actions that have actually been taken."[12] Parties are unlikely to sacrifice immediate self-

12. Robert Axelrod, The Evolution of cooperation 126, 140 (1984). Axelrod modeled the problem of cooperation as a repeated Prisoner's Dilemma game and found that a simple reciprocity strategy worked well so long as the game is repeated long enough and the discount rate for future pay-

interested behavior in one-time anonymous encounters, but regular interaction over a substantial period by identifiable individuals allows them to build a reputation that provides payoffs in the future.

While highly individualistic approaches (known as "rational egoist" models) suggest that individuals will not voluntarily contribute to public goods, Elinor Ostrom's studies of communities that manage common property informally and economic experiments show a more positive outcome.[13] In economic experiments with public goods, participants routinely contribute a portion of their income toward the public good, especially if they believe that other participants will contribute.[14] Ostrom's empirical studies of communities that successfully manage common property resources have generated several design rules for facilitating cooperation. One important generalization is that communities that design their own rules are more likely to follow those rules voluntarily than communities which are based on rules imposed by a higher level authority. A second important finding is that cooperation is improved when the community provides some kind of monitoring of how the members perform, with graduated sanctions for anti-social behavior that begin with mild reprimands and increase with repeated offenses.

The lessons of the economics literature suggest the following characteristics of an industry arbitration mechanism. The pool of

---

offs is low, making the future benefits of cooperation more valuable than the short-term payoff from defecting against a cooperating partner.

13. Elinor Ostrom, *Collective Action and the Evolution of Social Norms*, J. of Econ. Perspectives, Summer 2000, 137–158; Elinor Ostrom, Governing the Commons: The evolution of Institutions for Collective Action (1990).

14. A typical experimental design gives members of a small group a fixed amount of money and the opportunity to contribute to a public good or to retain the money for themselves. The total amount contributed is then doubled and divided equally among the members of the group. Group welfare is maximized if all contribute the full amount, but individual welfare is maximized by a contribution of zero. A common result is that participants contribute about half of the possible amount. See Charles Holt, Markets, Games & Strategic Behavior (2007), Chapter 14.

potential arbitrators should be designated in advance of any particular arbitration. It should consist of individuals who are willing to serve as arbitrators and who are recognized as experts in the details of interconnection and intercarrier compensation. There should be a rating mechanism by which an arbitrator's reputation for expertise and fairness can be either enhanced or impaired.[15]

When an actual dispute occurs, an arbitration panel of three members should be drawn from the pool, subject to the condition that no one associated with a company involved in the dispute may be on the panel.[16] The arbitration panel would hear the dispute and attempt through mediation to help the parties reach a voluntary solution. If that effort fails, the arbitration panel would issue a binding decision. The arbitration decision could be appealed to the FCC and then to the courts, but appeals should be discouraged by according arbitration decisions a strong presumption of validity. The details of the arbitration process should be worked out by the industry in accordance with the general finding that participants have more respect for self-developed rules than for externally imposed rules.

Pure bargaining and arbitration with no guidance can create high transaction costs as similar issues are negotiated and arbitrated multiple times. The goal is to focus negotiation and arbi-

---

15. A wide variety of reputation mechanisms have been used to increase the incentives of parties to perform well when there is little direct recourse for poor performance. A current example is the rating structure for independent online resellers that allows purchasers to reasonably expect honest performance from a person they have never met or done business with before. A historical example is the successful long-term operation of the Maghribi traders in the eleventh century Mediterranean world who entrusted their goods to unrelated agents who had the opportunity to steal the goods but were constrained by a reputation mechanism that determined future opportunities and increased the incentive to behave honestly. See Avner Greif, *Contract Enforceability and Economic Institutions in Early Trade: The Maghribi Traders' Coalition*, 83 Am. Econ. Rev. 525–548 (1993).

16. The panel size should be a small odd number larger than one, which suggests either three or five. A larger panel provides more diverse views but increases transaction costs.

tration on the specific details of the intercarrier compensation arrangement at issue and to avoid repetitive negotiation over broader principles and policies.[17] Therefore, the FCC should specify a general framework of presumptions and default arrangements to guide the parties. The presumptions would not be specific rules that parties are required to follow, but they would help shape the expectations of the bargaining parties as to the likely outcome if they fail to reach an agreement. Similarly, the arbitrators would not be bound by the presumptions if the circumstances of the individual case suggest that the presumptions should not apply. But they should expect the presumptions to apply in the absence of evidence that they are inappropriate.

The first presumption is that the exchange of traffic normally benefits both parties and therefore reciprocal compensation with zero per-minute rates (bill and keep) should be the default arrangement. The presumption should be that carriers find interconnection mutually beneficial and exchange traffic for each other's customers at little or no usage sensitive cost and, therefore, that bill-and-keep is the appropriate intercarrier compensation regime, as proposed by the staff of the FCC's Wireline Competition Bureau.[18] That presumption assumes that the cost of terminating traffic for another carrier is very low and that consequently the transaction costs of measuring traffic imbalances and charging a positive reciprocal compensation rate for the differential are high

---

17. In the early days of competition for switched local telephone service, the conditions for interconnection and intercarrier compensation were determined on a state-by-state basis through proceedings at each state regulatory commission. The same policy issues of whether competition was desirable and how it would affect existing subsidies were examined multiple times with effectively identical arguments in various states. The Telecommunications Act of 1996 standardized the basic framework and allowed further proceedings to focus on detailed implementation rather than general policy issues. Similarly, it is desirable to avoid repetitive negotiation over issues that routinely arise in intercarrier compensation.

18. Intercarrier Compensation Reform, Further Notice of Proposed Rulemaking, 20 F.C.C.R. 4685, at 4781 (2005), Appendix C, "A Bill-and-Keep Approach to Intercarrier Compensation Reform."

in relationship to the level of payments that would result. The presumption also assumes that each party is collecting payments from its own customers and exchanging traffic to allow customers of both companies to benefit from the ability to reach a larger network. It will not apply to all billing arrangements or all combinations of interconnecting companies. Arbitrators would be authorized to consider whether the characteristics of mutual benefit for interconnecting carriers are present or whether an arrangement functions more like a customer to carrier arrangement. Under this framework, for example, the long-standing controversy over intercarrier compensation to CLECs that primarily serve ISPs would be dealt with by a panel of arbitrators that presumably would find that the exchange of traffic between ILECs and CLECs serving only ISPs does not provide the level of mutual benefit that would justify reciprocal compensation.

The second presumption should be that intercarrier compensation should not be used to gain strategic advantage. Regulators routinely have intervened in interconnection and intercarrier compensation disputes in order to prevent dominant firms from using interconnection terms and intercarrier compensation rates to preserve or enhance their market power. As competition increases, the strategic opportunities are reduced but not eliminated. With multiple carriers of similar size, all have an incentive to interconnect voluntarily. But with very different sizes and types of carriers there may be incentives to refuse interconnection or to impose high compensation rates in order to promote dominant market power. Thus while bargaining is the starting point and preferred solution, arbitrators should take on the role played in the past by Congress and state and federal regulators of ensuring that interconnection and compensation terms are not designed to create or enhance market power.

Recommendations and Conclusion

Intercarrier compensation reform is long overdue. Access charges should be abolished. Subsidies should be clearly separated from intercarrier compensation arrangements. The reciprocal compensation structure currently used between LECs serving the same geographical territory should be expanded to a wide range of interconnecting carriers. The default intercarrier compensation method should be bill-and-keep. Strategic use of intercarrier compensation to gain competitive advantage should be prohibited. The preferred method of developing specific intercarrier compensation agreements should be private bargaining to reach a voluntary agreement. Private bargaining should be supported by an arbitration mechanism in which industry experts serve as the arbitrators.

CHAPTER 7

Delivering Media Content in a New Technological Environment: An Exploration of Implications for Television Policy

*Steven S. Wildman**

Introduction

Technological change, as manifest in the Internet, cheap home computing, consumer broadband, and rapidly declining digital storage costs, is transforming the way media content of all kinds is produced, distributed, and stored, and signs of upheaval in media industries are already apparent. In the face of competition from digital alternatives, both legal and illegal, newspaper and music industry revenues have been shrinking at alarming rates. Neither industry's efforts to counter with its own digital strategies have been sufficient to reverse this trend, let alone recapture lost ground. While some advertisers do report increasing the portion of their ad budgets committed to Internet promotion at the expense of television, television services have not yet suffered a comparable crisis of technology-driven declines in revenue. Nevertheless, signs of an industry in transformation are abundantly apparent. Video services indigenous to the Internet (most visibly

* I want to thank Pyeongseon Oh for assistance with the research that informed the argument presented in this chapter.

YouTube) have become immensely popular, and the traditional television networks are now actively promoting the distribution of their programs online, often through a combination of their own and third-party controlled websites.

Exploring the long-term implications of changing media technologies for media industries could easily occupy a book. In this chapter, my goals are more modest—to examine likely consequences for the television industry and television policy of an ongoing transition to what I will call server-based distribution systems. Server-based distribution systems are video distribution systems that allow viewers to select and play programs stored on a video server at times of their choosing. I will argue that server-based distribution gives rise to a set of economic incentives for video service providers very different from those that in the past influenced the programming strategies of television services relying on the traditional (pre-commercial Internet) distribution technologies of over-the-air broadcasting, cable television, and direct broadcast satellites (DBS). Because the principal policy rationale for television regulation is a belief that the incentives of commercial suppliers of television services do not align with important goals for media policy, the effects of a shift to server-based distribution on service provider incentives is a matter of considerable importance to the design of media policy going forward.

This chapter is organized as follows. The next section identifies critical technology-based features of traditional television services that are reflected in the laws and regulations that currently govern this industry. The section that follows describes the movement toward server-based distribution that is already underway and explains why this shift will dramatically change the nature of television service and critical incentives of television service providers. The final section explores implications of these changes for television policy.

Economics and Policy for Traditional Television Delivery Systems

Television services that rely on traditional distribution technologies deliver streams of programs via spectrum-using channels that are allocated one each to television networks (or stations) which select the programs to be shown on their channels and the unique time slots assigned to each program.[1] These traditional networks are now increasingly referred to as linear networks to distinguish them from their "nonlinear" online counterparts whose programs can be accessed at any time and in any order. Because they are commercial enterprises, the linear networks' selections of programs and the times they are shown are largely determined by economic considerations. Of particular importance is the fact that the number of spectrum-using channels available to deliver programs is limited by the amount of broadcast spectrum the government allocates to over-the-air broadcasters and the fact that channel capacity is costly to expand for cable systems and DBS services, a characterization that also applies in large part to the IPTV (Internet protocol television) services currently being deployed by telephone companies. While the correspondence is not one-to-one, the channel capacity of the distribution segment of the television industry effectively places a cap on the number of networks, which in turn limits the number of different programs that might be made available to viewers at any given time.

Even before Internet users began uploading the hundreds of millions of homemade videos now available through online video services like YouTube, the supply of programs vastly exceeded the number of slots in networks' schedules. This made networks first-level gatekeepers determining what programs would and would not be made available to American viewers, with television stations, cable operators, and DBS systems serving as second-level gatekeepers determining which networks were to be distributed in any given geographic region. Excepting public broadcasters, which are small in number in any locality, these decisions are all made by entities that are in the business for commercial gain. Whether

1. To simply the following discussion, I will treat over-the-air television stations as if they simply use their channels to retransmit programming delivered to them by broadcast networks. In reality, independent stations select their programs themselves and network-affiliated stations acquire programs to fill in gaps in their networks' schedules.

the private interests of television service providers align with some notion of a larger public interest has always been a matter of concern to communications policy makers. As this question is also a nontrivial challenge to economic analysis, starting in 1952 with a seminal paper by Peter Steiner,[2] economists have devoted considerable time and effort to empirical studies and the construction of economic models that might shed light on this relationship. However, there is general agreement that the commercial television system in the United States has the following economic characteristics:

- Television networks select the programs they offer viewers to maximize profits, based in large part on estimates of the revenues audiences attracted to different types of programs will generate.
- Viewers' choices among programs and program services are driven by comparisons of the personal consumption benefits anticipated from different viewing options.

---

2. Peter O. Steiner, *Program Patterns and Preferences, and the Workability of Competition in Radio Broadcasting*, 66 Q.J. ECON. 194 (1952). For more recent contributions to this literature, see Simon P. Anderson and Stephen Coate, *Market Provision of Broadcasting: A Welfare Analysis*, 72 R.E. STUD. 947 (2005); Brendan Cunningham & Peter J. Alexander, *A Theory of Broadcast Media Concentration and Commercial Advertising*, 6 J. PUB. ECON. THEORY 557 (2004); E. Kim and Steven S. Wildman, *A Deeper Look at the Economics of Advertiser-Supported Television: The Implications of Consumption-Differentiated Viewers and Ad Addressability*, J. MEDIA ECON. 55 (2006); and Roberto Rosson, *Price Discrimination and Audience Composition in Advertising-Based Broadcasting*, J. MEDIA ECON (forthcoming). Much of the earlier literature is reviewed in BRUCE M. OWEN AND STEVEN S. WILDMAN, VIDEO ECONOMICS (1992). Policy restrictions on the number of broadcast stations a single entity can own in a local market or nationally, and possible cross-media ownership combinations, have been debated (and modified) almost continuously from the early 1980s to the present. An FCC rule limits the number of subscribers served by a single multiple system cable operator to 30% of U.S. cable households. See Robert B. Horwitz, *On Media Concentration and the Diversity Question*, 21 THE INFO SOCIETY 181 (2005), for an excellent review of the history of media ownership policy up to a few years ago.

- Larger taste-defined segments of the aggregate television audience benefit from having more programs and more expensive programs produced to appeal to their tastes than are produced for smaller taste-defined groups of viewers.
- While not necessarily true, there may be circumstances for which jointly-owned networks and television distribution services (television stations or cable systems) may profit from denying competitors at the distribution stage of the industry access to co-owned networks' programs.

The major concerns with media content that have dominated the debate over television policy since the early 1950s and radio policy before that are direct reflections of these industry traits:

- That content that addresses important political and social concerns or is educational in character will be undersupplied and underconsumed relative to the social benefits it might provide because viewers do not internalize the benefits the rest of society would realize if they consumed such content and were better informed.
- That content with negative consumption externalities (say violent or sexually explicit programs) will be oversupplied relative to its benefits to society because behaviors changed by exposure to this content will create problems for society at large that viewers do not consider when deciding to watch it.
- That content highly valued by small numbers of viewers will be displaced by duplicative offerings of programs that appeal to the largest viewer taste segments.
- That distributors with ownership interests in highly popular programs (the prime time broadcast network programs of an earlier era) or the most popular cable networks may weaken actual or potential competitors by denying them fair access to those programs or networks.
- That concentrated ownership of distribution facilities will unduly limit the number of independent viewpoints presented to the American public.

Policymakers have used three general types of regulatory and legal interventions to address these concerns: (1) exclusionary restrictions and affirmative obligations that directly influence the mix of programs television service providers can and do offer viewers by prohibiting carriage of certain types of content and mandating carriage of others; [3] (2) caps on concentration in ownership of local media facilities; (3) and rules designed to ensure that owners of distribution facilities (television stations or cable systems) co-owned with television networks not weaken competitors by denying them access to their co-owned networks' content.[4]

The Very Different Economics of Server-Based Video Distribution

The television industry is now in the process of migrating toward a new distribution architecture that stores programs on video servers and delivers them on request to viewers. We see this hap-

---

3. Examples of exclusionary restrictions include the now defunct Prime-Time Access Rule, which prohibited network-affiliated television stations from broadcasting network-supplied programs during at least one hour of their daily prime time schedules to create a demand for independently-supplied programs, and the FCC's prohibition (under the Children's Television Act of 1990) on television stations broadcasting program-length commercials (television programs for children that air commercials featuring characters from the program). Examples of affirmative obligations include the requirement that television stations air three hours of approved children's programming weekly (also under the Children's Television Act of 1990) and cable systems' obligation to retransmit local broadcast stations signals (should stations elect mandatory carriage rather than try to negotiate a more profitable arrangement).

4. Under the Cable Television Consumer Protection and Competition Act of 1992, vertically integrated cable networks must be offered to satellite services and cable operators that compete with their co-owned cable systems. The Financial Interest and Syndication Rules, which were in effect from 1970 to 1995, were designed to prevent television networks from denying independent stations competing with network affiliates the opportunity to acquire network series once they went into syndication.

pening in a number of parallel, but loosely-linked, developments. One is the emergence of the Internet as a new channel for video distribution. This started with the creation of web-native services like YouTube and Yahoo! Video that made videos produced for web distribution by both amateurs and professionals available for streaming and downloads to personal computers. However, it was not long before players in the mainstream television industry began to look to the Internet as a new way to put their content before viewers. Television networks, both broadcast and cable, now make the vast majority of their programs available on their own websites and through a growing number of websites and web-based services maintained by third parties. For example, recent and back episodes of the Fox Network's popular series, *Prison Break*, can be streamed free to a desktop or laptop computer from Fox's own website and websites maintained by a large number of Internet services, including Yahoo!, Hulu, AOL.com, Veoh, and Fancast.com, to list just a few. This program can also be downloaded to a computer or handheld viewing device for a fee from iTunes.

The growth of the Internet as a distribution channel for television content is also being furthered by hardware developments. Apple, Microsoft, and other companies have developed home networks that link PCs to television sets, which make it possible for viewers to watch web-based video on standard television screens. But this may just be an intermediate step toward consumer adoption of television sets that a number of set manufacturers will be bringing to market soon that can be connected directly to the Internet. These developments will help eliminate disadvantages that smaller computer screens may pose to viewing Internet content, especially in social settings with multiple viewers. At the same time, cable operators and the new IPTV services are making server-based on-demand programming an increasingly important part of their competitive strategies and advertising campaigns, and it is widely believed that for both the telephone company and cable services the long-term technological trend is toward increasing reliance on server-based distribution.

For consumers, the advantages of these server-based options to services featuring traditional linear channels are substantial. As with digital video recorders (DVRs) like the TiVo, they can watch the programs they want at the times they choose, but with the added advantage of not having to program a recording device in advance. Also like DVRs, they can stop, rewind, and fast-forward programs streamed from servers. Experience to date with DVRs suggests that these capabilities have substantial impacts on viewing behavior. DVR penetration was reported at about 27 percent by early November 2008 and recent viewing statistics for the more popular of the broadcast networks' programs showed that the time-shifted DVR audience added between 20 and 30 percent to the audience watching at the time of the initial broadcast. For one program it was over one-third.[5]

Time-shifted shares of audience were even higher for younger viewers. Early evidence for web viewing of television programs shows a similar pattern. According to a recent report released by the Conference Board, a second-quarter 2008 consumer survey found that approximately 20 percent of households with Internet connections watch television online, with the convenience of being able to watch programs at times of their own choosing given as a primary reason for doing so.[6] Online viewing of standard-length television programs is still a relatively new activity and video players optimized for this experience are comparatively new and still evolving. As the technology improves and increasing numbers of consumers connect their TV sets directly to the Internet, we can expect to see viewers turn increasingly to online services for the programs they want to watch.

In the long run, as consumers take increasing advantage of the time flexibility of server-based video services, it is an open question whether networks' traditional linear program schedules will

---

5. Figures reported in Bill Gorman, *Bones Has Largest DVR Audience, Top Model Greatest DVR Increase*, TV BY THE NUMBERS, Sept. 22, 2008, *available at* www.tvbythenumbers.com/2008/09/22/bones-has-largest-dvr-audience-top-model-greatest-dvr-increase/5252.

6. The Conference Board, *Online TV Grows in Popularity*, September 4, 2008, *available at* www.conference-board.org/economics/consumerBarometer.cfm.

retain much value as guides to consumers' viewing options. Further, as the quality of the online viewing experience improves and viewers increasingly realize that at any given time there are vastly more programs available online than can be found clicking through the channels of their cable or satellite services, the value-added propositions of the multichannel subscription video services will look increasingly dubious. To retain customers, they will have to make more and more of their programming available on-demand. This process seems to be already underway, although today it is driven primarily by competition between cable operators and the telephone companies' IPTV services.

The decline and possible long-term demise of appointment viewing is only one consequence of a shift to server-based distribution. Server-based video services also have very different incentives when it comes to deciding what programs and how many to offer viewers. Of particular importance is that viewers only need a single channel to watch programs selected at a server. Unlike over-the-air broadcasting, cable TV systems and DBS services, for which increasing the number of programs available to viewers at any given time requires a commensurate increase in the number of channels delivered to their television sets, the number of programs a server-based video service can offer viewers is limited only by the storage capacity of its video servers. Therefore, it is the cost of adding storage capacity rather than the cost of increasing bandwidth that limits the amount of programming that might be offered. We know that at the margin this cost must be extremely low. If this were not the case, YouTube would not allow users to upload the equivalent in videos of 57,000 full-length motion pictures per week as was recently reported by its CEO Chad Hurley.[7] Because storage capacity is cheap, viewers prefer more choices to less, and the bandwidth cost of serving a video to a viewer is not increased if viewers are offered more options, the incentive is to continually

---

7. See *YouTube Compares Online Video to Early Television*, Informitv, October 15, 2008, *available at* informitv.com/articles/2008/10/15/youtube comparesonline.

add to the stock of programs available to viewers rather than engage in the stringent gatekeeping dictated by limited channel capacity for traditional cable, broadcast, and satellite services.

These differences between traditional and server-based distribution systems are illustrated in Figures 1 and 2 at the end of this chapter. The critical difference is the replacement of the multiple channels connecting a cable viewer's set top box to the system's head-end in Figure 1 by a single channel used to stream programs from a video server to a viewer's PC or TV set in Figure 2.

Implications of Server-Based Distribution for Television Policy

The economics of server-based distribution run counter to two of the basic tenets of U.S. television policy during TV's linear era. One tenet that is undermined is that lawmakers and regulators can influence the mix of programs supplied viewers through regulatory interventions aimed at influencing content choices made by owners of local television distribution facilities. IPTV operations and cable operators are offering server-based video-on-demand services as noted above. However, the most exciting innovations in the supply of video content have been taking place online, beginning with services like YouTube that initially offered short videos, and more recently have made full-length network television programs and even motion pictures available for both streaming and download online. For online video the relevant local distribution facilities are cable and telephone companies' local broadband networks, but these are passive conduits for content selected by viewers from online services whose business addresses are immaterial to the services they offer. The local ISPs connecting online viewers to the Internet play no significant role in determining the content options available online.

A second major tenet of U.S. television policy undermined by server-based distribution is the belief that the bandwidth employed to distribute television programs is a scarce resource limiting the supply of programs to viewers. Because service providers' natural inclination is to continue to add more content as long as it draws an audience, which is consistent with both the economic reasoning outlined in the previous section and the observed behavior of Internet video services, there is no longer reason for concern that the supply of policy-favored content will be restricted to make room for material that better serves the profit interests of service providers. If programs are produced, they likely will be offered to viewers.

Whether the television industry will spend enough on the types of programs favored by policymakers to meet their policy goals following a shift to server-based distribution is another matter. Policymakers were able to compel broadcasters to supply programs that otherwise would not have aired in the past because broadcasting was a profitable business and broadcasters were given limited term licenses with renewal conditioned on approval by the regulator. Similarly, carriage requirements for cable operators were sustainable policy interventions because it was possible to set subscription fees at levels that enabled operators to satisfy regulatory requirements dictating how some of their channels were to be filled while still turning a profit. It is hard to identify video services in the dynamic and shifting world of online video whose market positions are both sufficiently profitable and secure to warrant the imposition of similar programming obligations. Even if this were possible, the legal authority and mechanisms for doing so would still have to be established.

If in the long run consumers spend most of their television time watching programs streamed from the video servers operated by IPTV systems and cable systems, it is conceivable that regulators might impose programming requirements on the owners of these last-mile facilities. But this assumes that Internet-delivered video does not emerge as a credible, if not preferred alternative, to content residing on local servers. While the marginal cost of server capacity is low, the total cost of the servers required to store the video content available from Internet video services is huge. Economies of scale in video storage should thus favor Internet-based providers. Operators of local facilities would thus appear to have the upper hand as video service suppliers only if the technical quality of locally-streamed content was significantly better than that coming from Internet servers. The rapidly improving technical quality for Internet video suggests that this is not likely to be the long-term outcome. But this depends in part on the quality and pricing of the Internet connections that currently are supplied by the cable and telephone companies whose subscription television services would be the principal alternatives to Internet-delivered video. While competition for broadband customers creates countervailing incentives, policymakers should be sensitive to the possibility that local ISPs might strategically degrade the quality of their broadband Internet connections to further their interests in the business of content delivery.

In either case, the logic of server-based video distribution suggests that any policy concerns regarding content would best be addressed by focusing on improving users' ability to find the types of content that contribute to the larger social and political goals for television policy amid a myriad of digital options and finding effective ways to promote their consumption. The old strategy of restricting access through regulation to less favored types of content at certain times on certain channels is not an option.

If they want to continue to try to influence programming decisions, policymakers will have to find new ways to encourage the production of programs with substantial public interest benefits which, like educational children's programs today, are deemed to be undersupplied by the commercial television system. As a practical matter, it is hard to see how the old strategy of compelling some service providers to supply desired programming as a condition for doing business might effectively be implemented in a server-based television industry. The most direct approach would be for the government to subsidize the production of such programs, perhaps by expanding the mission of the public broadcasting system.

Recommendations and Conclusion

The shift to server-based distribution for media content is already well underway. In the process it is eliminating bandwidth as a constraint on the supply of content, spawning content suppliers whose incentives are to continually add rather than exclude content from diverse sources, and rendering anachronistic traditional policies aimed at compelling owners of local distribution facilities to supply regulator-favored content. Therefore, concerns that certain types of content may be undersupplied relative to their benefits to the public should be addressed in new ways. Subsidies paid to producers of undersupplied types of content would be the most direct approach, but incentives to produce policy-favored content might also increase through strategies that stimulate demand. Developing services that make it easier for consumers to find undersupplied types of content is one possibility. Policymakers might also consider advertising, a strategy long employed by commercial television services to promote their own programs. Advertising programs with positive spillover benefits could serve the dual purposes of increasing awareness of these programs and educating the public as to the benefits of watching them.

Finally, although there is no indication yet that this might be happening, because cable operators and telephone companies are also by far the biggest ISPs in most local markets, regulators should be sensitive to the possibility that they will limit the quality of the broadband Internet connections they offer subscribers to diminish the threat of Internet-delivered content to their own local television services.

Figure 1 Cable Television Structure

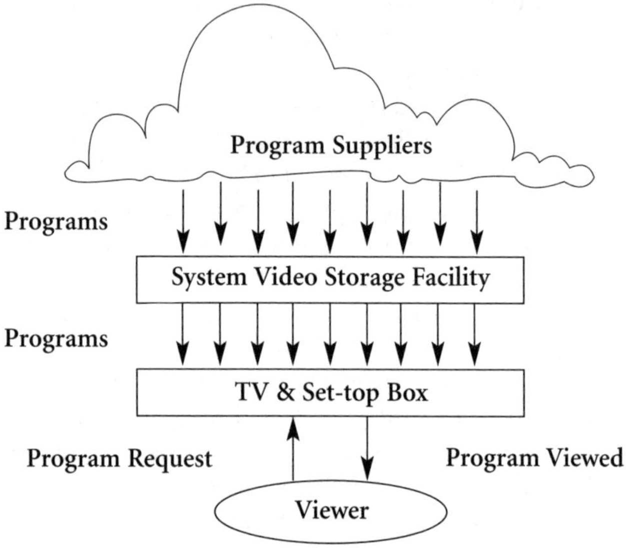

Figure 2 Server-Based Video Structure

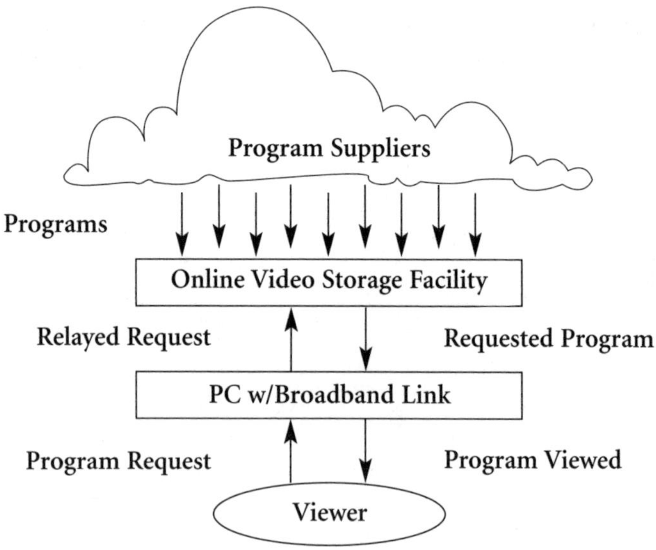

CHAPTER 8

Public Affairs and Private Employment: Some Unintended Consequences of the 1996 Telecommunications Act

Diane M. Disney

Some people of a certain age can easily recall the lessons of high school civics classes, while their slightly younger counterparts will remember that the televised *Schoolhouse Rock* explained "how a bill becomes a law." In real life, however, nothing is as clear-cut as the ways those processes were described. Inevitably, proponents laud intended benefits, opponents decry societal decrements, enterprising souls look for ways to hedge their bets and make money whatever the outcome, and insiders think about how to tailor implementing regulations to produce the results that they *really* want, regardless of the public rhetoric.

So it was with the Telecommunications Act of 1996, at least up to a point. Proponents projected such benefits as lower prices for long-distance calls, lower cable rates, higher levels of employment in telecommunications-related fields, greater diversity in information and entertainment, and much greater competition, which in turn would foster innovation and reduce prices. Opponents were relatively muted, and the public was essentially uninvolved, as the bill passed by overwhelming majorities (91 to 5 in the Senate and 415 to 16 in the House). The impacts, however, have gone far beyond what was publicly discussed, in ways that have adversely affected employment, failed to accommodate the pace of technological change, reduced public access to local information, and homogenized entertainment. Have there been benefits? Certainly, there have been. But the implementation has also brought some unintended and less optimal outcomes for individual families and communities. This essay focuses on two largely unrelated but nevertheless consequential results: diminished employment and related benefits and diminished availability of local broadcast access and programming.

Employment Realities

Technological change has driven a near-makeover in the telecommunications industry's employment, affecting not only job content and skill requirements but also location, competition, and benefits. "Webmaster," for instance, is a commonly accepted term today, but a decade or so ago, it would have referred to a spider or a spy rather than a telecommunications specialist. Individual consumers now plug in their own devices rather than rely on phone company installers. And the need for other types of positions has been overridden by technology that permits consumers to customize networks and determine what messages they will receive where and when. Employment changes in the industry, therefore, must be analyzed cautiously, as no single factor can account for a majority of changes.

Three decades ago, a Bureau of Labor Statistics economist explained how technological change was increasing productivity but reducing unit labor requirements in the telecommunications industry.[1] His *Monthly Labor Review* article cited the notable labor-management cooperation in the field, "where coverage of nonsupervisory workers by union contracts [was] estimated to be 100 percent."[2] While very few of the contracts mentioned technological change, the joint labor-management cooperation "successfully reduced permanent employment while holding layoffs to a mini-

1. Michael D. Dymmel, *Technology in Telecommunications: its Effect on Labor and Skills*, Monthly Lab. Rev., January 1979, at 13.

2. *Id.* at 19.

mum."[3] However, he projected, coming decades would see technological change going beyond the traditional areas to affect the more stable, highly skilled jobs, thereby creating enormous social and economic ramifications.

His prescience was underscored by the publication's assessment of employment changes a decade after the passage of the Telecommunications Act. Rather than focusing solely on what happened right after the act's passage, Christopher Carbone divided the 1990–2005 period into four phases:

- Early 1990s (January 1990—August 1993), when telecommunications employment fell 4.4 percent (34,000 jobs);
- Anticipated deregulation (August 1993—January 1996), when it grew 3.8 percent (36,000 jobs);
- Boom (January 1996—March 2001), which saw growth of 36 percent (352,000 jobs); and
- Bust (March 2001—December 2005), where employment fell 25.3 percent, or 337,000 jobs.[4]

Researchers for the U.S. Chamber of Commerce provided more insight into the "bust" period:

> Between March 2001 and May 2004, the telecommunications industry lost 380,500 jobs in the areas of telecom service, Internet service, and telecommunications equipment manufacturing. Voice, video, and data services were all affected. Overall, 29% of U.S. job losses during this period were in the telecommunications industry. And when overall employment increased by 1.4 million jobs between August 2003 and May 2004, telecom employment declined by another 23,000 jobs.[5]

---

3. *Id.*

4. Christopher C. Carbone, *Cutting the Cord: Telecommunications Employment Shifts Toward Wireless*, Monthly Lab. Rev., July 2006, at 28.

5. Thomas W. Hazlett et al., *Sending the Right Signal: Promoting Competition Through Telecommunications Reform*, A Report to the U.S. Chamber of Commerce, Oct. 2004, 1, *available at* http://www.uschamber.com/publications/reports/041006_telecomm.htm.

Most assuredly the 1996 Act's passage, along with the ensuing deregulation (which some would call "managed competition" or "micromanagement"[6]), and increased investment caused an employment boom for a few years, but this has since been reversed. In addition, what the gross figures mask is that the bulk of the employment gain was in the wireless sector, which saw jobs increase from 68,000 in 1995 to nearly 254,000 in 2006.[7] In other words, old jobs were vanishing, and the new ones created by technological advances could not quite take up the slack.

Some of the change pre-dated the 1996 Act. For example, AT&T had been known for having "good" jobs, ones with stability, decent pay, top-notch benefits, and opportunities for career growth. In implementing the 1982 antitrust consent decree between AT&T and the United States, however, the 1984 break-up of the integrated Bell System changed that world.[8] When its share of the long-distance market fell sharply, AT&T responded with downsizing and acquisitions. According to several industrial relations specialists, this strategy essentially "broke with its tradition of investment in its workforce and long-term employment."[9] By reinvesting in largely maintenance-free systems, the corporation replaced blue-collar positions with fewer white-collar positions requiring remote-testing computer skills but paying about 20 percent less than those existing before. In addition, the absence of regulatory restrictions permitted the company to consolidate operator and customer serv-

---

6. See, for example, ALFRED E. KAHN, WHOM THE GODS WOULD DESTROY OR HOW NOT TO DEREGULATE, American Enterprise Institute-Brookings Joint Center for Regulatory Studies, 2001. In his words, telecommunications "continues most dramatically to exemplify the perverse propensities of regulatory agencies to micromanage the process–indeed to regulate pervasively in the name of 'deregulation,'" *Id.* at 3.

7. CTIA-The Wireless Association, *Semi-annual Wireless Survey*, 2007, Table 1120.

8. AT&T v. United States, 552 F. Supp. 131 (D.D.C. 1982), *aff'd sub .nom.* Maryland v. United States, 460 U.S. 1001 (1983).

9. Matias Ramirez, Frederick Guy, and David Beale, *Contested Resources: Unions, Employers, and the Adoption of New Work Practices in US and UK Telecommunications*, BRIT. J. OF INDUS. REL., 495, at 503 (2007).

ice centers into fewer but much larger offices, effectively leaving thousands of employees behind. Downsizing soon became a routine approach to the need for change and growth.

Although AT&T did make some attempts to include unions in human resource planning through its *Workplace of the Future* initiative, efforts to use more flexible work hours as a way of forestalling the import of non-union labor failed, and labor-management relations deteriorated. Further, as the corporation moved from a unified organization to one with discrete business units, the common grading structure for positions was eliminated,[10] and the balance between flexibility and competence became harder to maintain. The blurring of lines across permanent, contingent, and outsourced labor had "become so unstable as to make medium-term manpower planning impractical."[11]

Because of AT&T's size and scope, its labor-management policies are ready targets of analysis. But what was happening there was replicated in the late 1980s and early 1990s in dozens of other firms that had arisen to compete in the expanding telecommunications field. Lacking the heritage of Ma Bell's protectiveness, though, many of them simply began with less structured ideas of employment and lower levels of commitment to employee benefits and retention.

The stage was set, then, for more profound changes when the Telecommunications Act was passed in 1996. This "opened the way for AT&T and other telecom firms to get into every part of the telecommunications market."[12] They did so with zeal, as mergers, acquisitions, and various other forms of realignment became the norm, with financiers, telecommunications lawyers, and executives making (and sometimes losing) fortunes. What was less obvious was the impact on ordinary telecommunications employees:

---

10. Grading structures are approaches used in the civil service and large nongovernmental organizations to ensure that comparable duties and qualifications are treated comparably across multiple units and locations.

11. Matias Ramirez, *supra* note 9, at 505.

12. David Masci, *The Future of Telecommunications*, CQ RESEARCHER, April 23, 1999, at 1.

- Job security was noticeably diminished, in part because redundancies created by corporate reshuffling led to layoffs, and in part because the pace of technological change put a premium on advanced skills that could not always be acquired in the short term. (Bell Atlantic did agree with the Communications Workers of America proposal to create a "technical telecommunications associate" position to keep represented members' skills current and to forestall the hiring of outside companies.[13] The CWA also convinced some other regional companies to adopt similar approaches. But the Nynex/Bell Atlantic merger in 1997 brought more corporate resistance to union involvement in growth areas and renewed interest in outsourcing.)
- Labor-management relations deteriorated, and unions lost strength. While the decline of factories had been depleting union strength for years, the new technology was "neither welcoming nor penetrable to organized labor."[14] Even when the CWA won a pay increase and the right to enlist wireless workers as a result of the 2000 strike against Verizon, many union members protested what they saw as CWA's failure to represent their particular interests. The union found it extremely challenging to try to "co-ordinate a diverse group of workers from different companies" in different regions that had only recently merged.[15] Solidarity was being swept away by the pace of organizational and technological change.
- Workplace discrimination complaints started rising. Even as a large field, telecommunications had accounted for less than 1.5 percent of the employment discrimination suits filed with the Equal Employment Opportunity Commission (EEOC). By 1999, though, this had risen to 2.0 percent, and the increase continues. Nynex and Bell Atlantic (now Verizon), Lucent, Nextel, and others have all faced increasing numbers of

---

13. Ramirez *et al*, at 507.

14. Stephen Handelman, *Unions Get Future Shock Plugging into New Economy*, Toronto Star, Aug. 29, 2000.

15. *Id.*

complaints as employees seek ways of redressing real and perceived grievances.[16]

- While salaries for some types of positions rose, typical compensation levels remained static or fell as positions were redefined, made contingent, or outsourced. Advanced technology permitted some services to require fewer workers, and those few tended to be more highly trained than their predecessors. Yet they were not necessarily added to a stable payroll. Contingent employment grew as temporary help agencies blossomed to help fill short-term vacancies. As one Verizon manager noted, temporary hiring "doesn't count against head counts. We do get consulting budgets. We don't pay for benefits or vacations or 401(k)s or any of those other perks. The company knows we're going to spend money on temporary help. As long as we stay within budget, it's okay."[17]
- The social policy impact of total compensation changes will become more evident in the next decade as more workers reach retirement age. Smaller firms have always been fairly unlikely to offer retirement plans; larger firms have increasingly been turning to temporary help and outsourcing to avoid paying for pensions; and among large employers, the past two decades have brought a general movement away from defined benefit pensions (which provide a lifetime benefit based on salary and years of service) to defined contribution plans (where the payout depends upon employee contributions and the success of the investment vehicles). In other words, the risk has been shifting from employers to employees across society as a whole.

---

16. See, for example, Jeffrey Bartash, *AT&T Faces Bias Suit Amid Job Cuts*, CBS Market Watch, Jan. 8, 2003; *Financial Wire, Equal Employment Opportunity Commission Sues Lucent*, Fin. Times, April 11, 2006; Diane E. Lewis, *Verizon Will Settle Major Pregnancy Bias Case*, Boston Globe, June 6, 2006; Seth Schiesel, *Workers Plan Bias Lawsuits Against Nextel*, N.Y. Times, June 20, 2000.

17. Kenneth Bredemeier, *Downsizing Means Gains for Temporary Workers*, Wash. Post, August 23, 2001.

How does this general movement affect telecommunications employees? First, it is important to note that "job tenure is longer for defined benefit participants than for either defined contribution participants or workers in general."[18] As telecommunications workers find themselves unable to stay as long as they would like at pension-offering firms because of mergers, acquisitions, and layoffs, few of them will be eligible for a defined-benefit pension even if they did manage to work for a company offering one. Second, more and more firms that once offered such plans are abandoning or "freezing" access to them. The latter approach either denies additional benefits to current plan participants, whether from raises or longevity, or denies new employees the opportunity to participate. "Hard" freezes were most likely to arise within firms of fewer than 100 employees, thereby limiting benefits among new competitors that might have arisen because of the deregulation.[19]

In a related move, many companies have begun moving toward "cash balance" plans, which operate like a hybrid between defined benefit and defined contribution models. Their portability may appeal to younger employees, but the change can amount to a retirement income cut for older employees. Already Sprint-Nextel, Bell Atlantic, and its successor Verizon Communications, among others, have announced such changes. The availability of pension plans in general is declining for telecommunications employees, as are medical benefits for retirees.[20]

Thus, contrary to many of the promises of those promoting the industry's deregulation, the reality is that the telecommunications jobs of today are fewer, on average less remunerative (though some positions do pay more than before), and less secure than those of years past. Yes, the increased competition and regulatory relief

---

18. Jack VanDerhei, *Defining Benefit Plan Freezes: Who's Affected, How Much, and Replacing Lost Accruals*, Issue Brief 291, Employee Benefits Research Institute, at 9.

19. *Id.* at 4.

20. Communications Workers of America, as referenced by Mike Causey, *Capitol Hill Full of Pension Allies: Retirement Plans Becoming Rare*, Wash. Times, Feb. 20, 2007, at A-9.

have had some positive outcomes (most notably greater choice and lower prices in some market segments), but these benefits have not come without cost to individual workers and their families.

Impacts of Media Consolidation on Local Communities

By any measure, the Telecommunications Act of 1996 loosened restraints and spawned ownership changes that could be called epochal. In the words of Federal Communications Commissioner Robert M. McDowell in his December 2007 Senate testimony:

> Just in the past decade, we have witnessed a brilliant technological explosion that has brought consumers five national broadcast networks, hundreds of cable channels spewing diverse cable content produced by more than 550 independent programmers, nearly 14,000 full-power radio stations, two vibrant satellite television companies, telephone companies offering video, cable overbuilders, satellite radio, the Internet and its millions of websites and bloggers, a myriad of wireless devices operating in a wonderfully chaotic and competitive environment, iPods, podcasts, and much, much more.[21]

While some might quibble over the use of some of the adjectives, probably everyone could agree with Commissioner McDowell's observation that "[w]e live in a media world that is far different from the one that existed even at the time of the 1996 Act."[22] Part of the difference stems directly from that act, but part stems as well from the interaction of its effects with activities that had been stimulated by the repeal of the Fairness Doctrine in 1987.

---

21. Robert M. McDowell, Testimony before the Committee on Commerce, Science, and Transportation, United States Senate, Dec. 13, 2007, pp. 1–2, *available at* http://hraunfoss.fcc.gov/edocs_public/attachmatch/DOC-278913A1.pdf.

22. *Id.* at 4.

Introduced in 1949 and incorporated into FCC regulations in 1967, the Fairness Doctrine did not require equal time for opposing views, but it did require that radio and television broadcasters present contrasting viewpoints.[23] Methods could include editorials, news segments, public affairs shows, and the airing of public service announcements. In *Red Lion Broadcasting Co. v. FCC*,[24] the Supreme Court upheld the Fairness Doctrine, but the 1980s brought decisions that raised questions about its limiting effect on free speech, particularly in light of the emergence of new communications technologies. Then in 1987, the FCC abolished the doctrine.[25] This article is not aimed at reinstating the Fairness Doctrine. Rather, it addresses two unfortunate, unintended consequences of its repeal, combined with the telecommunications deregulation of the 1990s, namely mass market programming homogeneity and the nonprofit sector's effective loss of access to the public airwaves.

Among other effects, that abolition effectively began the modern era in talk radio. Between 1990 and 2006, the number of stations with talk shows more than tripled, going from about 400 to some 1,400.[26] Leaving aside the political tenor of much talk radio, the salient point here is that it tends to be nationally syndicated, with relatively little attention paid to local viewpoints. From the purely entertainment side, the mergers and resulting central con-

---

23. In a spirited criticism of the doctrine, Adam Thierer, has said that "[w]ith the threat of potential FCC retaliation hanging over their heads, many broadcasters were more reluctant to air controversial opinions because it might require them to air alternative perspectives that their audience did not want to hear. On the other hand, they feared they would not be able to air enough, or the right type of, responses to make regulators happy." ADAM D. THIERER, MEDIA MYTHS: MAKING SENSE OF THE DEBATE OVER MEDIA OWNERSHIP, The Progress & Freedom Foundation, 37 (2005).

24. 395 U.S.367 (1969).

25. For a description of the doctrine, its impact, and its demise, see Syracuse Peace Council v. FCC, 867 F.2d 654 (D.C. Cir. 1989).

26. PROJECT FOR EXCELLENCE IN JOURNALISM, THE STATE OF THE NEWS MEDIA: AN ANNUAL REPORT ON AMERICAN JOURNALISM (2007), *available at* http://www.stateofthenewsmedia.com/2007/.

trol have also been replacing classical, jazz, and locally popular forms of music with "mass-produced tapes of homogenized, androgynous voices."[27] In the words of one analyst, this could lead to a situation where the country had "only one radio station and it [would] play only Celine Dion and Whitney Houston," or "All Celine, all the time."[28] Such was the result of nearly all radio markets being "dominated by just four radio companies, controlling at least 70 percent of the radio audience, with concentration even greater in smaller markets."[29]

Whether the focus is music, news, or opinion, though, the trend in mass media has been toward uniformity, with variety coming from alternative media with minimal audiences. One result has been fewer jobs in local media markets as stations rely on national feeds and eliminate local positions. Another has been the loss of broadcast information about causes and nonprofit organizations of importance locally. Going beyond news shows, this phenomenon is most obvious in the decline of public service announcements (PSAs).

The FCC had defined a PSA as an advertisement "for which no charge is made and which promotes programs, activities or services of Federal, State, or local governments or the programs, activities or services of nonprofit organizations or any other announcements regarded as serving community interests."[30] Prior to the late 1980s, television and radio stations were expected to maintain publicly available logs of the time donated to PSAs. Stations had discretion about which ones to air, and there naturally were specialists who helped organizations develop broadcast-quality material that would be readily acceptable and easily used. At a macro level, the best known provider of PSAs was the Advertising Council, which created such memorable campaigns as those featuring Smokey Bear (preventing forest fires), the crying Indian

27. Alice Mundy, *All Celine, All the Time*, MEDIA WEEK, Sept. 7, 1998.

28. *Id.*

29. Future of Music Coalition (2002), cited in Common Cause Education Fund, *The Fallout from the Telecommunications Act of 1996: Unintended Consequences and Lessons Learned*, May 9, 2005, at 10.

30. FCC Rules, Section 73.1810 (d) (4) (repealed).

(saving the environment), and The United Negro College Fund ("A mind is a terrible thing to waste").

The traditional PSA that educates people about important issues still exists, albeit in reduced number, frequency, and reach. But it has been supplemented and sometimes overshadowed by network or station promotions that feature their own employees talking about their personal involvement in such issues as breast cancer treatment (a major focus here being promotion of the stations' stars) and by cause-related marketing, such as Anheuser-Busch's paid ads that promote responsible drinking.[31] While these last two do provide some information, they do not conform to the Ad Council's definition of public service advertising: "that the spots be non-sectarian, non-commercial, and non-partisan."[32]

To determine what had happened with public service advertising, in the last quarter of 2005 the Kaiser Family Foundation studied "a full week of television content on affiliates of ten major broadcast networks: the four major broadcast networks; five basic cable channels that present news, sports, music, children's and general audience programming; and one Spanish language network." Researchers sampled local affiliates' programming in seven different markets (Atlanta, Chicago, Dallas, Denver, Los Angeles, New York, and Seattle), collecting 1,680 hours of television content.[33] Among the findings:

- Overall, the broadcast and cable stations in the study donated an average of 17 seconds an hour to PSAs.
- This represents one-half of one percent of all TV airtime on these channels (.5%). By comparison, 25 percent of all airtime was spent on advertising (21%) and promos (4%).
- From 2000 to 2005, the proportion of time donated to locally [as opposed to nationally] oriented spots decreased on both broadcast (from 33% to 25%) and cable (from 20% to 6%).

---

31. Ruth A. Wooden, *Education Should Be Sole Purpose of PSAs*, ADVERTISING AGE, May 19, 1997.

32. *Id.*

33. WALTER GANTZ, NANCY SCHWARTZ, JAMES R. ANGELINI, and VICTORIA RIDEOUT, SHOUTING TO BE HEARD: PUBLIC SERVICE ADVERTISING IN A CHANGING TELEVISION WORLD, The Kaiser Family Foundation, 4 (Jan. 2008).

- Donated PSAs were disproportionately placed between midnight and 6 a.m., a time when viewership—and advertising rates—are low.
- Thirteen percent of all donated PSAs featured a star or personality specifically associated with the network on which the PSA aired.

If the station or network marketing inherent in the spots mentioned in the fifth bullet were considered sufficient to disqualify the spots as PSAs, the amount of time donated to public education would be even lower than that reported in the first three bullets. These findings follow years of decline in the 1990s. A 1997 Ad Council report noted that PSA time had decreased in the three previous years "from 12 seconds in prime time each hour to just 5 seconds. In contrast, the amount of time TV devoted during prime time to promotional spots has ballooned in recent years to 12 minutes nightly [or] 4 minutes of each primetime hour."[34]

In the late 1990s, in an effort to guarantee exposure for the Clinton Administration's anti-drug message, Drug Czar Barry McCaffrey used congressionally approved funds to buy air time in an arrangement that required some donated time. Regrettably, this willingness of a sponsor to pay for air time for public service messages has worked to lessen the likelihood of stations' willingness to air spots without charge.[35]

A further reality is that 80 percent of donated PSAs identified by the Kaiser Family Foundation study could have aired anywhere, as they featured issues of importance countrywide. At the same time, however, they did "not feature local personalities or geographically specific elements in the message."[36] Both broadcast and

---

34. Wooden, *supra* note 31.

35. This venture began when Congress approved $1 billion in 1997 to buy anti-drug advertising if networks sold the time at half price. General McCaffrey made the project more palatable by trading some of the ad time for incorporation of anti-drug themes in prime-time shows. See Daniel Forbes, *Prime-time Propaganda*, Salon.com, Jan. 13, 2000, http://dir.salon.com/news/feature/2000/01/13/drugs/index.html.

36. See Gantz, *et al.*, *supra* at 18.

cable stations aired more spots with a national focus in 2005 than in 2000, and for each, the national orientation accounted for at least three-quarters of the spots. (For cable channels, the national focus reached 94 percent.)

The loss of local voice was further illustrated by a study commissioned by the Benton Foundation. Its study of 24 media markets in 2000 found an average of 1.1 hours of local public affairs programming over a two-week period. Put another way, only "0.3 percent of the total commercial broadcast time within these markets was devoted to local public affairs programming."[37] Nonetheless, broadcasters did see some competitive value in such programming, as the more stations there were in a market, the more likely a given station in that market was to broadcast a PSA. Adding local news to the equation raised the total devoted to local public affairs programming to 1.06 percent of total broadcast hours, less than a quarter of the average in the 1970s.[38] Also, "a random sampling of 285 full-power TV stations during a two-week period in 2003 found that four out of ten commercial TV stations aired no local public affairs programs during that time."[39]

Despite these data, most broadcasters adamantly maintain that they are doing enough to fulfill their obligations to their communities and reject calls for greater responsiveness to public needs. Indeed, the National Association of Broadcasters has asserted that "[e]ven in the absence of specific obligations, all radio and television stations already air a sufficient amount of news, public affairs and local non-entertainment programming."[40] Many local communities would disagree.

---

37. Philip M. Napoli, Market Conditions and Public Affairs Programming: Implications for Digital Television Policy 3 (2000).

38. William E. Kennard, Federal Communications Commission, Report to Congress on the Public Interest Obligations of Television Broadcasters as They Transition to Digital Television, 7 (2001).

39. Michael Yan and Philip Napoli, referenced in Common Cause Education Fund, 16.

40. National Association of Broadcasters, 2004 statement referenced in Common Cause Education Fund.

The problem is particularly acute with nonprofit organizations. This Third Sector (with government and business being the first two) is responsible for fulfilling so many of the tasks that society values but that entrepreneurs do not find profitable.[41] While many nonprofits now have websites to explain their operations and to seek essential financial support, they still need mechanisms for the public to know those websites exist. The loss of broadcast appeal via programming and PSAs has created great difficulties for such groups. It is the *reach* of the broadcast mass media that alerts the public to the existence of organizations and causes that they might find of benefit or interest.

At the same time that the 1996 Act set the stage for mass media mergers and greater message limitations through consolidation, though, it ignored the Internet, "except as a vector for pornography."[42] Even after the Act's technological shortcomings became clear, Congress continued to regulate the Internet as a medium for sexually explicit speech and shopping. It gave the FCC no tools for addressing Voice over Internet Protocol ("VoIP") or other Internet applications. Also, the devotion to free, advertiser-supported television effectively "negated policy options that might have had more beneficial impact on competition in mass media."[43]

Conclusions and Recommendations

Virtually any basic microeconomics text will observe that sometimes markets fail. And sometimes laws that purport to deregulate

---

41. See particularly the work of Lester A. Salamon, Founding Director of the Johns Hopkins Institute for Policy Studies, and notably the findings of the definitive Nonprofit Sector Study he directed for the Urban Institute with broad-based foundation support in the 1980s. Government Spending and the Nonprofit Sector in New York City, January 1986, with Alan J. Abramson.

42. Jim Chen, *The Echoes of Forgotten Footfalls: Telecommunications Mergers at the Dawn of the Digital Millennium*, 43 Hous. L. Rev. 1360 (2007).

43. *Id.* at 1363.

markets and stimulate competition can have deleterious effects as well as positive ones. So it has been with the Telecommunications Act of 1996.

In this case, the promise of employment growth was greatly oversold. Lawmakers failed to consider the pace of technological change, and the forces they set in motion were soon overtaken by events. Newly freed businesses behaved in their own self-interest, which was not exactly what all lawmakers had envisioned, and created a situation where there is still much innovation, but arguably more centralized control of content than before.

Phenomena such as the rise of a contingent workforce, the increase in outsourcing, and upgrading of jobs' skill requirements, and even the reduction in job-based social welfare protections (notably pensions and health insurance), are not confined to the telecommunications industry. Therefore, little could effectively be done to address them through telecommunications-focused legislation or policy. What lawmakers and policymakers should recognize, though, is that everything they do with regard to regulating or deregulating the telecommunications field will have employment consequences; care needs to be taken to avoid making these consequences unnecessarily painful.

As for the free flow of information and the best interests of local communities, however, concrete steps can be taken to halt the march toward national uniformity and what some have called a totalitarian approach to information. The first step would be to create some mechanism to require radio, broadcast television, and cable, to provide a certain minimum of locally focused PSAs to give the Third Sector access to the public airwaves. Because the term "Fairness Doctrine" generates such strong and stereotyped reactions, the approach will need greater focus and a new name. Perhaps "Nonprofit Access Mechanism" or some variant would be more precise and less inflammatory. The key is to provide a way to bring the local interests and local problem-solving organizations back to visibility in their communities.

Digital broadcasters could also be encouraged to use their multichannel capacity to offer airtime to local groups.[44] In addition, former FCC Chair Kennard has recommended that stations should be required to make their public service logs accessible to the community, with personnel "trained to respond to the public's request for access."[45]

Taken together, these recommendations would impose no particular hardship on any broadcaster, but they would work to combat the national homogenization and local subordination of broadcast programming, regardless of how the competitive entities reconfigure themselves.

44. Kennard. *supra* note 38, at 8.
45. *Id.* at 13.

CHAPTER 9

Charting a New Constitutional Jurisprudence for the Digital Age

*Randolph J. May**

Introduction

Communications law and policy would be much different today—and more suited to the now generally competitive and converging communications marketplace—if the Supreme Court's twentieth century jurisprudence had been different. As it was, the Court took an unduly restrictive view of First Amendment free speech rights and an overly broad view of the nondelegation doctrine. Thus, the Federal Communications Commission's (FCC's) Fairness Doctrine, requiring broadcasters to present both sides of controversial public issues, along with much other program content regulation, was upheld against First Amendment attack. And the FCC, the administrative agency charged under the Communications Act with regulating broadcasters, common carriers, and other communications companies, was given what at times amounted to unbridled discretion to regulate "in the public interest." Arguably, at times the Court also took a somewhat overly narrow view of Fifth Amendment property rights of communications service providers.

Some of the key Supreme Court decisions that established the parameters of twentieth-century communications law doctrine run

* Earlier versions of this essay appeared in the October 2008 edition of *Engage* (Volume 9, Issue 3), a publication of the Federalist Society, and the Winter 2009 edition of the Charleston Law Review.

contrary to fundamental tenets of our constitutional culture. This is especially so with respect to free speech rights which are essential to the robust exchange of ideas in a democracy and to separation of powers principles which are necessary to maintain democratic accountability. It is the jurisprudence implicating these free speech and separation of powers concerns that will be the focus of this essay, with greater emphasis on the First Amendment jurisprudence.

A persuasive case can be made that some of the key decisions discussed below ought to have been decided differently at the time as a matter of law. But in some ways, as a matter of communications policy, they at least reflected the tenor of the analog age. Until the past decade or two, most segments of the communications marketplace generally were characterized as monopolistic or oligopolistic, regardless whether one considered the then-separate "broadcast," "telephone," or "cable" market segments.

But at least since the Telecommunications Act of 1996[1] amended the Communications Act of 1934,[2] the communications marketplace environment has been characterized by increasing competition among a variety of media and service providers and also by a convergence of the services offered by media companies and telecommunications providers. Convergence has meant the blurring of formerly distinct service boundaries that were tied to what I have called "techno-functional constructs," because service classifications were based on technical characteristics or functional features.[3] It no longer makes sense to speak of the "telephone," "broadcast," "cable," or "cell phone" markets in the same way it did only a few short years ago. Telephone companies now provide video and Internet services in addition to voice; cable companies

---

1. Telecommunications Act of 1996, Pub. L. No. 104-104, 110 Stat. 56 (codified in scattered sections of 47 U.S.C.).

2. Communications Act of 1934, ch. 652, §602(a), 48 Stat. 1064 (codified as amended in scattered sections of 47 U.S.C.).

3. See Randolph J. May, *Why Stovepipe Regulation No Longer Works: An Essay on the Need for a New Market-Oriented Communications Policy*, 58 FED. COMM. L. J. 103, 104–108 (2006).

provide voice and Internet services; and wireless companies provide voice, video, and Internet services. Increasingly, people watch "television" programs on their "computer" screens, or even on their mobile devices.

The advent of competition and convergence is attributable in large part to the rapid technological developments accompanying the transition from analog to digital equipment and from narrowband to broadband services.[4] Much has been written about the marketplace transformation wrought by digital age competition and convergence. This is not the place to rehash the marketplace or technological developments which, in any event, often become outdated almost as soon as they are reported. Suffice it to say, for purposes of this essay, that the communications marketplace today bears little resemblance to that which existed at the time the Supreme Court rendered major communications law decisions of the twentieth century.

I am going to discuss some of these key twentieth-century decisions to show how they have shaped the existing jurisprudence defining the media's First Amendment rights. Most significantly, the import of these decisions is that broadcasters have been accorded decidedly less First Amendment protection than the print media, and even less protection than other forms of electronic media, such as cable television, which have received less protection than print publishers. I will also address the FCC's seemingly limitless authority, under prevailing Supreme Court decisions, to regulate under the public interest standard those media and telecommunications companies that are subject to its jurisdiction. Finally, I will suggest that, whatever the merits of these decisions at the time they were decided—and the merits are quite debatable —either through overruling or distinguishing them the Supreme Court should find ways to chart new jurisprudential directions that will comport more comfortably with important constitutional values.

---

4. See May, *supra* note 3, at 108–110. As for convergence, in 2004 the FCC explained how the greater bandwidth of broadband networks encourages the introduction of services "which may integrate voice, video, and data capabilities while maintaining high quality of service." IP-Enabled Services, Notice of Proposed Rulemaking, 19 F.C.C.R. 4863, at ¶ 16 (2004).

Indeed, as I will explain in the last section, the Court has been presented this 2008 Term with just such an opportunity to render a decision that comports more comfortably with our constitutional values. In *Federal Communications Commission v. Fox Television Stations, Inc.*, the Court is reviewing an appeals court decision holding that the FCC failed to provide a reasoned basis for a change in policy that led to sanctioning broadcasters for programs containing only "fleeting expletives" rather than non-isolated instances of what it considered to be indecent speech.[5] While the Second Circuit based its vacation and remand of the FCC's decision announcing its new broadcast indecency enforcement regime on traditional administrative law grounds, it did suggest in *dicta* that, in its view, the FCC's new, more stringent enforcement policy might well be unconstitutional. In their Supreme Court briefs, the broadcaster parties and others urge the Court to hold the FCC's new "fleeting expletives" policy unlawful not only on the basis that it was not adequately explained by the Commission, but also on the basis that it infringes the broadcasters' free speech rights. Should the Court take on the constitutional issue, it would have an opportunity to rationalize its First Amendment jurisprudence in a way that would accord all the electronic media the same high level of free speech protection that the print media has always enjoyed.

The Broadcast and Public Interest Models: Analog Era Regulatory Regimes

At the heart of twentieth-century media regulation discussed here is the "broadcast model" that took firm root before the rise of

5. Fox Television Stations, Inc. v. FCC, 489 F. 3d 444 (2nd Cir. 2007), *cert. granted sub nom.* FCC v. Fox Television Stations, Inc., 128 S. Ct. 1647 (2008). On April 28, 2008, as this book was being prepared to go to press, the Supreme Court handed down its decision in *Fox*. It reversed the Second Circuit decision on administrative law grounds and did not reach the First Amendment issue. FCC v. Fox Television Stations, Inc., 129 S. Ct. 1800 (2009). In his concurring opinion, Justice Thomas cited an earlier version of the article that appeared at 3 Charleston L. Rev. 373 (2009), in expressing his willingness to revisit the existing First Amendment jurisprudence.

successive newer media employing various technologies.[6] Under the traditional broadcast model, because the electromagnetic spectrum was considered to be a scarce physical resource that could support only a limited number of users at one time, the Communications Act's framers subjected over the-air-broadcasting to a regime under which the FCC assigns frequencies to selected licensees to operate for limited periods of time in the "public interest, convenience, and necessity."[7] And after initial award, licenses may not be renewed or transferred to a third party without an FCC determination that such renewal or transfer serves the public interest.[8] Thus, as a practical matter, FCC approval is required for mergers or other combinations of communications companies in which the transfer of control of a spectrum license integral to the companies' business is involved.

With the delegation of "public interest" authority in hand, the FCC proceeded to adopt licensing criteria for broadcasters based in part on the content of programming.[9] For example, the agency

---

6. Other scholars have used this "broadcast model" terminology. For a particularly cogent recent exposition of the role of the "broadcast model," see Christopher S. Yoo, *The Rise and Demise of the Technology-Specific Approach to the First Amendment*, 91 GEO. L. J. 245 (2003).

7. See 47 U.S.C. §§303, 307, 309. The literature describing the linkage between the theory of spectrum scarcity and the Communications Act's public interest standard is well nigh inexhaustible. For a good general introduction, with citation to many authorities, see THOMAS G. KRATTENMAKER AND LUCAS A. POWE, JR., REGULATING BROADCAST PROGRAMMING, AEI PRESS (1994) (see especially Chapters 2, 3, and 6). Two other good introductory articles concerning the theory of broadcast regulation arising from the claim of spectrum scarcity, each with ample citation of authorities, are: Glen O. Robinson, *Title I, The Federal Communications Act: An Essay on Origins and Regulatory Purpose*, in A LEGISLATIVE HISTORY OF THE COMMUNICATIONS ACT OF 1934, 3 (Max D. Paglin ed., 1989) and Thomas W. Hazlett, *The Rationality of U.S. Regulation of the Broadcasting Spectrum*, 33 J. L. & ECON. 133 (1990).

8. 47 U.S.C. §§308, 310 (d).

9. See KRATTENMAKER AND POWE, JR., *supra* note 7. The entire book concerns the regulation of program content by the FCC. For a description of the comprehensive nature of the FCC's early efforts to regulate broadcast pro-

required licensees to limit the amount of advertising material broadcast[10] and to limit network-produced programs broadcast during prime time.[11]

There are other examples of broadcast content regulation. Perhaps the most notorious example is the FCC's now-defunct Fairness Doctrine. Over time the Fairness Doctrine was subject to slightly different formulations, but this FCC statement from 1949 captures its essence as a component of broadcasters' public interest obligations:

> If, as we believe to be the case, the public interest is best served in a democracy through the ability of the people to hear expositions of the various positions taken by responsible groups and individuals on particular topics and to choose between them, it is evident that broadcast licensees have an affirmative duty generally to encourage and implement the broadcast of all sides of controversial public issues over their facilities.[12]

Thus, the Fairness Doctrine required broadcasters to cover controversial public issues and to do so in a balanced way. In the 1980s, the FCC began questioning whether, with the proliferation of additional media outlets, the doctrine was still in the "public interest." Ultimately, it concluded this government-mandated requirement of balanced programming exerted a chilling effect on broadcasters, creating incentives for licensees to broadcast less con-

---

gram content, see FEDERAL COMMUNICATIONS COMMISSION, PUBLIC SERVICE RESPONSIBILITIES OF BROADCAST LICENSEES (1946).

10. FEDERAL COMMUNICATIONS COMMISSION, PUBLIC SERVICE RESPONSIBILITIES OF BROADCAST LICENSEES 41 (1946).

11. Amendment of Part 73 of the Commission's Rules and Regulations with Respect to Competition and Responsibility in network Television Broadcasting, 23 F.C.C. 2d 382 (1970).

12. Editorializing by Broadcast Licensees, Report of the Commission, 13 F.C.C. 1246, 1251 (1949). See also The Handling of Public Issues Under the Fairness Doctrine and the Public Interest Standards of the Communications Act, Fairness Doctrine Report, 48 F.C.C. 2d 1 (1974). Krattenmaker and Powe, Jr., *supra* note 7, have extensive discussion throughout their book on the Fairness Doctrine, including all of Chapter 9 ("The Fairness Doctrine").

troversial public affairs programming than otherwise they would.[13] Although the Commission initially concluded only Congress or the courts could get rid of the doctrine, the D.C. Circuit disagreed.[14] With its authority clarified, the FCC acted shortly thereafter to jettison the Fairness Doctrine upon public interest grounds, and its decision was affirmed.[15]

Basing licensing decisions on programming content raises obvious First Amendment issues. Indeed, the Communications Act itself contains a "no-censorship" provision.[16] As a practical matter, it has never meant what its language, at least literally construed, seems to imply. Rather, its inclusion in the Act only calls attention to the tension the FCC's program content intrusions create with respect to licensees' free speech rights. The Supreme Court, early on in the development of radio and television broadcasting, adopted an approach permitting an intrusive government-supervised content regulatory regime applicable to broadcasters. In the landmark case of *National Broadcasting Co. v. United States*,[17] the Supreme Court in 1943 invoked spectrum scarcity in sanctioning a lesser degree of First Amendment protection for broadcasters. Upholding the first FCC regulations governing the relationship between new radio broadcasting networks and local affiliates, the Court declared: "Freedom of utterance is abridged to many who

---

13. Inquiry into §73.1910 of the Commission's Rules and Regulations Concerning General Fairness Doctrine Obligations of Broadcast Licensees, 102 F.C.C. 2d 143 (1985).

14. Meredith Corp. v. FCC, 809 F. 2d 863 (D.C. Cir. 1987) (The Communications Act does not mandate the Fairness Doctrine.)

15. For a description of the doctrine, its impact on broadcasters, and a history of its demise, see Syracuse Peace Council, 2 F.C.C.R. 5043 (1987), *aff'd*, 867 F. 2d 654 (D.C.Cir. 1989), *cert. denied*, 493 U.S. 1019 (1990).

16. Section 326 provides: "Nothing in this chapter shall be understood or construed to give the Commission the power of censorship over the radio communications or signals transmitted by any radio station, and no regulation or condition shall be promulgated or fixed by the Commission which shall interfere with the right of free speech by means of radio communication." 47 U.S.C. §326.

17. NBC v. United States, 319 U.S. 190 (1943).

wish to use the limited facilities of radio. Unlike other modes of expression, radio inherently is not available to all. That is its unique characteristic, and that is why, unlike other modes of expression, it is subject to government regulation."[18] The FCC's "chain broadcasting" regulations prohibited certain practices that restricted the affiliate's discretion to broadcast a non-network supplied program.

Aside from rejecting the First Amendment claim on the basis of spectrum scarcity, the *NBC* case is also notable because Justice Frankfurter's majority opinion gave the FCC such wide berth to regulate "in the public interest." Referring to what he called the dynamic nature of the new field of broadcasting, Frankfurter declared the Communications Act's public interest delegation gives the agency "expansive powers."[19] And quoting from his earlier opinion in *FCC v. Pottsville Broadcasting Co.*, Justice Frankfurter proclaimed the public interest standard "is as concrete as the complicated factors for judgment in such a field of delegated authority permit."[20]

In 1969, in *Red Lion Broadcasting Co. v FCC*,[21] the Court employed the spectrum scarcity rationale used in *NBC* to affirm the constitutionality of the FCC's Fairness Doctrine. The FCC had determined that a radio broadcaster had violated the fairness mandate by refusing to provide broadcast time for someone claiming he had been personally attacked in the station's programming. Rejecting a challenge that the doctrine violated broadcasters' free speech rights, the Court declared:

> Where there are substantially more individuals who want to broadcast than there are frequencies to allocate, it is idle to posit an unabridgeable First Amendment right to broadcast comparable to the right of every individual to speak, write, or publish.... Because of the scarcity of

18. 319 U.S. at 226.

19. *Id.* at 219.

20. *Id.* at 216, quoting FCC v. Pottsville Broadcasting Co., 309 U.S. 134, 138 (1940).

21. 395 U.S. 367 (1969).

> radio frequencies, the Government is permitted to put restraints on licensees in favor of others whose views should be expressed on this unique medium. But the people as a whole retain their interest in free speech by radio and their collective right to have the medium function consistently with the ends and purposes of the First Amendment. It is the right of the viewers and listeners, not the right of the broadcasters, which is paramount.[22]

With *NBC* and *Red Lion*, curtailment of broadcasters' free speech rights, justified on the basis of spectrum scarcity, was firmly embedded in constitutional jurisprudence. Despite some periodic teases, the Supreme Court has yet to overturn *Red Lion*,[23] even though today there are thousands more broadcasting stations on the air than in 1969, not to mention the proliferation of new media outlets that did not then exist, such as cable and satellite systems with hundreds of channels of video and audio programming, and DVDs, iPods, mobile devices, and the Internet.

Although claimed spectrum scarcity has provided the primary justification for the broadcast model's free speech curtailment, it is worth noting that the Supreme Court has employed another rationale. In 1978, in *FCC v. Pacifica Foundation*,[24] the Court, split

---

22. *Id.* at 388, 390.

23. For an early hint that the scarcity rationale might be undermined in the future, see CBS v. Democratic National Committee, 412 U.S. 94, 102 (1973) ("The broadcast industry is dynamic in terms of technological change" so that "solutions adequate a decade ago are not necessarily so now, and those acceptable today may be outmoded 10 years hence." (plurality opinion) and ("Scarcity may soon be a constraint of the past, thus obviating the concerns expressed in *Red Lion*. It has been predicted that it may be possible within 10 years to provide television viewers 400 channels through the advances of cable television." *Id.* at 158, n.8 (Douglas, J., concurring in the judgment.) For a later hint, see FCC v. League of Women Voters, 468 U.S. 364, 376 n.11 (1984) ("We are not prepared … to reconsider our longstanding approach without some signal from Congress or the FCC that technological developments have advanced so far that some revision of the system of broadcast regulation may be required.") See generally Yoo, *supra* note 6, at 245, 284–88 (2003).

24. 438 U.S. 726 (1978).

5–4, upheld in a narrowly-drawn opinion the FCC's determination that it could sanction a radio station that broadcast George Carlin's "filthy words" monologue, which the agency determined to be "indecent."[25] In rejecting the broadcaster's First Amendment challenge, the Supreme Court, citing *Red Lion*, pointed out that "a broadcaster may be deprived of his license and his forum if the Commission decides that such an action would serve 'the public interest, convenience, and necessity.'"[26] Then the Court offered two non-spectrum scarcity rationales. First, "the broadcast media have established a uniquely pervasive presence in the lives of all Americans.... Because the broadcast audience is constantly tuning in and out, prior warnings cannot completely protect the listener or viewer from unexpected program content."[27] Second, "broadcasting is uniquely accessible to children," unlike other forms of offensive expression that "may be withheld from the young without restricting expression at its source."[28]

The *Pacifica* Court did emphasize the "narrowness"[29] of the holding, one in which "context is all-important."[30] And Justice Powell, in his concurrence joined by Justice Blackmun, which supplied the two votes necessary for a majority, emphasized the "narrow focus" of the Court's opinion.[31] And relevant to the *Fox Television* case to be decided this Term in the Supreme Court, he pointed out that the offensive language in the Carlin monologue "was repeated over and over as a sort of verbal shock treatment."[32] Nevertheless, *Pacifica* cemented the notion that broadcasters enjoyed—or suffered—diminished First Amendment rights. As the *Pacifica* Court concluded: "[O]f all the forms of communication,

---

25. For authority, the FCC relied on the statute that prohibits the use of "any obscene, indecent, or profane language by means of radio communications." 18 U.S.C. § 1464.

26. 438 U.S. at 748.

27. 438 U.S. at 748.

28. *Id.* at 749.

29. *Id.* at 750.

30. *Id.*

31. *Id.* at 756.

32. *Id.* at 758.

it is broadcasting that has received the most limited First Amendment protection."[33] There you have a concise summary of the twentieth century's jurisprudence under the "broadcast model."

Not much has changed from a jurisprudential perspective since Justice Jackson observed in *Kovacs v. Cooper* that each of the different communications media represents a "law unto itself."[34] On the one hand, any speech restrictions affecting the print media receive very strict scrutiny. In the leading case of *Miami Herald Publishing Co. v. Tornillo*, the Court unanimously held that a Florida statute requiring a newspaper to publish a reply to an editorial criticizing a political candidate violated the First Amendment.[35] So *Tornillo* constituted an unequivocal rejection of the assertion that a *Red Lion*-like "right of access" regime, a fairness doctrine, if you will, should be applied to newspapers in the interest of enhancing the speech rights of newspaper readers. The Court had no trouble holding the Florida right of reply statute unconstitutional even as it declared that "[c]hains of newspapers, national newspapers, national wire and news services, and one-newspaper towns, are the dominant features of a press that has become noncompetitive and enormously powerful and influential in its capacity to manipulate popular opinion and change the course of events."[36] The "scarcity" rationale that served as the basis for curtailing the broadcasters' First Amendment rights held no sway with respect to newspapers.

On the other hand, in 1994 in *Turner Broadcasting System v. FCC*, the Court, in a 5–4 decision, rejected a First Amendment challenge to a "right of access" mandate.[37] Having in mind the government's argument that "free" over-the-air television service provided by local broadcast stations deserved special protection, the majority refused to invalidate, at least on its face, a law requiring cable operators to carry local broadcast signals. The Court acknowledged the "must carry" mandate directly implicated cable

33. *Id.* at 748.
34. 336 U.S. 77, 97 (1949) (concurring opinion).
35. 418 U.S. 241 (1974).
36. *Id.* at 249.
37. 512 U.S. 622 (1994).

operators' free speech rights.[38] Nevertheless, applying an "intermediate level of scrutiny,"[39] and asserting cable operators' possessed a marketplace "bottleneck" that allowed them to play a "gatekeeper" role with respect to programming entering subscribers' homes,[40] the Court rejected the argument that the *Tornillo* print model, with strict scrutiny applied to speech restrictions, should govern. It is important to note that in rejecting application of the First Amendment print model, the Court did not place any reliance on the spectrum scarcity rationale at the heart of *Red Lion.*

Finally, thus far at least, the Court has reviewed content-based restrictions applied to the Internet under a strict scrutiny standard akin to that applied to the print media. In the leading case, in 1997, *Reno v. ACLU,* the Court struck down on First Amendment grounds a law regulating "indecent" communications on the Internet.[41] In doing so, the Court declared, "unlike the conditions that prevailed when Congress first authorized regulation of the broadcast spectrum, the Internet can hardly be considered a 'scarce' expressive commodity."[42]

The Way Forward: A Constitutional Jurisprudence for the Digital Era

In today's competitive and converging digital environment, it is time for the Court finally to abandon the scarcity rationale used

---

38. *Id.* at 641.

39. This is not the place, nor would there be space, to discuss the Court's tortured constitutional "standards" of jurisprudence, even with respect to the First Amendment. Suffice it to say that in *Turner* a key to the employment of intermediate rather than strict scrutiny was Justice Kennedy's determination for the majority that the "must carry" requirement was content neutral. In dissent, Justice O'Connor argued the carriage requirement was in fact a content-based restriction because it was directed at "local" broadcast station content.

40. 512 U.S. at 656.

41. 521 U.S. 844 (1997).

42. *Id.* at 896.

in *Red Lion* to justify limited First Amendment protection for radio and television broadcasters. In *Red Lion's* place, the Court should articulate a jurisprudence that generally affords the various forms of electronic media the same strict First Amendment protection that newspapers receive under *Tornillo* and that the Internet receives under *Reno*. There will always be special considerations presented by laws or regulations defended on the basis they are intended to protect children from harmful content, and the government's interest in this respect certainly is legitimate. But in today's digital environment, much more so than in the past, parents have available easy-to-use filtering and blocking tools to screen out offensive content, whether such content is delivered via broadcasting, cable, satellite, or the Internet. The widespread availability of such screening tools surely constitutes a "less restrictive alternative" to content regulation that should render *Pacifica's* pervasiveness and uniquely-accessible-to-children rationales largely a historical relic. The *Pacifica* Court was wise at the time "to emphasize the narrowness" of its holding.[43]

The Public Interest Standard

Before elaborating more fully on the way forward for a new First Amendment jurisprudence for the electronic media, a word is in order concerning the public interest standard under which so much of the FCC's regulatory activity, including content regulation, takes place.[44] In the leading case of *J. W. Hampton, Jr. v. United States*, the Supreme Court, although there rejecting a non-delegation doctrine challenge to a tariff statute, declared: "If Congress shall lay down by legislative act an intelligible principle to which the person or body authorized to fix such rates be directed to conform, such legislative action is not a forbidden delegation of

43. 438 U.S. at 750.

44. Congress has directed or authorized the FCC to act in the public interest in nearly one hundred separate statutory provisions. See Randolph J. May, *The Public Interest Standard: Is It Too Indeterminate to Be Constitutional*, 53 FED. COMM. L. J. 427, 429 and Appendix A (2001).

legislative power."[45] Although the Court has not held a statute unconstitutional on nondelegation doctrine grounds since 1935, when it did so twice,[46] it has continued to maintain that, in order not to violate fundamental separation of powers principles, there must be an "intelligible principle" set forth in every statute delegating congressional authority.[47]

With respect to the Communications Act's "public interest" delegation, the Supreme Court's jurisprudence is incongruous and unsatisfactory. In *Mistretta v. United States*, Justice Scalia, in dissent, proclaimed: "It is difficult to imagine a principle more essential to democratic government than that upon which the doctrine of unconstitutional delegation is founded: Except in a few areas constitutionally committed to the Executive Branch, the basic policy decisions governing society are to be made by the Legislature."[48] Nevertheless, he observed, without expressing disapproval, that the "vague" public interest standard has withstood constitutional challenge.[49] And, in *Whitman*, now writing for the majority, Justice Scalia once again cited the public interest standard as an indication of how far the Court has been willing to go in sustaining vague delegations.[50]

The fact is that it is difficult, if not impossible, to square the indeterminate public interest standard, with the "intelligible principle" requirement to which the Court continues to pay lip service. Shortly after the passage of the Federal Radio Act, upon which the Communications Act was modeled, the agency's first general counsel stated: "'Public interest, convenience, or necessity' means about as little as any phrase that the drafter of the Act could have used...."[51] Another way of expressing, accurately, the same thought

---

45. 276 U.S. 394 (1928).

46. Panama Ref. Co. v. Ryan, 293 U.S. 388 (1935); A.L.A. Schechter Poultry Corp. v. United States, 295 U.S. 495 (1935).

47. See most recently, Whitman v. American Trucking Assn., 531 U.S. 457, 472 (2001).

48. 488 U.S. 361, 415 (1989).

49. *Id.* at 416.

50. 531 U.S. at 474.

51. Louis G. Caldwell, *The Standard of the Public Interest, Convenience or Necessity as Used in the Radio Act of 1927,* 1 Air L. Rev. 295, 296 (1930).

is to say the standard means whatever a majority of the agency's commissioners says it means on any given day.

I have argued in a much more extensive treatment that the public interest delegation ought to be held unconstitutional as a violation of the nondelegation doctrine's requirement that Congress lay down an intelligible principle, and I refer the reader to that article.[52] Constitutional law scholar Gary Lawson has called the public interest standard, "easy kill number one," as an example of a provision that should be held unconstitutional on nondelegation grounds.[53] At its next opportunity, the Court should reconsider those cases that have held the public interest standard constitutional. Doing so would force Congress to provide more policy direction for a so-called independent regulatory agency increasingly at sea in the new digital environment. And, in furtherance of the separation of powers principles which underlay the nondelegation doctrine, doing so would make Congress more politically accountable for establishing—or, perhaps, for failing to establish—sound communications policy direction.

Defining a New First Amendment Paradigm for the Electronic Media

Red Lion's scarcity rationale was suspect in one sense on the day it was rendered and in another not long thereafter. As Ronald Coase explained in his famous article ten years before *Red Lion*, all resources, not just spectrum, "are limited in amount and scarce, in that people would like to use more than exists."[54] Indeed, the extent to which spectrum is more or less scarce is impacted greatly by the government's regulatory decisions in allocating frequencies. As Christopher Yoo puts it nicely, "because the amount of spectrum available at any moment is itself a product of regulation, any

52. See May, *supra* note 44, at 443–452.

53. Gary Lawson, *Delegation and the Constitution*, 22 REG., No. 2, 1999, at 23, 29.

54. R.H. Coase, *The Federal Communications Commission*, 2 J. L. & ECON. 1 (1959).

reliance on spectrum scarcity in effect allows the regulation to serve as a constitutional justification for other regulations."[55] As Coase and many other scholars have pointed out, the so-called spectrum scarcity problem underpinning the *NBC* and *Red Lion* decisions would not exist, at least in the sense asserted, if Congress did not prohibit the emergence of an enforceable property rights regime. Under a property rights regime, claims concerning spectrum interference would be resolved through established marketplace mechanisms or through litigation resolving contract or tort-like claims. Then the notion of spectrum scarcity as a justification for the government to regulate program content under the indeterminate public interest standard would be eviscerated.

Even putting aside the classical Coasian economic argument against spectrum scarcity,[56] the communications marketplace has changed so radically since *Red Lion* was decided that the scarcity rationale should be jettisoned as a justification for continued diminished First Amendment protection. The *Red Lion* Court itself acknowledged the pace of "technological advances," but thought it "unwise to speculate" as to how such advances might alter the scarcity calculus.[57] The fact is, as a practical matter, technological advances have rendered obsolete the notion of a scarcity of media outlets. We live in an age of media abundance rather than an age of scarcity.

Without trying to paint a complete landscape here,[58] consider this. When *Red Lion* was decided in 1969, in addition to the daily

---

55. Yoo, *supra* note 6, at 251. See also Thomas W. Hazlett, *The Rationality of U.S. Regulation of the Broadcast Spectrum*, 33 J. L. & ECON. 133 (1990).

56. It is pertinent to point out here that the Court in *Red Lion* based its decision firmly on what it referred to as "a technological scarcity of frequencies," thus allowing it to avoid dealing with the "economic scarcity" argument. See 395 U.S. at 401, n. 28.

57. 395 U.S. at 397.

58. There is simply not space to do so. The figures presented in this paragraph are well-known. For a book with lots of facts and figures and tables and charts documenting the extent to which the media landscape has changed since *Red Lion*, see Adam D. Thierer, Media Myths: Making Sense of the Debate Over Media Ownership, The Progress & Freedom Foundation, 2005. For

newspaper and other print media, most Americans got their news and other information from the over-the-air broadcast stations affiliated with the then-three major networks, ABC, CBS, and NBC, and a few other television and radio stations serving their communities. In 1970, one year after the *Red Lion* decision, there were 875 television stations and 6,751 radio stations. In 2005, there were 1,747 television stations and 13,476 radio stations.[59] Today, over 90 percent of Americans subscribe to either multi-channel cable or satellite services, on average receiving over a hundred separate information and entertainment channels. There are over three hundred different national program networks from which cable and satellite subscribers may choose. In addition to cable and satellite television, there is now satellite radio, which offers hundreds of information and entertainment program channels. As the FCC said back in 2003, "[w]e are moving to a system served by literally hundreds of networks serving all conceivable interests."[60] Since then, more individual networks have emerged. The switch-over to digital television will lead to still more over-the-air television program channels. And, of course, today's broadband Internet services are a key development in terms of further enhancing access to thousands of additional information sources. We truly live in an age of information abundance.

The Roberts Court should seize the first opportunity to chart a new jurisprudential course that provides broadcasters, as well as other electronic media, including cable, satellite, wireless, and broadband Internet providers, with First Amendment protections that are on par with those traditionally enjoyed by the print media. In other words, government content restrictions applicable to the various electronic media, regardless of the technological platform used to deliver content, would be subject to the same strict scrutiny the Court employed in *Tornillo* in holding unconstitutional a

much data on the increasing number of information sources since *Red Lion*, see especially Chapter 1 ("Death of Diversity or Age of Abundance").

59. Adam D. Thierer, *supra* note 58, at 31, Table 5.

60. 2002 Biennial Regulatory Review of the Commission's Broadcast Ownership Rules, FCC 03-127, June 2, 2003, at 48–49.

newspaper "right of reply" mandate. This would mean, whether explicitly or in some less direct fashion, overturning *Red Lion* and *Turner Broadcasting*. With the availability of today's various parent-empowering blocking and filtering technologies, including, for example, the V-chip now embedded in every television set, it would not be difficult for the Court, were it so inclined, to acknowledge *Pacifica's* "uniquely pervasive" and "uniquely-accessible-to-children" rationales have much diminished force as justifications for content regulation.

A few times since *Red Lion*, the Court has indicated receptivity to revisiting the decision. For example, almost a quarter a century ago, in *FCC v. League of Women Voters*, the Court acknowledged, "[c]ritics, including the incumbent Chairman of the FCC, charge that with the advent of cable and satellite television technology, communities now have access to such a wide variety of stations that the scarcity doctrine is obsolete."[61] But on this and other occasions, while taking note of the doctrine's possible obsolescence, the Court has refused to bury it. It is time to do so. The Court could recognize that it erred in a fundamental way at the time, and before, in not recognizing that spectrum, in an economic sense, is no scarcer than other resources. Or perhaps more palatably, it could acknowledge that advances have rendered obsolete the "tech-

---

61. 468 U.S. 364, 376, n.11 (1984). In 1998, yet another FCC Commissioner (and soon-to-be FCC Chairman) declared: "I believe that any attempt to consider how changes in technology and the regulatory environment affect public interest obligations, necessarily must include a review of the underpinnings of current First Amendment jurisprudence.... I submit the time has come to reexamine First Amendment jurisprudence as it has been applied to broadcast media and bring it into line with the realities of today's communications marketplace." "Willful Denial and First Amendment Jurisprudence," Remarks by Michael K. Powell, Commissioner, Federal Communications Commission, before the Media Institute, Washington, DC, April 22, 1998. Commissioner Powell went on to state: "Most importantly, advances in technology have been astonishing since the time of *Red Lion*. Digital convergence, rather than reinforcing the unique nature of broadcasting, has blurred the lines between all communications medium [sic].... Even this brief overview of the marketplace makes the reasoning of *Red Lion* seem almost quaint...." *Id.* Remember, these remarks were delivered over a decade ago.

nological scarcity" upon which *Red Lion* was premised. In either case, the Court would acknowledge that the scarcity rationale's obsolescence means that content regulation based on it cannot withstand First Amendment challenge.

And, fortuitously, the opportunity to emphasize the limited continuing relevance, if not outright irrelevance, of *Pacifica* may be at hand. In March 2008, the Supreme Court granted certiorari to review the Second Circuit's decision in the *Fox Television* case holding that a new FCC policy sanctioning "fleeting expletives" is arbitrary and capricious under the Administrative Procedure Act for failure to articulate a reasoned basis for the change in policy.[62] Prior to announcing its new policy, the agency required more than fleeting or isolated use of expletives such as "fuck" and "shit" to find a violation of the indecency statute. Under the new policy, isolated uses of these words were presumptively subject to indecency sanction, with the broadcaster bearing the burden to show that they were not.

While the court of appeals based its decision on traditional administrative law grounds, it went on in *dicta* to "question whether the FCC's indecency test can survive First Amendment scrutiny."[63] The court stated "we are sympathetic to the Networks' contention that the FCC's indecency test is undefined, indiscernible, inconsistent, and, consequently, unconstitutionally vague."[64] Taking note that new filtering and blocking technologies might provide "less restrictive alternatives" to achieve the government's interest in protecting children than outright banning of speech, the Court observed "we would be remiss not to observe that it is increasingly difficult to describe the broadcast media as uniquely pervasive and uniquely accessible to children, and, at some point in the future, strict scrutiny may properly apply in the context of regulating broadcast television."[65]

62. See Fox Television Stations, Inc. v. FCC, 489 F. 3d 444 (2nd Cir. 2007), *cert. granted*, 128 S. Ct. 1647 (2008). The case was argued in the Court on November 4, 2008.

63. *Id.* at 463.

64. *Id.*

65. *Id.* at 465.

The government asserts in brief that the Second Circuit's decision conflicts with the breadth of the FCC's authority recognized in *Pacifica* to enforce the statute prohibiting "indecent" broadcasts,[66] and that, because the adequacy of the Commission's explanation was the only issue on which the appellate court based its reversal, there is no need for the Supreme Court to reach the constitutional issue.[67] But Fox Television and other parties urge the Court to address head-on the First Amendment issues the Second Circuit discussed. Fox states:

> While petitioners would have the Court ignore those issues, the regulation of "indecent" speech necessarily implicates core First Amendment values, and the administrative law analysis simply cannot be divorced from the constitutional one. A change in policy that results in the restriction of a greater amount of speech–as the change in this case undoubtedly does–must be justified not only by a "reasoned explanation," but also by proof that the policy represents the "least restrictive" means to address a real, established harm.... In the 30 years since *Pacifica*, legal and technological developments have eroded the underpinnings of the *Pacifica* decision, which make an expansion of the indecency regime especially suspect.[68]

Interestingly, an *amicus curiae* brief submitted by a group of former FCC officials, including three former FCC Chairmen and one former FCC Commissioner, urges the Court to affirm the Second Circuit's decision.[69] They, too, urge the Court to reach the First Amendment question:

---

66. See note 25 *supra*; 18 U.S.C. §1464.

67. Brief for the Petitioners, FCC v. Fox Television Stations, Inc., No. 07-582, June 2008, at 19. ("And there is no reason for this Court to depart from its customary practice and reach out to decide constitutional questions not passed on below.")

68. Brief for the Respondent Fox Television Stations, Inc., No. 07-582, August 1, 2008, at 17–18 (internal citations omitted).

69. Brief for Amicus Curiae Former FCC Commissioners and Officials in Support of Respondents, No. 07-582, August 8, 2008. Two of the former

> Further, we do not believe the question of administrative arbitrariness can be isolated from the deeper free speech issues that lie at the heart of this controversy. The Government's attempt to frame the issue before this Court as simply one of administrative procedure ignores what the court of appeals made clear: the issue of reasoned analysis is inextricably bound up with a fundamental constitutional question. While the court labeled its treatment of the First Amendment issue as *dicta*, it clearly expressed its judgment that the FCC's failure to offer a reasoned explanation for its new 'fleeting expletive' regime was not merely a procedural defect but was a constitutional defect as well.[70]

Of course, it is not clear now whether the Court will reach the First Amendment question in deciding the *Fox* case. Despite the pleas to the contrary, it is certainly possible it could dispose of the case without doing so.[71] But if the Court does reach the constitutional issue, in my view it should use the opportunity to further restrict *Pacifica's* already narrow holding. The Court has an opportunity to restore at least some, if not all, of broadcasters' long lost free speech rights.

As for cable operators, whatever *Turner Broadcasting's* merits when it was decided, cable (and satellite operators) now should receive full First Amendment protection. Recall the Court freely acknowledged cable operators' free speech rights were implicated by the "must carry" mandate.[72] But in ultimately refusing to hold the

---

commissioners joined in the FCC's original *Pacifica* decision that was ultimately affirmed by the Supreme Court.

70. *Id.* at 4.

71. As this book was going to press, the Supreme Court decided the *Fox Television* case. See 129 S. Ct. 1800 (2009). The Court ruled that the FCC's actions were not arbitrary and capricious and did not reach the First Amendment issue. In a concurring opinion, however, Justice Thomas, citing an earlier version of this essay which appeared at 3 Charleston L. Rev. 373 (2009), indicated he is prepared to reconsider the existing First Amendment jurisprudence applied to the electronic media.

72. See note 38 *supra* and accompanying text.

mandate unconstitutional after a fact-finding remand, the Court relied heavily on Congress's judgment that local stations providing "free" over-the-air television deserved special economic protection.[73] Today, with many more media outlets available, along with the Internet, the justification, if ever there were any, for providing special protection to local broadcasters at the expense of cable operators' First Amendment rights is even more problematic. In *Turner*, the Court viewed cable operators as possessing a control different in kind than the "monopoly status" it acknowledged in *Tornillo* that most newspapers enjoyed in increasingly prevalent "one-newspaper towns."[74] The *Turner* Court stated: "[T]he physical connection between the television set and the cable network gives the cable operator bottleneck, or gatekeeper, control over most (if not all) of the television programming that is channeled into the subscriber's home. Hence, simply by virtue of its ownership of the essential pathway for cable speech, a cable operator can prevent its subscribers from obtaining access to programming it chooses to exclude."[75]

Although it is doubtful that by the mid-1990s cable operators continued to have such dominance as to justify the "bottleneck" or "gatekeeper" tag, it is simply not the case today that they can control the video programming that enters a subscriber's home. Cable competes vigorously with satellite operators providing hundreds of channels, and, increasingly with "telephone" companies that now offer hundreds of channels of programming over high-capacity networks. And the Internet is the source of virtually unlimited information sources, including audio and video. More and more people watch the latest "television" programs on their "cell phones." *Turner* was a 5–4 decision. When the occasion next arises, the Court should indicate, in light of the changed communications marketplace, that the decision's rationale has been undermined and cable operators are entitled to enjoy the same First Amendment rights as newspapers.

---

73. Turner Broadcasting Sys. v. FCC, 520 U.S. 180 (1997).

74. See note 36 *supra* and accompanying text.

75. 512 U.S. at 656.

Recommendation and Conclusion

While not likely any time soon, perhaps one day the Supreme Court will breathe some new life into the nondelegation doctrine by holding that the indeterminate public interest standard, which is at the core of the Communications Act and much communications policymaking, does not contain the requisite "intelligible principle" to guide agency action. And perhaps one day in the not-too-distant future, Congress will pass a new Digital Age Communications Act that will replace the statute's ubiquitous public interest standard with a competition-based one.

Hopefully, sooner rather than later, the Court will revisit *Red Lion*, *Pacifica*, and *Turner* in order to establish a new First Amendment paradigm for the electronic media, one that is much more in keeping with the Founders' First Amendment vision. It is possible it could move in this direction this Term in deciding the *Fox Television* case.

In short, the Supreme Court should seize the first opportunity to chart a new jurisprudential course that provides broadcasters, as well as other electronic media, including cable, satellite, wireless, and broadband Internet providers, with First Amendment protections that are the same as those traditionally enjoyed by the print media. Laws or regulations applicable to the various electronic media that have the purpose or effect of restricting program content should be subject to the same strict scrutiny the Court employed in *Tornillo* in holding unconstitutional a newspaper "right of reply" mandate. It should make no difference what type of technological platform is used to deliver the content. Thus, either explicitly or in some less direct fashion, *Red Lion* and *Turner Broadcasting* should be overturned.

Perhaps it was predictable, maybe even likely, that the First Amendment's protections would be limited substantially during the twentieth century's analog age. After all, for the most part, during the analog age the communications marketplace tended towards monopoly or oligopoly, and the lack of effective competition was not irrelevant to the outcome of major cases like *Red Lion* or *Turner*. But, now, in the face of proliferating competitive alternatives and media outlets spurred by profound marketplace and technological changes, it ought to be considered predictable, and, yes, even likely, for the Court to establish a new First Amendment jurisprudence befitting the media abundance of the twenty-first century's digital age.

CHAPTER 10

A Fresh Start in Communications Policy: Two Modest Reforms

*Bruce M. Owen**

A country that leads the world in the development of the technologies that have revolutionized communications services should not have a second-rate system for regulating those services. Our communications policy is an embarrassment to the United States and a bad example to other countries. Fixing the economy, Social Security, and the health care system may be more pressing, but repairing America's communications policies should be on the agenda as well. The new President and Congress should try to make America's communications policy worthy of America's communications technology and its people. But that will not be easy.

This brief essay offers an overview of what needs fixing and why, and of the obstacles to reform. I suggest two specific policy initiatives, both aimed at loosening the persistent grip of obsolete decisions on current policy. One useful reform would be to permit spectrum users to resell or repurpose their frequencies, so long as no new interference is created for other users. A second helpful reform would mandate that all individual rules and regulations contain provisions for automatic expiration after a term of years.

* I am grateful to Roger Noll and Greg Rosston for helpful comments.

What's Wrong?—*The Process*

"Communications policy" refers to how we regulate electronic mass media, Internet and telephone services. American communications policy is a mishmash of laws, rules and regulations—over 300,000 words of statutes alone and five printed volumes in the *Code of Federal Regulations*, accumulated over the past century. In addition, the fifty states each have their own sets of communication policies and local regulations.

Communications policy is not just law and regulation; it is also the daily bread of a *community* made up of thousands of specialized lawyers, lobbyists, labor unions and industry associations, consultants, regulators, and congressional staffers. The community has its own daily newspapers, weekly magazines, online pundits and blogs; and its own argot. In principle the community helps the government decide what communication policies are in the public interest. In practice the cost of joining and participating in the community is prohibitive for all but relatively small groups with strong economic interests. The interests of ordinary citizens as taxpayers and consumers are not well represented, except by single-issue activists, usually from ideological polar regions. Non-participation by individual consumers and voters is rational. None of this is unusual in Washington; similar communities exist for transportation, health, environmental, energy, financial, and tax policy.

Communications policy is made, of course, by commissioners, senators and representatives heading relevant committees or subcommittees, presidents, judges, and by their staff advisors, interacting with each other and with the greater communications policy community. The formal interactions are governed by laws and procedural rules known as "administrative law." Decision-makers hear daily from highly paid, skilled advocates, none representing the ordinary consumers who often bear the costs of regulatory goodies over which the economic interest groups are tussling.

None of the players in this game pursues Platonic ideals. There is no way to understand our current communications policies except as the outcomes of complex bargaining among industry groups competing for government favors. The reality is that communications policy consists of compromises, brokered by public officials, among the various economic and political interest groups, heavily weighted in favor of the best-financed, most articulate and politically influential. These outcomes have been worked out over the past century and are now embedded in laws, regulations, and legal precedents, much of which survives today.

Taking a wider view, our political system can be viewed as an elaborate game in which elected officials pursue political advantage by catering to the economic and other goals of competing interest groups—what the Founders called "factions." It is necessary to keep these factions in the game in order "preserve the Union," meaning the coalition of interests that constitutes our nation. Key factions and potential coalitions of factions must believe that they are better off being part of the system than out of it; compromise must seem preferable to the costs and risks of some form of secession. Our system is structured to reward politicians who respond to the incentives created by interest group competition and the art of compromise. The system has been remarkably successful, producing only one bloody civil war in more than two centuries; that war is a useful reminder that the alternative to compromise can be very costly.

Keeping the coalition intact is a praiseworthy endeavor, and the politicians who work to do so should be praised. But human nature seems to require more than the considerable gift of political stability, a condition that is frankly boring and sells no newspapers. We crave high ideals and lofty rhetoric—the dangerous cant of extremist true believers—for which the slogans of work-a-day politicians may seem an unsatisfactory substitute. Hence the importance to these officials of the myths that the system is designed, and that politicians are obliged, to seek "the public interest" at the expense of the "special interests." The truth is that the system, broadly speaking, serves the public interest by keeping the special interests in the game. Unfortunately, the contrast between the rhetoric and the reality probably contributes to the general disrepute of elected officials.

The accumulation of compromises would make for an even less coherent and stable set of policies than we have were it not for the role of the federal courts in supervising regulators. Generally, of course, courts do not recognize "compromise among interest groups competing for government favors" as sufficient justification for regulations. Most policies must be couched or defended in terms of the Communications Act's prevailing "public interest" standard. The courts seek consistency, insisting that new compromises be capable of rationalization in ways consistent with prior rationalizations. New regulatory actions also have to be articulated in the language of the underlying assumptions and precedents of communications policy—what I call the community's "foundational myths."

Like many nations and indigenous peoples, the communications policy community does have foundational myths. One is the idea that the enterprise is concerned directly with the public interest, as opposed to the political regulation of the pursuit of economic advantage.

Many other basal myths, particular to communications policy, are mostly mistaken or outdated—but precedent-setting—assumptions about the technology of telecommunications, such as the notion that the radio waves are uniquely scarce, the idea that television is still the only medium for political ideas to reach the public, or the idea that telecommunications companies retain intractable monopoly power. Obeisance to these myths sometimes restricts the ability of government officials to broker compromises, and often preserves obsolete laws and regulations—that is, policies that reduce consumer welfare and are no longer relevant to a compromise among contending interest groups.

What does it mean for a policy to be "bad," given the preceding understanding of the political process? The answer is simple, at least from an economic perspective. Among politically feasible compromises, we should choose those that make consumers as well off as possible. If a policy harms consumers and is not required to achieve or sustain the resolution of a significant conflict among current interest groups, it should be abandoned. In forging solutions to political conflicts, no more consumer welfare should be sacrificed than necessary to resolve the problem. This is common sense and obvious to all, but too little observed.

What's Wrong?—*The Outcomes*

Example: Phone Service

Behind the facade of public interest rhetoric, foundational myths, and techno-babble argot, the big picture of current communications policy is easy enough to understand. Let's start with the telephone business. The federal and state governments regulate telephone service because telephone service used to be a monopoly. During the monopoly period the FCC, Congress, and the old Bell System connived to create valuable perks for various special interests, such as low rates for citizens of rural states.

The old monopoly Bell System had no interest in providing rural telephone service—it left that to hundreds of small companies and cooperatives. Nevertheless, the Bell System did promote rural telephone service by agreeing to charge its urban customers prices higher than the cost of service, and using the extra revenue to subsidize prices charged to rural telephone companies in exchange for protection from competition itself. The money for the rural state special interests was extracted from other phone customers, by charging them higher prices. Urban telephone customers, rich and poor alike, paid higher rates so that telephone service in, for example, Oklahoma, could be cheap for rich and poor alike. The slogan for all this cross-subsidization was "universal service," the idea that it would be a good thing if everyone, however remote, who wanted a telephone should have one, whatever the cost to other telephone customers.

All of this may have made political sense during the period between the two world wars, a period when rural life was particularly brutal and rural telephone suppliers were at odds with the Bell System monopoly. Such subsidy schemes cannot be sustained in a competitive market, because consumers have choices. When competition finally arrived in the telephone industry a generation ago, the obvious policy would have been to abolish the universal service subsidy, which by then was producing much cheap multi-line telephone service for the rural vacation homes of the urban rich. Today, the character and size of the rural population and the structure of the telephone industry no longer require a "universal service" subsidy. Assuming that the reality of the cross-subsidies and the rhetoric of universal service was a satisfactory solution to a conflict of interest groups in the 1920s and 30s, it cannot be so today. Why is the system still in place?

Congress made the "universal service fund" into law as part of the Telecommunications Act in 1996, mandating subsidies not only for rural telecommunications services but also for rural health and education providers. Congress also expanded the definition of telecommunications to include Internet service, and to pay for all this, it decreed, not that the government would pay, but rather that everyone who was not on the list of those subsidized would pay—through higher rates for telephone and Internet service.

None of this makes the slightest economic policy sense. Alaska has now become the poster child for the absurd set of cross-subsidies that benefit all rural states. It is one thing to help poor people, it is another to help Senator Ted Stevens (who happened to chair the relevant Senate subcommittee) get reelected by subsidizing citizens of a state that distributes, at present, $1,700 in surplus oil royalties to every resident. Poor people, whether rural or urban, can be helped far more effectively with targeted direct subsidies.

The new tax scheme requires that regulation continue, even though monopoly has disappeared and most of rural America has been depopulated. As a result the FCC and the states continue to supervise a telephone industry that is increasingly competitive. Most Americans already can buy telephone service from five or six independent providers. Telephone service prices are so low that long distance service is now effectively a commodity item—but nevertheless priced higher for most customers than it would be without regulation. The mere existence of continued regulation offers opportunities for the FCC and Congress to pander to new special interests.

Perhaps the simplest explanation is that it was far easier for Congress in 1996 to cater to the relatively weak economic political interests still benefiting from the obsolete universal service system than to abolish the system. The beneficiaries of abolition (ordinary telephone customers) had little or no political muscle, or even awareness of the issue, and hence were weaker still. The status quo had acquired its own unfortunate inertia.

Example: Mass Media

The background story with mass media service is much the same as with phone service. As everyone knows, America started out with a great idea: freedom of the press from government censorship. But the Supreme Court later decided that censorship of broadcasters was okay because stations were using the government-owned radio spectrum, and there wasn't enough of that commodity to go around. The FCC took on the task of regulating the content of radio and TV stations, and later of broadcast networks. In the days when most citizens received their information and embedded social cues from programming provided by just three radio or TV networks, many believed this policy a sound one. After all, in the 1930s and 40s the reputation of government was much improved, relative to business, and the excesses of George III and Lord North a distant memory. And in any event the *printed* press was still free of censorship.

But the same technological revolution that hit the telephone industry also transformed the electronic mass media. In place of three television networks we now have hundreds. Thanks to the Internet, information and social cues no longer are under the control of any small group of suppliers. Mass media content today is even more responsive to consumer demand than it was in the days when only three networks sold eyeballs to advertisers. And even totalitarian governments have failed in efforts to control use of the Internet by ordinary citizens.

Still, we continue to regulate electronic media content. Why? Some on the left advocate continued regulation of electronic mass media because they see media "moguls" still deciding the content of what the public views. These advocates confuse cause and effect. At any given time a huge fraction of the public demands whatever is popular, but what is popular by definition changes constantly. Fashion is driven by random events, creative effort, marketing skill and consumer demand, not mogul power. The moguls are merely the alertest imitators, forced by competition to drive what is popular out of fashion. Anyone who complains about mass media content is complaining about the public's tastes, and media moguls' forced pursuit of it.

Advocates on the right reach the same policy conclusion—that federal regulation of media content is righteous—but they do so by a different route. They place all their emphasis on the single issue of "family-friendly" media content. The right seems unmoved by the contradictions between this position and its traditional distrust of government and emphasis on literal constitutional interpretation.

In spite of extremist support for government regulation of the electronic media, it seems very doubtful that either Congress or the courts today would *initiate* (or permit) such intervention, were it not already in place. A policy that began as a political compromise involving a minor industry (radio broadcasting in the 1920s) has been preserved long after the relevance of the compromise has faded.

Thus, pointless FCC regulation of broadcast content continues, focused on such silliness as penalties for out of bounds football half-time entertainment and radio shock jocks. More seriously, the courts and Congress so far have consented to the expansion of FCC content regulation to the new mass media. Given the decline and likely demise of printing as a technology of mass communication, it seems we will eventually have no medium of expression to which the press freedom of the First Amendment applies. The Supreme Court will have a chance in the 2008 term to rethink the whole matter when it hears Fox's Television's challenge to one of the FCC's recent acts of broadcast censorship in the name of indecency regulation.

Solutions—*Overcoming Gridlock*

Communications regulation is carried out by the FCC. The agency has a lot of discretion, but it does not set communications policy by itself. Congress tells the FCC what policies to pursue, and the federal courts also are in the game. Appellate courts have very little respect for the FCC's ability to make sound policy judgments, and FCC decisions are frequently second-guessed and overturned. Liberal judges overturn Republican policies and conservative judges overturn Democrat policies. Communications policy is gridlocked because so many players have a veto, because most issues seem arcane and technical to the public, and because almost any proposal for change threatens the profits of favored industry groups while stimulating frantic lobbying by potential beneficiaries or victims of change.

The President has the power to appoint a majority of the FCC commissioners and to name the chairman, though in most administrations the President's role in communications policy has been small. But any President can choose to be a communications policy leader, and when that happens, real change can occur. For example, the Nixon administration blocked a move by Comsat and the FCC to monopolize domestic communications satellites. The result was healthy open satellite competition in the delivery of video programming to broadcast stations and cable TV systems, and later, direct to homes. This was key to the creation of dozens of competing video networks. The Nixon administration also set the groundwork for the antitrust case that led to the breakup of AT&T. Earlier, President Lyndon Johnson played an important role in the creation and federal funding of the public broadcasting system, at a time when the number of commercial broadcast channels was strictly limited by FCC policies.

Not all presidential interventions are as high-minded or as successful as those of Johnson and Nixon. President Reagan, acting at the behest of his old friends in Hollywood, intervened at the FCC to stop a reform of outdated broadcast regulations that threatened the profitability of the movie studios. The reform had to wait another decade. President Clinton's vice president, Al Gore, played an unusual direct role in policymaking at the FCC and participated in forging the 1996 Telecommunications Act. The 1996 Act made it the law of the land that the communications business should be opened up to more competition and deregulated. The FCC was directed to pursue that goal. But more than ten years later, nothing of the sort has taken place. Instead, the Republican FCC, members of both parties in Congress, and several federal courts have blocked deregulation and even proposed creation of new regulations. Wholesale reform simply failed. Too many interests benefit from regulation or would be out of work in an open market.

This experience seems to indicate that a President can achieve significant improvements in communications policy by targeting a few key issues and using the power and prestige of the presidency to bowl over the normal Washington resistance to change. It is tempting to propose another attempt at wholesale reform, but that seems quixotic, and most of the hot-button issues of today—net neutrality, bundling, universal service, various mergers and ownership issues—are meaningful only within a regulatory system that is dysfunctional at a much larger scale. Instead, I propose two reforms. I believe these reforms have the potential to make significant, long-run improvement, mainly by undermining the power of inertia to preserve obsolete policy.

Recommendation 1

Resale: Permit licensees to use or sell their spectrum for any purpose that does not interfere with others

The use of spectrum today is mostly determined by dead people. Right now, all spectrum users, even those who paid billions for their licenses in FCC auctions or by purchasing from prior licensees, must continue to use their slices of spectrum as originally intended. If someone holds a radio broadcast license first awarded in 1936, that's all it can be used for today—radio broadcasting at a given frequency on the AM band at a certain location with a specified number of watts, and so on. Never mind that the spectrum assignment could be used far more productively for cell phone service, wireless Internet access, or something else without causing interference with other users. The licensee today can sell its spectrum assignment to anyone it wishes (except felons or foreigners), but the new owner can only run an AM radio station. This makes no sense. There actually is an ancient principle in trust and estate law called the "Rule Against Perpetuities," which limits the ability of dead people to control the use of property forever, from the grave.

The historical reason for this really bad rule restricting spectrum use is the assumption that the late FCC engineers and commissioners got it right when they decided in the 1930s and 40s how much of the then-usable spectrum should be used for, say, AM broadcasting as opposed to taxicab radios. Common sense tells us that the decisions they made, even if sound at the time, cannot possibly still be correct today. But the FCC sticks with the status quo, meaning that any potential improvements in the efficiency of spectrum use must take place, willy nilly, only as new technology opens up room at higher and higher frequencies, and others cannot take place at all.

The benefits of this initiative go far beyond efficiency in spectrum use. A major economic benefit is that anywhere suppliers of communications service are overcharging customers, entrants can get the spectrum they need to build new capacity, driving down the prices consumers have to pay for service. A major political benefit is that industry participants with existing licenses are no longer bound to spend millions to block reform; now they can put their spectrum to its most valuable use. Even federal government spectrum users, such as the Department of Defense, for which huge swaths of spectrum are now reserved, would benefit. The department could sell off its unused spectrum to help fund other defense communications activities, and it could buy spectrum for any new needs that arise, just as it procures other goods and services.

What's not to like about the initiative? The only obvious problem is the interference issue. Suppose someone claims that interference is taking place. How will we deal with such disputes? It turns out that we already have a solution. Engineers can (and already do) measure interference—it is nothing more than the profile of the licensee's signal (frequency, power, etc.) at specific locations. To achieve optimal levels of interference (which are not zero), simply set the level of interference that currently exists as the norm. More interference than that requires the licensee either to stop the interference or to negotiate a deal with anyone who complains. A right to be free of interference could be enforced by civil proceedings at the FCC or in the courts, using the existing tools for real property rights. The vast majority of interference claims would be settled out of court.

Recommendation 2

Sunset: Terminate rules that embody obsolete political compromises

It is a healthy thing, in general, that Washington produces political compromises. But political compromises when embodied in law or regulation have a downside. They stay in place long after the politics and economics that produced them are long forgotten. Legislative and administrative procedures make it much harder to get rid of old policy than to enact new policy. The need to respect founding myths gets in the way of house cleaning. The experience with the 1996 Telecommunications Act illustrates this point dramatically. Even an Act of Congress is powerless to force regulatory reform at the FCC.

There is only one way to solve this problem: "sunset rules." If every component of the entire corpus of communications regulation automatically expired by law at a certain date after adoption, at least the rules would reflect current political compromises, rather than old ones. Moreover, rather than requiring an effort and a majority of the FCC or of Congress to get *rid* of a bad rule, an effort and a majority would be required to *keep* a bad rule. This is potentially a big difference.

Congress, in 1996, passed up its chance to rely on sunsets. Instead, the FCC was ordered to review its rules at regular intervals and to deregulate gradually, as increased competition reduced the need for regulation. Although not explicit in the language of the Act, the implicit message was that old, obsolete regulations must go. That sounds sensible enough. Why didn't it work?

It turned out that most FCC rules (and many provisions of regulatory statutes) simply don't make sense to begin with, except of course as compromises among competing interests. For example, the FCC sought to ease a rule limiting the number of TV stations one company can own. But because the original rule was itself arbitrary from a rationalist perspective, the Commission could not come up with a legally-sustainable "rational basis," either for the original standard or the new one. One standard was an old political compromise; the other standard was a new political compromise. The courts keep overturning FCC attempts to "adjust" such limits as arbitrary and capricious. The result is that the old rule remains in place. This reinforces the status quo bias of other features of administrative law.

Establishing a sunset regime for existing rules and statutes doesn't automatically eliminate policies that injure consumers. There is a sunset rule in place now, for example, for the regulation that requires many program producers not to sell on an exclusive basis to cable systems (as opposed to satellite broadcasters or other multichannel video services). Every five years or so, the FCC must review the rule, and so far has renewed it each time. The non-exclusivity rule is bad for consumers because it reduces the incentive of the various video services to develop new programming as a means of competing for viewers. As a result, the programming by cable and satellite operators is pretty much the same. First enacted back in the early 1990s when satellite broadcasting was relatively new, the non-exclusivity rule was intended to protect satellite broadcasters from being outbid for programming by cable operators. Satellite broadcasters are no longer new entrants requiring such protection from competition.

Still, the possibility of sunset keeps hope of reform alive. Every five years the satellite broadcasters' arguments for protection get weaker, and a majority of the FCC gets harder to obtain. The lesson of the example is that policies harmful to consumers may survive the political bargain that gave rise to them, even with sunset provisions, because their rents continue to generate economic incentives for political action.

Recommendations and Conclusion

It is often laudable and no evidence of corruption or incompetence that politicians use compromise to resolve conflicts among economic interest groups, even if they do so at the expense of consumer welfare, because consumers also have an interest in "preserving the Union" in the sense of preserving a system that is able to maintain political stability. We need to accept that the policy-making regime produces policies that cannot be explained rationally as supporting a narrow consumer welfare objective. But keeping the coalition intact is not the only legitimate task of government. Consumer welfare should not unnecessarily be sacrificed to resolve current conflicts, and consumer welfare losses attributable to policies that resolved obsolete conflicts should be stemmed. Foundational myths that no longer serve a useful purpose should not be allowed to prevent improvements in consumer welfare that threaten no extant political interest.

In communications policy we can take two modest steps, steps that will permit technological progress and shifting industrial structure to improve consumer welfare more quickly than will otherwise be possible. First, we can permit spectrum users to do what they like with their spectrum, subject to the usual competition laws, so long as they create no new interference with other users. Second, we can create a presumption in the law that any regulatory provision becomes defunct after a number of years fixed at the time of enactment, unless its proponents can convince the majority anew that the provision makes sense. These steps, like the Rule Against Perpetuities, would improve the lot of the living, and provoke only the dead.

Notes

Resale of spectrum rights

Using markets to allocate the radio spectrum has long been advocated by economists. Ronald Coase, *The Federal Communications*

Commission, 2 J. L. & ECON. 1 (1959); Pablo T. Spiller and Carlo Cardilli, *Toward a Property Rights Approach to Communications Spectrum* 16 YALE J. ON REG. 53 (1999). A market of sorts in spectrum rights was developing prior to nationalization of the spectrum in 1927; see Thomas W. Hazlett, *The Rationality of U.S. Regulation of the Broadcast Spectrum*, 33 J.L. &ECON.133 (1990). A Johnson administration task force on communications policy commissioned a study of how salable spectrum rights might best be defined; see Arthur De Vany, et al., *A Property System for Market Allocation of the Electromagnetic Spectrum: A Legal-Economic-Engineering Study*, 21 STAN. L. REV. 145 (1969). A principal barrier to adoption of a property rights system in spectrum is the implied legitimization of scarcity rents in the hands of existing rights holders, an outcome offensive to many. But the offense is based on a misconception. The scarcity rents accrued to the original license holders many years ago. Most licenses today are held by parties who purchased them directly or indirectly from the original holders for prices that included the value of the scarcity rents. Thus, spectrum resale creates no windfall for current licensees.

Sunset provisions

Sunset provisions have been around for a long time. The Roman republic automatically terminated delegations of dictatorial and military powers at the conclusion of the terms of the Consuls. Thomas Jefferson wrote that every law "naturally expires at the end of 19 years. If it be enforced longer, it is an act of force and not of right." Thomas Jefferson to James Madison, September 6, 1789, enclosure in Jefferson to Madison, 9 January 1790, in Julian P. Boyd ed., 15 THE PAPERS OF THOMAS JEFFERSON 392–97 (Princeton, 1958). Political scientist Theodore J. Lowi more recently explored use of sunset provisions in his well-known book THE END OF LIBERALISM: IDEOLOGY, POLICY, AND THE CRISIS OF PUBLIC AUTHORITY (Norton, 1969). See also MARK R. DANIELS, TERMINATING PUBLIC PROGRAMS: AN AMERICAN POLITICAL PARADOX 34 (1997); Bruce Ackerman, *Sunset Can Put a Halt to Twilight of Liberty,* L.A. TIMES, Sept. 20, 2001.

Behavior of reviewing courts

See Thomas J. Miles and Cass R. Sunstein, *Depoliticizing Administrative Law*, HARVARD PUBLIC LAW WORKING PAPER No. 08-16, June 26, 2008.

About the Authors

Gerald W. Brock is Professor of Telecommunication and of Public Policy and Public Administration at The George Washington University, where he also serves as Director of the Master of Public Policy Program. Prior to joining the GW faculty in 1990, Professor Brock served as Chief of the FCC's Common Carrier Bureau. His research interests include telecommunications and Internet policy and the inter-relationship of regulation and technological progress, and he is the author of four books and many articles on these subjects.

Diane M. Disney is Professor of Management at Pennsylvania State University, where she has been Chancellor of the School of Graduate and Professional Studies and Dean of Commonwealth College. Formerly, she was Director of the University of Rhode Island Research Center in Business and Economics. Professor Disney served as Deputy Assistant Secretary of Defense (Civilian Personnel Policy) from 1994 to 2001, where she oversaw the development and implementation of policies for managing DoD's workforce. She also was Director of the University of Rhode Island's Research Center in Business and Economics. Professor Disney has written and testified widely on workforce development, human resource management, and defense issues, and has served on several international commissions.

Richard A. Epstein is James Parker Hall Distinguished Service Professor of Law at the University of Chicago, where he has taught since 1972. He has also been the Peter and Kirstin Bedford Senior Fellow at the Hoover Institution since 2000. He is also visiting professor at New York University Law School. Professor Epstein, one of the nation's most influential public law scholars, has been a member of the American Academy of Arts and Sciences since 1985. He is the author of numerous books and scholarly articles covering a wide range of legal and interdisciplinary subjects.

Randolph J. May is Founder and President of the Free State Foundation, an independent, non-profit, free market-oriented think tank. From 1999–2006, May was a Senior Fellow and Director of Communications Policy Studies at the Progress & Freedom Foundation. He has practiced communications, administrative, and regulatory law as a partner at major national law firms. Mr. May has served as Associate General Counsel at the Federal Communication Commission. He is a past Chair of the American Bar Association's Section of Administrative Law and Regulatory Practice and a member of the ABA House of Delegates. He is a Fellow of the National Academy of Public Administration and has served as Public Member of the Administrative Conference of the United States. He is an adjunct professor of law at George Mason University. Mr. May has published more than one hundred articles and essays on communications, administrative and constitutional law topics. In addition, he is the co-editor of two books, NET NEUTRALITY OR NET NEUTERING: SHOULD BROADBAND INTERNET SERVICES BE REGULATED? and COMMUNICATIONS DEREGULATION AND FCC REFORM.

John W. Mayo is Professor of Economics, Business and Public Policy at Georgetown University's McDonough School of Business. He previously served as the School's Dean. A prolific contributor to the economics, law and policy journals, he has also participated in a number of regulatory and antitrust proceedings. He has frequently testified before state and federal legislative and regulatory bodies on matters including monopolization, price fixing, mergers, and regulatory pricing policy.

Bruce M. Owen is the Gordon Cain Senior Fellow at the Stanford (University) Institute for Economic Policy Research. He is the Morris M. Doyle Professor in Public Policy and Director of the Public Policy Program at Stanford and also a professor, by courtesy, of economics. Previously, Professor Owen was the chief economist of the Antitrust Division of the U.S. Department of Justice and, earlier, of the White House Office of Telecommunications Policy. Professor Owen's research is in the areas of competition and regulation policy, law and economics, and mass media.

Glen O. Robinson is David A. and Mary Harrison Distinguished Professor of Law Emeritus at the University of Virginia. He served as a Commissioner of the Federal Communications Commission from 1974–1976 and as U.S. Representative to the World Administrative Radio Conference in 1979. Professor Robinson has taught and written extensively in a number of fields, including administrative law, antitrust, communications, intellectual property, property, and torts.

James B. Speta is Professor of Law at Northwestern University School of Law. He teaches in the Law School and in the Joint Program in Law and Business operated by the Law School and the Kellogg School. His research interests include telecommunications and Internet policy, antitrust, administrative law, and market organization. Professor Speta clerked for Judge Harry T. Edwards on the U. S. Court of Appeals for the D.C. Circuit and, before joining the Northwestern University faculty, he practiced appellate, telecommunications, and antitrust law.

Dennis L. Weisman is Professor of Economics at Kansas State University. Professor Weisman is on the editorial board for the *Review of Network Economics*, the *Journal of Regulatory Economics*, and *Information Economics and Policy*. His primary research interests are in strategic behavior, government regulation and antitrust. He is the author or co-author of numerous articles, books and book chapters, including DESIGNING INCENTIVE REGULATION FOR THE TELECOMMUNICATIONS INDUSTRY and THE TELECOMMUNICATIONS ACT OF 1996: THE "COSTS" OF MANAGED COMPETITION. Professor Weisman's work has been cited by the Supreme Court.

Steven S. Wildman is Co-Director of the Quello Center for Telecommunication Management and Law at Michigan State University and holds the James H. Quello Chair of Telecommunication Studies. His research interests include economics and policy for mass media industries, institutional underpinnings of law and regulation for communication industries, and universal service policy.

Professor Wildman has published broadly in scholarly and professional journals and is the co-author or co-editor of five books.

Christopher S. Yoo is Professor of Law at the University of Pennsylvania Law School and Professor of Communication at the Annenberg School for Communication. He is Founding Director of the Law School's Center for Technology, Innovation, and Competition. He has written prolifically and testified before Congress and federal agencies on communications law, government regulation, and intellectual property. Professor Yoo clerked for Judge A. Raymond Randolph of the U.S. Court of Appeals for the D.C. Circuit and Justice Anthony Kennedy of the Supreme Court of the United States.